Lyric, Meaning, and Audience

in the Oral Tradition of Northern Europe

Poetics of Orality and Literacy

general editor

John Miles Foley

Lyric, Meaning,

AND

Audience

IN THE

Oral Tradition

OF

Northern Europe

THOMAS A. DuBOIS

University of Notre Dame Press

Notre Dame, Indiana

Manufactured in the United States of America

Library of Congress Cataloging-in-Publication Data

DuBois, Thomas A. (Thomas Andrew), 1960–
Lyric, meaning, and audience in the oral tradition of Northern Europe /
Thomas A. DuBois.
p.   cm. — (Poetics of orality and literacy)
Includes bibliographical references (p.   ) and index.
ISBN-13: 978-0-268-02589-2 (pbk. : alk. paper)
ISBN-10: 0-268-02589-4 (pbk. : alk. paper)
1. Folk songs—Europe, Northern—History and criticism.
2. Lyric poetry—History and criticism.   I. Title.
ML3580.D83   2006
782.420948—dc22

2006024211

CONTENTS

I have always wondered what songs are about. This book seeks to answer that question by offering an overall framework and applying it to a variety of lyric songs and song genres from northern Europe. It may seem that I have taken a very simple thing and made it quite complicated. But I hope that, by the end of this book, it will seem that I have taken a complicated thing and made it at least a little simpler.

I would like to thank the many people who have contributed vitally to this study. My teachers Kenny Goldstein at the University of Pennsylvania and Leea Virtanen at the University of Helsinki introduced me to the issues at the core of this study, helping me to appreciate the excitement of a topic that they sincerely loved and knew backwards and forwards. I would not have written this book without their help. I am also grateful for the guidance and advice I have received over the years from Margaret Mills, Dell Hymes, and Roger Abrahams; their influence is evident in these pages. I owe a special debt of gratitude to John Miles Foley. I had the good fortune to begin this project while attending a National Endowment for the Humanities Summer Seminar titled "The Oral Tradition and Literature" that John hosted at the University of Missouri at Columbia in 1994. I remember fondly sharing with John my first attempts at diagramming my ideas about lyric interpretation, drawn with my young son's crayons on a hot afternoon. In the years since, John has remained solidly enthusiastic and supportive of the project. I am delighted that this book appears in his series with the University of Notre Dame Press.

Many others have contributed thoughts and advice as I worked on this book: Gerry Philipsen and Guntis Šmidchens at the University of Washington, Seattle; Jim Leary, Scott Mellor, and Jack Niles at the University of Wisconsin–Madison; and Ríonach ui Ógáin, Joe Harris, Senni Timonen, Lauri Harvilahti, Anna-Leena Siikala, Richard Jones-Bamman, Harald Gaski, and Krister Stoor. The two anonymous reviewers who read my manuscript for the University of Notre Dame Press provided me with much wise advice, which I have tried to incorporate in the present work. I also thank Barbara Hanrahan at the Press for her enthusiastic support of this project through the publication stages. I am grateful to all these people for their insights and patience, and I apologize in advance for the errors in my study, all of which I acknowledge as my own.

I thank the libraries of the University of Washington, Seattle, and the University of Wisconsin–Madison for their sustained devotion to a set of texts and topics that form the heart of this study. And I also gratefully acknowledge the support and honor I received from the National Endowment for the Humanities, the John Simon Guggenheim Memorial Foundation, and the Graduate School Research Committee of the University of Wisconsin–Madison.

I could not have brought this book to completion without the generous help of Michael and Lizzy Lyne or the good-humored patience of my family, Wendy Vardaman and Conor, Greer, and Brendan DuBois. I thank them for making this possible.

Introduction

Lyrics and the Issue of Meaning

Will no one tell me what she sings?—
Perhaps the plaintive numbers flow
For old, unhappy, far-off things,
And battles long ago;
Or is it some more humble lay,
Familiar matter of today?
Some natural sorrow, loss or pain,
That has been, and may be again?
William Wordsworth, The Solitary Reaper (1807)

For the speaker of William Wordsworth's classic poem, as for romantic intellectuals in general, the folk songs of ordinary peasants fell into two broad categories: the ballad, a narrative song recounting "old, unhappy, far-off things and battles long ago," and the lyric, "some more humble lay, familiar matter of today." Focusing not on an explicit plot but rather on descriptions, situations, characters, and feelings, the lyric becomes more familiar to its audiences and yet more elusive. A song's character may display sentiments or attitudes immediately comprehensible to an audience, and yet that audience may still not know much about the speaker whose feelings are described, or the circumstances alluded to in the song, or when the events took place. Indeed, as Wordsworth's speaker laments his incomprehension, he likewise gives voice to centuries of scholarly frustration at the seeming simplicity and yet persistent opacity of the lyric genre. How is one to interpret a lyric in the absence of a stated narrative? Must one find a plot submerged in its lines, or can other frameworks supply meaning as well? The answer to this question—the focus of this study—is, I argue, as much a part of what the lyric is all about as are its words or images or form. Communities, I posit, share norms for interpreting lyrics just as surely and as readily as they share the songs themselves. These interpretive frameworks, this native hermeneutics, can be gleaned from ethnographic evidence sometimes hinted at in song texts or melodies but often lying outside the songs entirely. Anchored in specific cultural traditions and practices, these frameworks are nonetheless comparable and to a certain degree predictable from culture to culture.

Below, I introduce the central questions and methods of this study through the examination of three lyric songs. Viewed within their ambient frameworks of performance and interpretation, these three lyrics sketch the variety of interpretive practices that exist in connection with the lyric genre, even while the lyrics themselves may seem outwardly similar in terms of form or image. To illustrate and account for this range of interpretive possibilities, I first introduce some key terms that are used throughout this study.

A TYPOLOGY OF INTERPRETIVE STRATEGIES

Lyric interpretation, I argue, traditionally proceeds through varying recourse to three different interpretive axes: the generic, the associative, and the situational. Along the first of these, the generic, aspects of the lyric genre itself—both its typical content and its typical contexts for performance—serve as keys to the song's meaning. A song's details, potentially startling or novel to a listener from outside of the tradition, become familiar and easily comprehended by an audience knowledgeable in the genre as a whole. Certain ways of approaching lyric topics are normative in a given locale or tradition, just as certain commonplaces exist in terms of performance style, melody, word choice, and theme. We can talk about more or less standard lyric topics in given periods or locales, for example, the complaints of an unhappy wife or the laments of a jilted lover, two themes that proved especially popular throughout the region from the medieval period onward. And we can recognize certain contexts in which lyric songs are particularly appropriate, for example, in courtship, or when recalling a deceased friend, or even while doing certain kinds of work. While some of these norms show remarkable consistency across northern Europe, others are characteristic of particular cultural areas or subgenres of lyric. An audience listens to any new performance from within a set of locally and historically shaped "generic" expectations, shaped by past performances and a tradition of interpretation in the locale.

Along the second axis, the associative, interpretations depend on associating the song with a particular person, place, or thing. This meaning-bearing entity may be oneself (personalization), an inscribed interlocutor (invocation), or a third party (attribution). In personalization, one sees a song in relation to one's own life and experiences, or remembers the personal moments in which the song played a part ("They're playing *our* song!"). Perhaps the song stirs memories of childhood, or of coming of age in a village from which one has long since departed, or of an especially important personal relationship in one's life. In invocation, one envisions a person or being to whom the song's lines are addressed, a recipient whose very existence makes the song a purposeful communication. The invocation may be purely imaginative, but in many cases in the oral tradition of northern Europe, the invocation is seen as mystically functional, a means of calling upon a friend, or deity, or entity important in one's life: "I miss *you,* I need *your* help, I am thinking of *you* . . . " In attribution, the song becomes meaningful by association with a composer or performer connected with the song, or a narrative character mentioned in the song's text. Perhaps the song was composed by a well-known performer of the past, someone about whom lots of stories are told. Perhaps the song is said to have arisen at a particular moment in the life of a narrative character, someone about whom broader narratives are told. The song then becomes a slice of life, a souvenir from another's world of experiences.

Finally, along the situational axis, a song becomes meaningful through reference to its inscribed situation, be it described narratively (as something that has occurred to a specific individual at a certain place and time) or proverbially (as something that typically happens to people in certain common situations, e.g., separation from a lover, an unhappy marriage, the state of orphanhood). As I shall show, Irish and Scottish lyric traditions often have long and detailed narratives that were associated with particular songs, supplying details that sometimes lie entirely outside of the lyric's text itself. In Finnish tradition, in contrast, songs often were seen as reflecting whole classes of people (e.g., the orphan, the daughter-in-law) rather than any specific person. Although this axis comes the closest to what we find in narrative genres like the ballad, it is important not to assume that its significance is the greatest of the three. Rather, all three axes come into play in each act of lyric interpretation, and specific norms within cultures impinge on how an audience approaches the challenge of finding meaning in a song. These interpretive possibilities can be represented diagrammatically, as in figure 1.1.

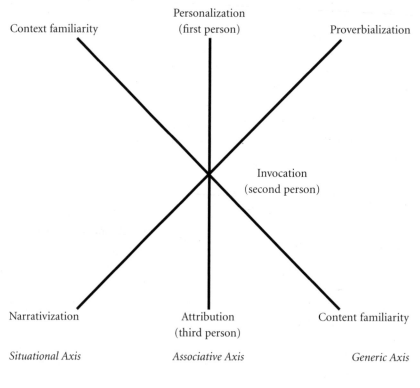

FIGURE 1.1

In Olaus Sirma's Kemi Sámi *Moarsi fávrrot* (Song for a Bride), we see an interpretive tradition that relies heavily on both the generic and associative axes. In Henrik Gabriel Porthan's transcription of the Finnish *Jos minun tuttuni tulisi* (If the One I Know Would Come), we find, in contrast, a song that was interpreted predominantly along the generic and situational axes. And in Douglas Hyde's approach to the Irish *Casadh an tSúgáin* (Twisting of the Rope) we see a situational interpretation that favors narrativization over proverbialization. Any given song or tradition, I argue, may use various of these axes of interpretation at the same time. Nonetheless, norms exist in each culture for how an audience usually deploys interpretation along each axis and which axis usually predominates. It is the purpose of this study to explore these interpretive traditions comparatively across northern Europe. In a sense, I hope to answer the impassioned questions of Wordsworth's speaker by turning to the singer herself and her knowing traditional audience and letting them explain what the song is about.

By way of introduction, however, I also examine in this chapter how scholarly interpreters have tended to overlook traditional hermeneutic practices, preferring instead to offer theories of meaning that reside in other notions: abstracted concepts of human sentiment, for instance, not rooted in the specificities of cultural practice, or an idealized national character, or a reconstructed textual history. Johan Scheffer, and the many scholars and poets who came after him, saw in Sirma's *Moarsi fávrrot* proof that even "primitive" people have finer sentiments. They reproduced, translated, and adapted Sirma's lyric repeatedly in their fascination with this discovery. Porthan, and the many scholars and poets who came after him, found in *Jos minun tuttuni tulisi* the expression of a nation, one with its own unique viewpoint and destiny. Hyde, and the actors and audiences of the Irish Abbey Theatre, celebrated in the play *Casadh an tSúgáin* the ebullience of Irish tradition and the potential that a community could will to retain its traditions, thereby regaining its cultural—and political—viability.

Moving from these early approaches to scholarship of the past century and a half, I survey briefly the ways in which later scholars have approached the folk lyric. I focus on the theorists and methods that have helped to shape this study. Finally, this chapter introduces the chapters that follow, sketching the set of issues and examples explored in each. The chapters are not intended as an exhaustive look at every aspect of lyric and its interpretation in northern Europe. Rather, I adopt an approach reminiscent of lyrics themselves—allowing particular moments and examples to come into focus as evocative of greater wholes. Together, I believe, the various moments and cases surveyed provide a glimpse of the richly nuanced and effective repertoire of interpretive strategies that communities recognize, assert, and maintain alongside the songs they perform. Sometimes consciously enunciated, sometimes unquestioningly felt, these strategies help to anchor and sustain lyric traditions over time and space.

Case 1. *Moarsi fávrrot*

Pastos päivä kiufwrasist jawra Orrejaura!

Jos koasa kirrakeid kornagadzim
ja tiedadzim man oinämam jaufre Orrejawre,
man tangaszlomest lie sun lie,
kaika taidä mooraid dzim soopadzim,
mak taben sadde sist uddasist,

ja poaka taidä ousid dzim karsadzin,
mack qwodde roannaid poorid ronaidh.

Kulckedh palvaid tim suuttetim,
mack kulcki woasta jaufrä Orrejaufrä.

Jos mun tåckå dzim kirjadzim sååst worodze sååst!

Ä muste lä såå dzigä såå, maina tåckå kirdadzim,
äka lä julgä songiaga julgä, äkä lä siebza,
fauron siebza, maan koima lusad dzim norbadzim.

Kalle lu läck kuck madzie wordamadzie
morredabboid dadd päiwidad, linnasabboid
dadd salmidadd, liegäsabboid, waimodadd.

Jus kuckas sick patäridzik,
tannagtied sarga dzim iusadzim.

Mi os matta lädä sabbo karrasabbo
ku lij paddä saanapaddä, ia salwam routesalwam,
käck dziabräi siste korrasistä
ja käsä mijna täm oiwitäm, punie poaka
tämä jurdäkitämä.

Parne miela piägga miela,
Noara jorda kockes jorda.

Jos taidä poakaid läm kuldäläm,
luidäm radda wära radda.

Oucta lie miela oudas waldäman;
nute tiedäm pooreponne oudastan man kauneman.[1]

———

Let the sun shine bright on the lake, Lake Orra!
If I were to climb to spruce tops

and I knew I saw the lake, Lake Orra,
in whose heather valley she is, she is,
all those trees I would fell
which have started growing there lately,
and all those branches I would cut away
which have sprouted shoots, good shoots.

Blowing clouds I have followed
As they blow toward the lake, Lake Orra.

If only I could fly there on wings, a crow's wings!

I have no wings, a duck's wings,
with which I could fly there,
nor do I have feet, a goose's feet,
nor do I have heels, fine heels,
with which I could head to your side.

Long indeed have you waited,
through the brightest of your days,
the softest of your eyes,
the warmest of your heart.

No matter how far you were to flee,
I would soon catch you.

What can be stronger, tougher,
than a rope, a sinew rope,
or a chain, an iron chain,
which bite hard
and bind our heads,
twisting all our thoughts?

A boy's will, a wind's will
a young man's thoughts, long thoughts.

If I were to listen to them all
I'd take the road, the wrong road.

One will alone is there for me to choose;
now I know the better one I will find before me.

Preserved in a language that has since disappeared, translated into Latin and published in Frankfurt in the seventeenth century, *Moarsi fávrrot* depicts the musings of a young man in love. Through his eyes, we see a sun-drenched lake, Oarrejávri, on whose heathery banks his love resides. The song's speaker declares that he would gladly cut away any trees that would obstruct his view of the lake or don wings to fly to its shores. Yet, as the Sámi critic Harald Gaski (1996: 13–14) has noted, the song implies as well that the speaker has actually kept his beloved waiting for some time: "through the brightest of your days, the softest of your eyes, the warmest of your heart." And after ambivalent images of chains that both bind and chafe, the speaker admits frankly the fickle nature of youth: "A boy's will, a wind's will, a young man's thoughts, long thoughts." Realizing that his imaginings may lead him astray, the speaker seems in the end to resolve on a better course of action, presumably to journey to the side of his beloved forever more.

How are we to understand this lyric song, a work grounded not in an explicit narrative plot but in characterization, description, emotion? How are we to make sense of its content, appreciate its integrity, and evaluate its effectiveness as a communication or as a work of art? Fortunately, in approaching these questions, we can ask the singer himself. For we know that *Moarsi fávrrot* was performed in 1672 by Olaus Sirma, a young Sámi theology student from the Kemi region of northern Finland, then part of the Swedish empire. Sirma had come to the university at Uppsala that same year to study for the ministry, a calling that he eventually lived out in his home from 1676 until his death in 1703 (Henrysson 1993: 86). At the request of his German-born teacher Johan Scheffer, he sang, recorded, and rendered the song in Swedish along with one other lyric. Sirma did more than merely perform and translate his song: he also wrote an explanation of the musical tradition it represented. His words, written in Swedish and preserved in Scheffer's notes, are as follows:

> These songs begin in this and other ways. Some sing more, others less, according to their own inclinations to create and compose. At times they repeat the same song over and over. Nor do they have any set tune but sing or *joik* this song, which is called *Moarsi fávrrot,* the bride's song, according to their custom and as it seems best to them to sing. (Quoted in Kjellström, Ternhag, and Rydving 1988: 11)

It is clear from this description that Sirma is describing the highly improvisational, melodically variable *joik* tradition, which is examined in more detail in
chapter 3. In *joik* tradition, the same song could be sung with or without words,
or with substantial variation in melody or style. In his brief description, Sirma
seems intent on clarifying this aspect of *joik* for the reader of his song, and he
uses the Sámi verb *joiga* (modern Northern Sámi *juoigat*) to distinguish the tradition from that of Swedes or Finns. The song had, in other words, a particular
meaning as an exemplar of a specific musical genre known and valued by Sámi
people. It was a genre that carried with it norms of style, content, and context. Of
its stylistic features, we can survey today only those that left tangible marks in
Sirma's text, for example, the artful way in which a word is first introduced in a
general manner and then immediately followed up by a specification: "lake, Lake
Orra," "wing, a duck's wings," "rope, a sinew rope." Undoubtedly, such typical
turns of phrase, vocal performance style, and improvisational freedom were all
readily identifiable features to Sámi audiences. Many of these same features persist in Sámi *joik* communities today.

In terms of typical context, as Sirma explained further in his notes to Scheffer, songs like *Moarsi fávrrot* were performed in the summer, in particular, when
young men were staying in the mountains with their reindeer herds. Indeed, he
termed the song explicitly a "summer song," contrasting it with his other lyric,
which he termed a "winter song." For Sirma, this summer context seems to have
been important in his understanding of the song and relates as well to the situation it describes in its lines. These generic considerations, then, in terms of style,
content, and context, comprise a key interpretive axis by which a Sámi audience
was able to place and appreciate the song, as Gaski's (1996) insightful reading
of the text illustrates.

At the same time, it is clear that Sirma's song—like other exemplars of
the *joik* genre that have been collected and discussed since Sirma's time—also
accrues meaning through association with certain persons or beings. In Sámi
tradition, people tended to sing about entities or individuals with whom they
had a personal relationship. Thus, a song that mentions Oarrejávri in particular would most likely be sung by someone who knew the lake and its environs
well or could in some way claim a personal connection to it. Oarrejávri, today
known principally by its Finnish name Orajärvi, is a sizable lake to the east of
the Tornio River. To its north are a series of mountains that served as grazing
lands for reindeer herds. The lake's shores, forest area, and marshes supplied a
variety of needs for the Kemi Sámi community as well. The meaning of the *joik*

as Sirma would have performed or experienced it in his life in the Kemi region would have emerged from an audience's appraisal of the relation between the singer and the song's named entities. This tendency is perhaps reflected obliquely in Sirma's remark, "Some sing more, some less, according to their own inclinations": one's personal input in a song was crucial for its outward form as well as its received meaning. These interpretations can be described as lying along the second axis of interpretation, the associative.

In addition to such personal associations, however, there is a further interpretive potential along the associative axis: that of second-person association, invocation. The great Sámi writer Johan Turi (1910: 91) described *joik* not as simple song but as "okta muitim konsta" (a way of recalling). To "recall" in this tradition was both to remember a being and to make it spiritually and imaginatively present to the performer and the audience for the duration of the song. It was to call the being back, and thus *joiks* frequently shift from third- to second-person address, as in *Moarsi fávrrot*. At times, the lyric speaker describes himself and his feelings or relates the beauties of the lake and bride in first-person or third-person terms. At other times, it is clear that he addresses her directly, for example, when he declares, "No matter how far you were to flee, I would soon catch you." The speaker now confronts the woman and conveys to her his strong feelings, despite the intervening space that separates them from each other. The song thus comes to function as a message, a communication. And this interpretive tendency too, as is discussed in chapter 3, was typical of Sámi *joik*.

Finally, *Moarsi fávrrot* can be examined along the third axis of interpretation, the situational. The inscribed situation here is of a speaker separated from his love and wishing to see her again. Ethnographically, we know that during the summers in the Kemi region, men were often engaged in herding, fishing, or hunting in the mountains, while women remained in the valleys, devoting their time and energy to the other farming or gathering activities essential to the community's survival. The welfare of the community necessitated periods of absence, but these were not always easy for young people in love. Sirma's song recalls this situation, allowing it to act as a source of meaning. Its images of surmounting obstacles, boundless yearning, cold feet, and impassioned resolve thus make more sense when one contemplates a speaker separated from his love by seasonal duties, though these were not without their own appeal. Together with the summer context for this song, it is easy to see it as a potential tool in courtship, and indeed, Scheffer published it not in a chapter on music per se but rather in a description of Sámi courtship and marriage (see Scheffer 1704: 284–88). We have no way of knowing whether this song describes one specific man's lovesick musings (narrativization) or that attributed to young men in general in such a situation (proverbialization). Yet in either case, the situation itself would have helped a Kemi audience interpret and appreciate the song.

In short, then, the meanings of *Moarsi fávrrot* are arrayed along all three axes: the generic, the associative, and the situational. In each case, the song's text (and presumably also its vocal and other performance features now lost to us) were interpreted through reference to norms regarding how one sings, about whom, and about what. The range of feelings and ideas expressed in the song are complex and nuanced but also predictable and comprehensible to an audience that possessed a competence in the genre it exemplified.

Yet even while helping to preserve this song and ethnographic information, Sirma's German-born teacher seems to have missed much of its interpretive significance. Scheffer had asked his student for information on the musical traditions of the Sámi people because he was preparing a book he had been asked to write by the French-Swedish aristocrat Magnus de la Gardie. Sweden's warlike lord chief justice wanted a treatise that would inform Europeans about the true culture and customs of the Sámi, commonly rumored in the courts of central Europe to be supplying the Swedish Crown with supernatural aid in its various military exploits. Scheffer's tome *Lapponia* brought ethnographic knowledge of Sámi culture—and the texts of the two songs performed by Sirma—to the reading public of educated Europe; it appeared in Latin in 1673, in English in 1674, in German in 1675, in French in 1678, and in Dutch in 1682 (Kjellström, Ternhag, and Rydving 1988: 106).

Through Scheffer's text, as Kjellström and colleagues note (110), *Moarsi fávrrot* became one of the first pieces of Swedish literature widely known outside of Sweden. Richard Steele composed a new English-language translation in 1712, complete with rhyme, iambic meter, and regular stanzaic form, bringing it in this manner to the general readership of the immensely popular London periodical, the *Spectator* (Wretö 1984: 49). There it was described as "a Lapland lyric not unworthy of old Greece or Rome," an indication that the translator and his colleagues recognized some thematic or even formal link between this Sámi song and the lyric poetry of Mediterranean antiquity. The Scottish literary critic Hugh Blair, writing in praise of James Macpherson's newly published *Fragments of Ancient Poetry* (1760), praised Sirma's songs enthusiastically:

Surely among the wild Laplanders, if any where, barbarity is in its most perfect state. Yet their love songs which Scheffer has given us in his *Lapponia* are proof that natural tenderness of sentiment may be found in a country, into which the least glimmering of science has never penetrated. (Blair 1765; Gaskill 1996: 351 n 9)

For Blair, then, such songs were useful not as signs of a complex interpretive tradition operating in Sámi song tradition but rather as signs of a "natural tenderness" that all human beings—even "primitives"—possessed. They proved that barbarity was "not inconsistent with generous sentiments and tender affections" (351). Such a proof was important in a European intellectual climate that was for the first time truly contemplating the diversity of human cultures, both in the distant continents now becoming known to Europe and on the very fringes of the Continent itself. With similar wonderment, Voltaire and Lessing wrote their own approving characterizations of Sirma's songs (Kuusi 1963: 540). And the Baltic German literary critic and philosopher Johann Gottfried von Herder included his own translation of *Moarsi fávrrot* as the second piece in his seminal *Stimmern der Völker in Liedern* (The Voices of Peoples in Songs, 1778–79: 3). Placed after a Greenlandic Inuit song and before an Estonian one, *Moarsi fávrrot* was intended to illustrate the national character (*Volksgeist*) of the far northern peoples and to awaken in Europe's intelligentsia the realization that beautiful thoughts and sentiments lived in the breasts of even the cold-benumbed nature-folk of the north.

If imitation is the sincerest form of compliment, then it is noteworthy that admiring readers created their own renderings of Sirma's song. The Finnish poet Johan Runeberg penned a Swedish translation in his *Färden till den älskade* (Journey to the Beloved One), and Goethe and Kleist mined the song for inspiration in their own poetry (Kuusi 1963: 540). In Henry Wadsworth Longfellow's 1855 *My Lost Youth*, the song becomes an ironic rejoinder to the musings of an aging New Englander:

And a verse of a Lapland song
Is haunting my memory still:
"A boy's will is the wind's will
And the thoughts of youth are long, long thoughts."
(Longfellow [1855] 1985: 1285–86)

Moarsi fávrrot became the stuff of literary acknowledgment and allusion, yet the world chose to overlook the important question of how Sámi people interpreted it. Opting instead to use the song to answer questions of their own, scholars assimilated *Moarsi fávrrot* into a foreign interpretive framework built of notions of transcendent human sentiments and the search for the existence of these finer emotions among even the least of humankind. Had they attended to the interpretations that Sirma could provide, they would have discovered not only fine feelings but also sophisticated hermeneutics among the Sámi of Sirma's day.

Case 2. *Jos minun tuttuni tulisi*

Jos mun tuttuni tulisi,
Ennen nähtyni näkyisi,
Sillen suuta suikkajaisin,
Olis suu suen veressä;
Sillen kättä käppäjäisin,
Jospa kärme kämmenpäässä.
Olisko tuuli mielellissä
Ahavainen kielellissä,
Sanan toisi, sanan veisi,
Sanan liian liikuttaisi
Kahen rakkaan välillä.
Ennempä heitän herkku-ruat,
Paistit pappilan unohtan
Ennenkuin heitän herttaiseni,
Kesän keskyteltyäni,
Talven taivuteltuani.
    (Apo 1981: 60)

———

If the one I know were to come,
Were I to see the one I've seen,
Upon his lips I'd press a kiss
Were his mouth filled with wolf's blood;
To him I'd stretch out my hand

Were a snake coiled in his palm.
If the wind could understand,
If the harsh wind had a tongue,
It would take a word, bring a word,
Carry an extra word
Between two loves.
I would sooner throw aside choice foods
Forget the roasts of the parsonage
Than throw aside my love,
The one I spoke with in summer,
The one I persuaded in winter.

Inspired by the publication of Macpherson's *Fragments of Ancient Poetry* and intent on describing the poetic traditions of the Finnish peasantry, Henrik Gabriel Porthan (1739–1804) wrote down the above lyric twice from women in northeastern Finland in 1765 (Hautala 1954: 62–66). As in *Moarsi fávrrot,* the song's speaker laments the distance that separates lovers and pledges devotion to her beloved come what may. Nothing, it would seem, can come between them, except the much-lamented physical space that currently intervenes. The song's images of devotion are startling even by twenty-first-century standards, as we hear an unknown subject filled with powerful emotions: longing, desire, defiance.

As with *Moarsi fávrrot,* we can examine the ways in which this song was interpreted along the generic, associative, and situational axes. Yet here the relative importance of each axis shifts somewhat, as we move from one culture of interpretation to another. On the generic axis, Porthan reported that *Jos minun tuttuni tulisi* was characteristic of a particular genre of singing and a particular performance context and presented a portion of the song in Latin translation in the second volume of his dissertation, *De Poësi Fennica* (On the Poetry of the Finns; [1766–78] (1983): pt. xii, 83–86). He had heard both versions of the song as *jauhorunot,* work songs sung singly or by pairs of women as they performed the long, tedious, tiring work of operating millstones for grinding flour, a labor only then becoming replaced in Finland by water-powered mills. He writes: "The grinders sing songs to divert their minds in a particularly effective manner and to forget their heavy labor" (83). He noted that such songs are slow, and in content they vary from serious moral explorations to treatments of legendary or folktale motives. A great many treat of love, "as this occupies an important place in the thoughts of this sex" (84).

Later scholars collected the song throughout Finland and notated a variety of different melodies for it. D. E. D. Europaeus included a melodic transcription in his 1847 collection of Ingrian songs *Pieni Runon-seppä* (The Little Song-Smith) (Example 1.1, as reproduced in Ala-Könni 1986: 186).

EXAMPLE 1.1

Europaeus's transcription has seven beats per poetic line, obliging the singer to repeat the last part of each line when singing, as is evident in Example 1.1. More typical for songs in the trochaic tetrameter ("Kalevala meter") of Finland, Karelia, and Ingria, however, were melodies of four or five beats per line (Lippus 1995), as illustrated in a transcription A. Lähteenkorva collected of the song in the Karelian village of Tiiksjärvi in 1877 (Example 1.2, as reproduced in Launis 1930: no. 626, 225).

EXAMPLE 1.2

From the village of Liperi, Lähteenkorva collected another melody (Example 1.3, as reproduced in Launis 1930: no. 618, 222).

EXAMPLE 1.3

Erkki Ala-Könni (1986: 186–87) suggests that Europaeus substituted the melody of the trio section of a popular Ingrian polska to provide his song with what he regarded as a more appealing tune. Perhaps Europaeus found the slower, more plodding, more typical four- or five-beat tunes too simple or monotonous for a lyric of such inherent beauty and power, despite their usefulness for women engaged in grinding flour. His substituted melody transforms the song essentially from a work song to a dance tune.

Porthan's views regarding the verbal text of the song were readily mined and paraphrased in Giuseppe Acerbi's remarkably successful *Travels through Sweden, Finland, and Lapland to the North Cape in the Years 1798 and 1799* (Acerbi 1802: 517–19). Acerbi draws on Porthan's text as a source and provides both a literal and a poetic translation of *Jos minun tuttuni tulisi*:

> No inconsiderable number of runic songs, and those not of the least merit in point of composition, are of the production of the class of Finnish peasantry. Before the general use of wind and water-mills, corn was reduced to flour by the labour of the hands, either by pounding in mortars, or by grinding betwixt two stones. This was a daily task, and it fell to the woman's lot to perform it in Finland, as in other countries. During the long and dreary winters of that climate, they were engaged in this work at home, whilst their husbands abroad were either in pursuit of game, employed in the necessary business of seeking wood, forage, etc. To cheer their minds, and beguile their labour, such of the women as were unable to invent songs, studied the composition of new ones; whilst others who were not so happy as to possess that talent, sung those they had learned, whether new or old. In one of these a female peasant describes herself at work in these words
>
> Paiwat pyörin perkeleissa
> Kiwen puussa kükuttelen.
>
> ────
>
> Fix'd to this mill all day I stand,
> And turn the stone with patient hand.
>
> These songs, called *jouho runot,* or mill songs, are for the most part sung to a slow plaintive air. If two women are employed at the mill, they are sung in parts by both of them; but when they relieve each other, she only sings who works. These songs are composed on a variety of subjects; sometimes grave

and serious, at other times ludicrous and satirical; one a love story, and not infrequently the praises of some heroic action. Love which is the great business of their sex, is, as may well be supposed, the topic upon which the energies of the Finnish poetess are chiefly exercised; it is, however, not an easy matter to procure specimens of these songs, to which men are rarely or never admitted. (314–17)

While these generic considerations certainly helped to shape the song as Porthan experienced it, we may conjecture from Europaeus's melody, as from other ethnographic reports from later periods, that *Jos minun tuttuni tulisi* was not limited to flour-grinding contexts alone. And further, the situation inscribed in the song does not appear explicitly linked with that of grinding in the same way that the situation in *Moarsi fávrrot* could be seen as related to the condition of summer mountain sojourns. Rather, the situation at the core of this song revolves around protracted male absence, the reasons for which are not made explicit. Perhaps the song related the specific experience of a particular woman whose beloved was separated from her for some long period for reasons known through an accompanying narrative. Such would be likely were this an Irish lyric. In examining interpretive tendencies within Finnish folk song tradition, however, it seems more likely that the song relates the typical—the proverbialized—experience of women in general who find themselves bereft of loved ones, due to conscription or disease or economic necessity or other unhappy circumstance. Leea Virtanen (1994: 338) has noted that such proverbialized meditations of sorrow were popular in Finnish folk song tradition and that explicit accounts of personal sorrows were far less common (see also DuBois 1996: 246). Senni Timonen (2004: 308 ff.) has characterized such tendencies as instances of collective emotion: generalized feelings that subsumed the personal into a powerful contemplation of the typical and collective. Village culture strongly shunned open complaint as injurious and unwise, and thus personal or specific misery often found expression in proverbial guise.

Porthan's notes seem to indicate that he assumed songs such as *Jos minun tuttuni tulisi* had personal associations for his female informants. Yet, even while making this assumption, he laments his difficulty collecting examples of such songs from women, noting that he had success in this area only when approaching more mature farmwives. From a woman he describes as "elderly and childless, the wife of a bowlegged man," he collected a song that contains a few of the same lines as the above-quoted version but avoids altogether its images of unstoppable love. From an exceptionally generous performer he describes only as "a bride," he collected the more detailed version above. These difficulties collecting songs may reflect the same kind of self-censorship described above, as women who were young (and therefore more likely to be equated with the lyric speaker) avoided singing such songs to a man, lest they be accused of complaining about their own lots. In contrast, older women could sing the songs with more impunity, presumably because the possible linkage between their personal situations and those of the lyric speaker would have diminished over time. But even while surmising such personalization, Porthan does not appear to have asked his informants what they thought about the matter.

From the point of view of interpretive tendencies, then, *Jos minun tuttuni tulisi* would seem to have been understood through interpretation along both the generic and the situational axis, that is, as a typical lyric song of unhappy separation and as the purported expressions of a woman in one such situation. In contrast, the associative axis (except, perhaps, through muted self-reflection) seems little used in this case. We find little indication in the song of the identity of the speaker or of the lover, and Seppo Knuuttila and Timonen (2002: 256) have even pointed out that we cannot be certain of the speaker's sex. If we assume the speaker is female (as did Porthan), then we must make that assumption on the basis of generic tendencies alone and not from any concrete evidence in the song itself. The associative axis, then, so prominent in the Sámi understanding of *Moarsi fávrrot*, seems barely used. Such was not always the case in Finnish folk song, however; attribution was occasionally operative in Finnish lyrics, as, for example, in the case of the famed traditional singer Larin Paraske (Timonen 1982; DuBois 1996: 255). Yet in terms of dominant tendencies, there is a markedly different hermeneutic strategy in Finnish lyric interpretation than in Sámi.

While these specific interpretive norms can be seen in this, as in many other, Finnish lyrics, Porthan, Acerbi, and those scholars who came after them approached the song's meaning in decidedly different ways. Rooting their analyses largely or entirely in a reading of the song's text, they found an endless set of possible interpretations (Knuuttila and Timonen 2002). Porthan, for his part, was not actually interested in exploring deeply the emotional lives of peasant singers. Rather, he was intent on describing the *poesi fennica*—the poetry of the Finnish people as a whole. He opines that some of the songs performed by peasant women are "inherited from our forefathers, while some have been composed at a later time" ([1778] 1983: 83). For him, as for romantic nationalists in the next century, folklore became the collective property of a nation, the inheritance from common "forefathers" along with contributions from later members of the nation as well. When Acerbi arrived in Åbo in search of adventure and exotica, Porthan's student and friend Bishop F. M. Franzén enthustiastically penned a Swedish translation of the song to share with him as an example of "Finnish song." Acerbi took it as such, although also attributing it to a specific peasant author:

> Mr. Franzen, of Åbo, presented me with a song, the composition of a country girl, a native of Ostro-Bothnia, and the servant of the magister or the clergyman of the village, where she had constantly resided. It is composed on the occasion of her lover's absence, in a style of natural simplicity, strong sentiment, and bold figure, to attain which, more cultivated understandings sometimes labour in vain. The thought in the second stanza, if not altogether new to poetry, has something in it very striking, is prettily introduced and well turned. This little piece, considered: as the production of a girl who could neither write nor read, is a wonderful performance. It is nature's poet delivering the dictates of her heart in the words which love has suggested, and "snatching a grace beyond the reach of art." This Finnish Sappho, amidst all the snows of her ungenial climate, discovers all the warmth of the poetess of Lesbos. (1802: 317–18)

The struggle between assumptions of national origin for songs and the equally compelling notion of individual creation was to rage in folkloristic scholarship for much of the next century.

For some, like Porthan, the mournful but defiant speaker of *Jos minun tuttuni tulisi* became a specifically "Finnish" voice, a trope of national distinctiveness that obscured any reference to local or lived realities. The national imprint of *Jos minun tuttuni tulisi* remains evident in Johann Goethe's literary translation of the song in 1810. Goethe titled his poem *Finnisches Lied* (Finnish Song), placing it alongside similarly reworked songs from German, Swiss, Sicilian, and Romany.[2] The national significance is also evident in the Swedish writer C. G. Zetterqvist's odd literary tribute to the lyric. Zetterqvist, clearly transfixed by the song and intrigued by the notion of translating it, set out during the years 1842–59 to create an anthology of translations of the text into all the world's languages; he amassed some 467 translations before abandoning the project in exhaustion (Kuusi 1963: 389).

As poets enshrined the song's lines as embodiments of the Finnish character, composers made similar bows to its melody. Collections of folk songs, arranged for piano accompaniment and published under national rubrics, became popular items for the bourgeois or aristocratic sitting rooms of Europe. Europaeus's appealing Ingrian melody was soon being performed heartily as a "Finnish melody" in Finland, Sweden, and Denmark and found its way into a variety of parlor and school anthologies, including H. A. Reinholm's *Suomen Kansan Laulantoja* (1834–76) and Karl Collan and colleagues' *Valituita Suomalaisia Kansan-Lauluja, Pianon muka-soinnolle sovitettuja* (1857–71). This national function of music has by no means ended, in Finland or elsewhere in northern Europe. In the case of Finland, Tina Ramnarine's fine study *Ilmatar's Inspirations* (2003) charts the continued nationalizing functions of contemporary folk-derived music in the ongoing construction of a modern Finnish identity, and similar observations could be made in connection with music in many other parts of northern Europe (e.g., Goertzen 1997). The effects of such music publications on folk musicians during the era in which folk songs were first being recorded—a crucial element in this case—is examined in detail in chapter 6.

Jos minun tuttuni tulisi thus became an emblem of a Finnish national character, a tool in "imagining" a community that would eventually become its own nation-state (Anderson 1983). One of the great architects in this process, Elias Lönnrot, included a version of *Jos minun tuttuni tulisi* in his 1840–41 anthology, *Kanteletar* (Bk. II, no. 43), a lyric sequel to his seminal epic *Kalevala* (1835). Describing the composition of lyric songs in general, he wrote: "They are not made, but rather they make themselves, forming, maturing, and acquiring their final appearance without the attention of any single composer" (1841: "Alkulause," iii). As the song reflects a national consciousness, in other words, so it also arises from a collective creation, one that makes the folk song truly the property of the nation as a whole. In Lönnrot's view, individual ideas and impressions pass from one person to the next like water vapor in the air, until, at last, they coalesce, falling to the earth, like rain, in the form of a completed song. The theory of "communal creation" would remain central in folk song scholarship for the rest of the century, gaining an authoritative garb in the writings of Francis B. Gummere (1901). Still, in 1915, John Lomax could describe the folk songs he collected unproblematically as the collective creations of the young American nation. Crucially, this collective view contained within itself a nascent theory of folk reception: the song is purportedly formed by the collective aesthetic and formal decisions of the community at large, not by the conscious decisions of a singular composer.

Acerbi's musings on the Finnish Sappho, however, also had their followers. The communal creation theory gradually came under fire. In the historical-geographic research that followed, the question of reception became obscured, as scholarship shifted toward reconstructing the identity, era, and circumstances of the putative composer(s) of each item of folklore. This shift toward origins became a grounding principle in studies of the first half of the twentieth century, rendering audiences and their reception of songs merely imperfect implements of "transmission." In the area of Finnish lyric research, Väinö Salminen (1917) initiated this trend in his study of western Ingrian wedding songs. He attempted to determine the place of origin and historical development over time for each song in his study. Kaarle Krohn applied his historical-geographic method to lyric only late in his career, after extensive work on epic, folktales, and charms. His 1931 work, *Tunnelmarunojen tutkimuksia* (Studies in Lyric Poetry), focuses on songs about the act of singing and posits origins for them in either western Finnish clerical circles or among illiterate southern Finnish and Estonian peasant women. With respect to *Jos minun tuttuni tulisi*, Matti Kuusi (1963: 391) compared the characteristics of a wide array of versions to conclude that its composer was a well-educated female poet of the late medieval period. Kuusi argued for according lyric composers the respect that they deserve as artists: where nineteenth-century scholars saw pure unlettered emotion, Kuusi discerned artful authorial choice. Yet the historical-geographic method left little room for valuing folk audiences, which became synonymous with processes of distortion and decay.

Case 3. *Casadh an tSúgáin*

Chorus:
Má bhíonn tú liom, bí liom,
    A ghrádh gheal mo chroidhe
Má bhíonn tú liom, bí liom,
    Do ló gus d'oidhch,'
Má bhíonn tú liom, bí liom,
    Gach orlach ann do chroidhe

’S é mo leun a’s mo lom
nach liom trathnóna thu mar mhnaoi.

An g-cluin tu mé a ghiolla, tá ag iarraidh grádh,
Fill a-bhaile arís a’s fan bliadhain eile mar táir,
Tháinig me asteach i dteach a raibh grádh geal mo chroidhe
A’s chuir an chailleach amach ar chasadh an tsugáin mé.

B’ait liom bean a d’fhanfadh a bliadhain le n-a grádh
B’ait liom bean a d’fhanfadh bliadhain uile agus a lá,
Níor bh’ait liom an bhean bheidheadh leat-sa agus liomsa arís ar ball.
’S í mo ghrádh an bhean a d’fhanfadh ar an aon stáid amháin.

A’s cad é an cat marbh do sheól ann san tír seó mé
A’s a liacht cailín deas d’fhágbhaidh mé mo dhéigh,
Ni truimide mise sin, s ni buaileadh orm é,
A’s gur minic do bhain bean slat do bhuailfeadh í féin.

A’s shíos i Sligeach chuir me eólas ar na mhnáibh,
Agus shias i nGaillimh d’ól mé leó fá mo sháith etc.

————————

Chorus:
If you are mine, be mine,
    White love of my heart;
If you are mine, be mine,
    By day and by night;
If you are mine, be mine,
    Every inch in thy heart,
And my misfortune and misery
That you are not with me in the evening for wife.

[The maiden answers:]
“Do you hear me, gilly, who are seeking love?
Return home again, and remain another year as you are.”

[The harper says:]
"I came into a house where the bright love of my heart was,
And the hag put me out a-twisting of the suggaun.

I would like a woman who would wait her year for her love;
I would like a woman who would wait a whole year and her day;
I'd not like the woman who would be with you and again,
     on the spot with me:
My love is the woman who would remain in the one state only.

And what was the dead cat which guided me into this country,
And the numbers of pretty girls I left behind me?
I am not the heavier for that, and I was not beaten by it,
And sure a woman often cut a rod would beat herself.

And down in Sligo I gained a knowledge of women,
And back in Galway I drank with them my enough, etc.
     (Hyde 1893: 74–75)

Under the title *An Suísín Ban* (The White Coverlet) Douglas Hyde provides the first translation of a lyric that was to play a key role in the dramatic and literary history of Ireland. His notation, included in Hyde's seminal work, *Love Songs of Connacht* (1893), is not, however, the song's first instance in print. James Hardiman had included a transcription of several of its verses in the first volume of his 1831 *Irish Minstrelsy; or, the Bardic Remains of Ireland* ([1831] 1971: 195–96). The song there is placed in an addendum to a lengthy account of the life and repertoire of the famed Irish harper Carolan (see chap. 6). After discussing itinerant music making and gentlemen poets in some detail, Hardiman closes his addendum with this statement: "From among the many sprightly songs which once were favorites with the roving fraternity . . . the following are selected for the Irish reader" (194). After providing three verses of *Casadh an tSúgáin*, Hardiman adds: "The foregoing are given only as specimens of a class of song formerly fashionable with the 'Ranting Irishman,' a character somewhat resembling the 'Drunken Barnaby' of our English neighbours, but now rather rare in Ireland." It is clear from these statements that Hardiman sees the song as belonging to a specific thematic group within Irish lyrics and as integrally associated with a particular kind of wandering musician-performer. This is, in other words, an attributive interpretation, finding meaning through associating the song with a particular poet or type of performer. Presumably the viewpoint within the song—its inscribed speaker—refers to that sort of character, one whom Hardiman describes elsewhere in his study:

> A race of gentlemen, as they call themselves, who, too poor to support themselves, are, however, much above any commercial or manufacturing profession. I have known some of them without home, wander for months together from house to house, without the ceremony of an invitation. They ate and drank freely every where, and it would be deemed a great infraction of hospitality to shew them by any indication that they were not welcome. ([1831] 1971: 170).

Hardiman attributes this negative view of itinerant gentlemen to a "modern writer," refraining from identifying the person specifically. It would seem that he assumes that the class of men he describes, as well as their favorite lyrics, are very familiar to his Irish-speaking audience. And in this light, the importunate tone of the song's text takes on deeper meaning, as we hear both the demands and the boasts of a speaker who seems to hold himself in particularly high regard but who does not seem to be finding a welcome in his present situation.

In contrast to Hardiman's cursory and rather cryptic remarks, Hyde's account provides substantially more discussion of the song and its meaning. In his translation, Hyde breaks up one of the stanzas into a dialogue, labeling the interlocutors "The maiden" and "The harper." He also provides a narrative explanation of the situation in the song:

> Tis the cause of this song—a bard who gave love to a young woman, and he came into the house where she herself was with her mother at the fall of night. The old woman was angry, him to come, and she thought to herself what would be the best way to put him out again, and she began twisting a suggaun, or straw rope. She held the straw, and she put the bard a-twisting it. The bard was going backwards according as the suggaun was a-lengthening, until at last he went out on the door and he ever-twisting. When the old woman found him outside she rose up of a leap and struck the door to in his face. She then flung his harp out to him through the window, and told him to be going. (1893: 75–77)

Here, then, we are given a narrativized interpretation that subsumes Hardiman's more general attribution under the rubric of a particular narrative figure, an unwelcome harper. Specific textual details in the account match specific details in the song: we know through the prose account who the "hag" is (i.e., the disapproving farmwife) and why she set the speaker to twisting a hay rope (i.e., as a ploy to get him out of the house). Some details remain unclear—for example, "the dead cat which guided me into this country," why the woman must resort to such an elaborate ruse to rid herself of the guest, and what sort of maiden it is he is courting. Yet the specificity of the narrative is such that it seemingly trumps all more general interpretive avenues, leading one to feel that herein lies the *real* meaning of the song, even if, in some ways, the explanation raises as many questions as answers.

Casadh an tSúgáin is a favorite instrumental piece as well, and many performers, past and present, play its air, or one of several airs that go by the name, without any recourse to the song text. Geraldine Cotter (1983: 40), for instance, provides the following transcription of the tune for the tin whistle (Example 1.4).

EXAMPLE 1.4

Richard Robinson (2004) offers a somewhat different version of the air in his collection of folk song melodies (Example 1.5).

EXAMPLE 1.5

The piece is popular among Irish fiddlers as well, as Hugh Shields (1993: 71) notes in his study of Micky Doherty, a twentieth-century performer from Donegal. Although Doherty did not know any words to his air, he did know a story about it, one very similar to the explanation that Hyde provided. Shields summarizes the tale as follows:

> A traveling fiddler—an undesirable guest in a house with only two women—was got rid of before nightfall by their asking his help to twist a rope, giving him the end that made him back out of the door as the rope got longer, and shutting it on him once he was outside. (1993: 71)

Shields notes that Doherty regularly told this tale whenever he performed the air. In a performance situation that included only the melody, then, the narrative was still offered as a means of understanding and appreciating the song. Even when the words that would help to elucidate it are absent, in other words, Irish performers and their audiences found narrative explanations important to provide. It is also interesting to note that Doherty and his narrative's hoodwinked fiddler share the same profession. This may indicate some degree of personalization in Doherty's experience of the song, recourse to the associative axis that would complement but not displace the narrativized interpretation on which it relies.

These observations regarding the interpretation of *Casadh an tSúgáin* map well, in fact, the hermeneutic norms operative in Irish lyric tradition. As Shields has pointed out (1991; 1993: 58 ff.), Irish lyric singers and audiences—both in English and in Irish—relied heavily on the situational axis of interpretation, especially on narrativized explanations. Songs such as *Casadh an tSúgáin* were assumed to relate to some story, termed variously *míniú* (explanation), *brí* (force, meaning) or *údar* (authority), which could be solicited from the performer before or after the song itself (Shields 1991: 48). The associated narrative makes sense of the song's details, explicating, as the collector Enrí Ó Muirgheasa put it, "all the circumstances which are merely hinted at in the verses" (Shields 1993: 71). Often, the narrative contains details that go well beyond what one could reasonably glean from the song text alone: for example, the names and homes of the characters may be specified, their precise relations described, the events leading up to the lyric moment or following it recounted. A good audience— like a good performer—is expected to know the tale behind a song. And if audience members do not, they should know to ask, so as to become properly informed. So intimately associated are song, melody, and commentary that Shields describes them not as separate entities but as a single unity, a chantefable (58 ff.). It is a unity, however, in which the commentary need not be enunciated at the time the song is performed; it is enough that the commentary exists, and that people know it—or know to expect it—when listening to the song.

This robust reliance on narrative interpretations is shared in varying degrees by a number of other lyric traditions in northern Europe, including Scottish Gaelic, as I discuss later. The title of John Shaw's (2000) fine study of the Gaelic songs of Lauchie MacLellan is illustrative in itself: *Brìgh an Òrain: A Story in Every Song*. It is also easy to imagine, as Shields (1993: 58–69) demonstrates in his study, that prose commentaries could develop within a lyric tradition as a formerly narrative song evolves toward lyric content and form. As details of plot give way to a more heightened focus on characterization, emotion, or dialogue, an accompanying narrative could furnish the elements of the story no longer evident in the song. In his 1957 study of the Anglo-American ballad *Mary Hamilton,* Tristram Coffin theorizes that ballads undergo such evolution from their original compositions to their eventual attainment of aesthetic "perfection." In the initial stage, a ballad could be seen as an individual's creation, possessing some valuable or lasting elements and a clear plot but also possessing "frills of a poetic style that are too 'sophisticated' for the folk" (313). In the second stage, oral transmission by successive singers "wears away" that which is substandard, creating an aesthetically honed, effective work. In the process, narrative detail is lost, while "emotional core"—or lyric quality—is enhanced, so that a ballad "embodies a basic human reaction to a dramatic situation" (311). In the final "degenerate" stage, the ballad develops into either a full-blown lyric or a nonsense song, its narrative core too "decayed" to balance its emotional content. Coffin sought in his theory to chart a middle way between the outdated notion of communal creation and the equally confining focus on textual history alone. The strength of his theory lies in its integration of individuals and tradition: both play a part in the evolution of a folk song. And integral to his model is the notion that audiences shape content, if only through how they reperform the songs that they hear.

While Coffin's theory may work for ballad in some cases, the Irish tendency toward narrativization appears less compensatory than compulsory. Shields (1993) makes several points that illustrate the prominence of this interpretive strategy in particular. He recounts cases in which a spoken commentary accompanies a song even when the text of the song (e.g., a ballad) is entirely comprehensible on its own (64). And he notes a case in which his informant felt compelled to improvise a commentary where he did not know one before (72). Such details indicate a view in which song and narrative are seen as inextricably linked, twin embodiments of the Irish ideal of traditional knowledge, *seanchas*.

In contrast to the first two cases presented in this chapter, the scholarly interpretation of *Casadh an tSúgáin* appears, as the above accounts of Hardiman and Hyde indicate, to follow the established folk hermeneutics rather closely. Where *Moarsi fávrrot* and *Jos minun tuttuni tulisi* were subjected to markedly different interpretive regimes by elite scholars, scholars of *Casadh an tSúgáin* appear to have been content to quote or summarize the tales told to them by performers and audiences, embroidering them only somewhat. Perhaps this openness derived from the later era of their studies (the late nineteenth century as opposed to the mid-eighteenth century), or the Irish nationalist interest in celebrating collective wisdom and heritage as an emblem of national worth. Perhaps, too, the readiness of performers to supply such explanations and the seeming aptness of the narratives as keys to understanding otherwise cryptic song details played a role as well. Whatever the case, we find scholarly and artistic renderings of *Casadh an tSúgáin* more in line with the notions of pastiche or reproduction than with more extensive processes of reinscription or co-optation.

William Butler Yeats adapted the song's narrative background as the basis for his short story *The Twisting of the Rope* (1897). From the very beginning of his career, Yeats took a powerful interest in the figure of the Celtic bard, as the title of his first collection of poems—*The Wandering of Oisin and Other Poems*—makes clear (Forkner 1980: 79). In his 1897 short story, the bard becomes embodied in the figure of Red Hanrahan, an incorrigible drinker and womanizer who nonetheless holds a mystical power in his poems. Hanrahan arrives at a house where he is greeted by the farmer but immediately distrusted by the farmer's wife. The local populace fears Hanrahan's temper and the damage he can do through his vituperative poetry (an allusion to medieval accounts of bardic satires and later continuations of that tradition, as discussed in chapter 6). Hanrahan makes a beeline for the farmer's lovely daughter, Oona, who is soon beguiled by his dancing and fair words, as he recounts for her the story of Deirdre and the Sons of Usna (see chap. 2). After more of Hanrahan's words of romance and his recitation of a fine love lyric, Oona is completely taken in. As if to answer the incompleteness of the typical narrative explanation, Yeats has Oona's vexed mother and her friend enunciate the reason for the clever ruse that will finally rid them of the bard:

> Oona's mother was crying, and she said, "He has put an enchantment on Oona. Can we not get the men to put him out of the house?"
>
> "That is one thing you cannot do," said the other woman, "for he is a poet of the Gael, and you know well if you would put a poet of the Gael out of the house, he will put a curse on you that would wither the corn in the fields and dry up the milk of the cows, if it had to hang in the air seven years." (Yeats [1897] 1980: 79)

Fearing this supernatural repercussion—which appears to hold only if the poet is bodily expelled from the house rather than stepping outside of his own accord—the women hatch the hay-rope ploy. The entire household plays along as the farmwife asks Hanrahan for help in twisting a rope to repair some thatch on the farm's haystack. Wishing to further impress his Oona, Hanrahan twists his rope prodigiously until he finally crosses the threshold. The farmwife slams the door in his face as thanks. Yeats writes:

> He sat down on a big stone, and he began swinging his right arm and singing slowly to himself, the way he did always to hearten himself when every other thing failed him. And whether it was that time or another time he made the song that is called to this day "The Twisting of the Rope," and that begins "What was the dead cat that put me in this place," is not known. (81)

In the end, Yeats depicts Hanrahan resisting the advances of the queen of the fairies at Slieve Echtge, a sign of his high intrinsic worth but also fated ill luck in his dealings with human women.

Yeats's rendering depicts the bard as a good deal more mystical and serious than he appears in the narrative explanations quoted above. Nonetheless, it is clear that Yeats relies on the folk tradition for the core of his story. His portrayal of the duped suitor as a powerful poet parallels the personalizing tendency of the fiddler Micky Doherty to see the suitor as a fiddler: that is, Yeats's story uses the character and narrative to aggrandize his own calling as a poet. In this way, Yeats seems to elide folk and elite interests into a single interpretive community, a single tradition: an act that itself had profound implications not only for the study of Irish folklore but also for the political and cultural aspirations of the Irish nationalists.

This program of embracing Irish folk tradition, even among Anglo-Irish intellectuals who may have had little prior knowledge of these materials, came to a head in the works of Yeats, Hyde, and Lady Gregory and the founding of the Abbey Theatre. It was in the interest of creating the new theater's first play that Hyde—later president of the Republic of Ireland—read and adapted Yeats's story into his own *Casadh an tSúgáin* (1901). In Hyde's play, Hanrahan and Oona are joined by a jealous suitor, Sheumas O'Heran, who helps the farmwife (Maurya) and her friend to carry out their plan against Hanrahan. Maurya's husband, on the other hand, is now dead, as she explains. In fact, the old bond of friendship between the husband and Hanrahan is what has drawn the poet back to the locale. Drawing in part on stray details from other versions of the song *Casadh an tSúgáin*, Maurya declares (in Lady Gregory's translation):

> He was a schoolmaster down in Connacht; but he used to have every trick worse than another; ever making songs he used to be, and drinking whiskey and setting quarrels afoot among the neighbours with his share of talk. They say there isn't a woman in the five provinces that he wouldn't deceive. He is worse than Donal na Greina long ago. But the end of the story is that the priest routed him out of the parish altogether; he got another place then, and followed on at the same tricks until he was routed out again, and another again with it. Now he has neither place nor house nor anything, but he to be going the country, making songs and getting a night's lodging from the people; nobody will refuse him, because they are afraid of him. He's a great poet, and maybe he'd make a rann [doggerel] on you that would stick to you for ever, if you were to anger him. (Hyde [1901] 1903: 204–5)

Hanrahan and Oona perform an extended poetic dialogue full of elaborate compliments for each other (and drawn from other lyric songs Hyde had collected), while the frustrated Sheumas and Maurya look on. In the end, however, Hanrahan falls for the trick, walks through the doorway and is shut out as a result. Oona is distressed, but will feel better tomorrow, all agree, once the poet's spell has worn off. As with Yeats's version, then, Hyde's play adds details to fill out the story, yet it introduces relatively little that lies outside of either the song text or the usual narrative explanations. Significantly, however, as in Yeats's rendering, the song itself is not included in the play: narrative, melody, and song text can seemingly all be simultaneously invoked by mention of any one of the three.

Toward a Receptionalist Approach to Folk Lyric

As the three cases discussed above amply illustrate, lyric interpretation varies considerably from culture to culture, while relying ultimately on a limited number of interpretive axes. Norms exist within communities as to which axis of interpretation takes precedence and how the axes interrelate. A knowledgeable audience learns how to interpret a lyric properly within its culture just as it learns how to appraise the song's outward form and verbal or musical details. In a certain sense, all lyrics are what Shields (1991) refers to as chantefables: complex works that encompass both a fixed text and performance style and a more nebulous background and meaning that accompanies the song. The exact content of this background follows traditions within the community that performs and values the lyric.

The approach to the lyric presented here draws on the research findings of many scholars. On a certain basic level, it relies on the structuralist explorations of scholars of the 1970s and after who sought to uncover the stable, predictable elements of verbal art. Aili Nenola (1974) offers a Proppian analysis of elements in Ingrian wedding laments, and Vaira Vikis-Freiburgs (1989) analyzes Latvian lyrics to discover their formula types. Lauri Harvilahti's (1992) study of generative formulas within the Ingrian lyric tradition demonstrates the ways in which recurrent structures can give rise to new structures in the same vein. Further structural studies present typologies of depicted situations and speakers in the songs (Krnjević 1991; Propp 1993) and investigate the possible relation between the lyric's speaker and its probable composer (Bragg 1993). Formal characteristics, such as the use of first-person pronouns, have also received careful and enlightening examination (e.g., Harvilahti 1992; Timonen 1989). While these studies focus primarily on outward form or textual logic of the performed lyric rather than delve into its interpretive apparatus, they demonstrate cogently the orderly and coherent manner in which folklore is constructed and handled within living communities. If a song's very structure is shaped by tradition— as these studies clearly indicate—then we should not find it surprising to discover that its interpretations are likewise determined by traditional norms.

This structuralist approach can be combined with an earlier scholarly interest in function, a topic that brings the relations of performer, folklore, and audience into sharp focus. Functionalist scholars of the twentieth century maintained that folklore operates in the context of performer-audience interactions, in which both sides may use the item of folklore to exert control or influence over the other. Elsa Enäjärvi-Haavio (1935), Lauri Honko (1963, 1974), and Aili Nenola (1974, 1982), for instance, contribute valuable perspectives on the performance and functions of lyrics within Finnish, Karelian, and Ingrian communities. From this perspective, it is not hard to arrive at the idea that audiences possess interpretive norms for evaluating folkloric performances, norms that help to determine their responses and shape the roles that such performances could play. The current study seeks to chart more particularly the shared aesthetic and hermeneutic values that help performer and audience to make sense of each other and of their lyrics as they perform them.

The attention to the meaningfulness of lyrics in performers' personal lives signaled by a number of researchers (e.g., Abrahams 1970; Porter 1976; Pentikäinen 1978; Renwick 1980; Timonen 1989, 1990; Ilomäki 1990) provides a further valuable foundation for a broader receptionalist approach to lyric meaning. Given that a performer is in a very real sense also an audience member, one who expresses an evaluation of a song simply by performing it, such a focus brings to light wider issues of interpretation and hermeneutics. Thus, such examinations not only highlight the personalizing interpretations of the associative axis, they also open the door to the study of interpretation in general, as I show. These folkloristic works join a vein of analysis initiated earlier in medieval studies, for example, Dorothy Whitelock's perceptive *The Audience of Beowulf* (1951). Whitelock sought to use the medieval text as a key to making judgments regarding the creator of the poem and his audience. Although later scholars (e.g., Baum 1960) took issue with Whitelock's conclusions, the notion of reconstructing audience knowledge became an accepted part of medieval scholarship.

These various strands of ethnographic inquiry have been united powerfully in the works of John Miles Foley, a folklorist, classicist, and medievalist who has written a broad range of studies in the area of oral tradition. In his seminal work, *Immanent Art: From Structure to Meaning in Traditional Oral Epic* (1991), Foley develops a set of terms and methods that make the receptionalist study of oral tradition possible. While looking at the structurally stable formal elements of oral epic traditions—recurrent formulas and story patterns, memorable characters around whom certain kinds of narratives cluster, and so on—Foley recognizes a rich stock of associations or understandings that an audience may bring to bear on a given song's content or devices. The very mention of a name within a song, or the use of a typical turn of phrase, may set off a process of association in the minds of knowledgeable audience members that deepens and adds nuance to the performance. Foley terms this set of interpretive resources *immanence* and its application to any particular instance of song *traditional referentiality*. By attending to aspects of meaning that may be triggered by song content but that ultimately reside in the audience's competence in receiving the song, Foley's work calls for serious attention to the question of how one should "read an oral poem," a notion he explores in a more recent study of that title (2002).

While Foley's overarching theories provide an ideal foundation for my study, the work of scholars engaged in the analysis of particular song traditions have proved invaluable for examining lyric interpretation in northern Europe. Especially noteworthy in this respect are the fine works of Hugh Shields (1981, 1991, 1993) and Senni Timonen's (2004) comprehensive study of lyrics in the Kalevala meter. Shields documents with great precision and interest the hermeneutic practices of Irish lyric tradition, providing a framework that can be compared fruitfully with the song traditions of other areas. Timonen examines in detail the layers of personal and communal meaning associated with lyric songs in Karelia and Ingria, furnishing insights and examples that have greatly enriched this study. While my work differs from these in its comparative perspective, it relies on the culture-specific studies of earlier scholars in the area of folklore studies, ethnomusicology, and medieval studies. With these various studies in hand, we are able to examine lyrics cross-culturally from the perspective of folk reception, that is, to examine the sophisticated and nuanced ways in which traditional audiences in northern Europe have made sense of traditional songs.

The chapters that follow, then, draw on this rich tradition of research to explore lyric interpretation in a variety of places and times. Each chapter, just as each case above, illuminates different aspects of the generic, associative, and situational axes of interpretation, thereby underscoring the specificity of interpretive traditions in various cultures. At the same time, the perspectives together suggest a range of choices within which lyric interpretation may occur, sketching a delimited field of meaning-making common to northern Europe lyric traditions in general.

Chapter 2 looks at lyric songs, in particular, formal laments, as they appear in medieval manuscripts containing prose or epic poetry. I argue that the relations of these lyric "interludes" and their surrounding narratives act as models of norms for lyric interpretation existing in the medieval era. Interestingly, despite outward similarities in both the laments and the kinds of heroic narrative in which they are found from culture to culture, these interpretive norms seem to vary, with strongly narrativized lyric hermeneutics in medieval Scandinavian and Irish texts but more proverbialized understandings in Old English. Further, by looking transhistorically at Irish materials, we are also able to gauge the degree to which such lyrics and their associated narratives could exist independent of one another. Rather than see lament and narrative as integrally and inextricably linked, in other words, we find that the two elements could become uncoupled over time, with new lyric interludes or new narrative contexts substituted in response to changes in the form or content of the surviving element. What this situation suggests is the existence of norms of interpretation that helped medieval compilers and their audiences to *expect* varying kinds of linkages between lyric and narrative. The relation endured, while the specific components linked in the relation could change.

Chapter 3 looks at lyrics of varying kinds that contain second-person address forms, what I have termed *invocation.* Looking at the interpretation of such typically invocational lyric genres as the Sámi *joik,* I survey their complex meanings and mechanisms. I also compare them to other types of vocal communications in northern European tradition, for example, stylized calls used by Scandinavian and Karelian herders to communicate over long distances and ubiquitous magical charms intended to compel entities to behave in ways advantageous to the human performer or a client. Mourning laments addressed to the deceased and wedding songs addressed to bride, groom, or other family members are also discussed. Finally, the Scottish *piobaireachd* is compared to *joik.* Here we find again a highly lyrical, emotive variety of invocation but one understood typically via a narrativized rather than a proverbialized interpretation. Together, the various kinds of invocational lyric explored in this chapter shed light on the nuances of direct address as an aesthetic choice, communicative device, and mystical act.

Chapter 4 draws on the observations of the previous chapter to examine a body of lyric songs related directly to Christianity in northern Europe. The religious lyric, which diffused into northern Europe from the south along with the Christian faith itself, possessed its own complex norms for interpretation. In early medieval hymns, this hermeneutic is largely narrativized or attributional, but gradually more proverbialized interpretations come to dominate. The individual experience, as well as the individual entreaty, is couched in the collective through the shaping words and images of the lyric. Following the arguments of medievalists in the well-documented area of the English religious lyric, I suggest that these norms of interpretation diffused into secular lyrics as well, creating new possibilities and new expectations within the secular song traditions of the region. The rich cross-fertilization between religious and secular lyric in late medieval music is surveyed as a measure of the spread of both aesthetic form and interpretive norms in musical traditions.

Chapter 5 examines interpretation along the generic axis. I argue that the highly predictable formal and thematic features of medieval and postmedieval secular lyric—its recurrent images, standardized descriptions, and stereotyped speaker personae—could actually constitute a powerful and effective interpretive framework in which to locate any given performance or version of a song. I look for the ways in which audiences of the Elizabethan era were expected to receive and interpret such lyrics by examining the musical interludes and their functions in the plays of William Shakespeare. Shakespeare uses characters' attitudes toward lyric songs as a key means of shedding light on their personalities, foibles, and convictions. His lyrics, some already familiar to his audience from contemporary song culture, others apparently composed specifically for the play, set the tone for scenes and advance the narrative in certain directions. In so doing, I argue, Shakespeare provides both positive and negative models for how persons *ought* to relate to lyric songs in the estimation of a playwright who made his living playing to the aesthetic and emotional tastes of his audiences.

Chapter 6 examines figures of third-person attribution from the medieval down to the early modern era in a range of northern European cultures. Medieval bard figures such as the Welsh Taliesin or Dafydd ap Gwilym or the Irish mad Suibhne are compared to the Swedish troubadour Carl Michael Bellman,

the Irish harper Toirdhealbhach Ó Cearbhalláin (Carolan), the Irish fiddler Antoine Ó Reachtabhraigh (Raftery), and the Finnish kantele player Kreeta Haapasalo. The discussion explores how each of these figures used interpretive norms
within their respective musical traditions to maintain and propel their careers,
while their audiences drew on interpretive norms of attribution to comprehend
and appreciate their songs. As in the previous chapter, we find stylization here
not as a source of falsity or inferior quality but rather as a powerful and effective means of evoking meaning in a performer-audience situation unfolding in
briefer encounters and tied to the exchange of hospitality or remuneration.

Finally, chapter 7 allows us to return to the issue of personalization and
its relation to other kinds of interpretation in the performance and experience
of lyric songs. By looking at the songs of one traditional singer, Michael Lyne
of Tandragee, West Meath, Ireland, and the ways he and his wife, Lizzy, discuss
his songs, I am able to suggest some of the rich complexities of personalization as
a process in lyric interpretation. Personal meanings underscore certain aspects
of a song and realign some of its details, sometimes to the point of contradicting
the song's text. While intensely personal, these meanings are not necessarily private, nor are they necessarily fleeting or temporary. Rather, they may act as a
foundation from which all other aspects of the song's meanings are viewed, jus-
tifications for the hard work of building, maintaining, and performing a repertoire of songs over time.

In a field that has privileged narrative genres—epic, ballad, legend, tale—the
question of interpretation of non-narrative genres offers interesting alternative
avenues for the exploration of the workings of folklore in daily life. Lyric songs
in northern Europe are no simple matter, even if their outward form sometimes
makes claims for simplicity, transparency, and spontaneity. In fact, as I hope the
following chapters demonstrate, lyric songs possess their own complex rules not
only for composition and performance but also for interpretation, rules that
competent performers and audiences alike acquire as they become familiar with
the genre. These traditions, these norms for receiving and evaluating lyric songs,
operate as ambient systems of meaning, common ground from which individual
performances arise and through which each individual performance is understood. Ranging from the medieval to the modern, and from Ingrian to Irish, the
lyrics surveyed in this study serve as illustrations of a wider reality: the com-
plexity and nuance of meaning-making in oral tradition.

Pausing in a Narrative's March

The Interpretation of Lyrics within Epics

Blíadain di-ssi trá i fail Chonchobuir ocus risin ré sin ni•tib gen
ngáire ocus ni•dóid a sáith do bíud na cotluth ocus ni•túargaib
a cenn dia glún. In tan didiu do•mbertis na hairfiti dí, is and
as•bered-si in reicni sea sís.

Vernam Hull, ed., *Longes Mac n-Uislenn* (1949)

———

Deirdre spent the year following Noísiu's death with Conchubur,
and, during that time, she neither laughed nor smiled, nor did she
ever have her fill of food or sleep. She never lifted her head from
her knee, and, whenever musicians were brought to her, she recited
this poem.

Jeffrey Gantz, *Early Irish Myths and Sagas* (1981)

Typically, I have argued, lyrics are interpreted through some combination of the
generic, associative, and situational axes, but emphases vary depending on culture, period, or variety of lyric. Here I explore more thoroughly the workings of
the associative and situational axes by comparing lyrics that belong to a single
genre, the formal lament. We will see that even when generic and associative
norms appear very similar across three cultures, interpretive factors along the
situational axis may vary greatly. Further, I hope to demonstrate methodologi-
cally the ways in which textual evidence—in this case, prose and poetic texts
from the medieval period—can shed light on past norms of interpretation. By
attending to the representation of interpretive acts within these texts, as well
as the relation of the laments themselves to the narratives within which they
occur, we can glimpse the workings of lyric hermeneutics from centuries past.

This glimpse allows us to examine the degree to which some interpretive norms may endure over long periods within a single culture.

Some of the earliest lyric songs recorded in northern Europe appear within the textual fabric of prose or poetic narratives. Long narrative lays regarding heroes of the past—exemplars of the epic genre—were once broadly distributed throughout many parts of Europe. Northern Europe was no exception, and in its most peripheral and linguistically distinctive areas, the tradition has survived even into the present. The heroic lay (Irish and Gaelic *laoi[dh]*, *duan*) in Irish and Gaelic bears thematic and even musicological resemblance to the *virret* or *runot* of Balto-Finnic peoples of the eastern Baltic (Shields 1993: 10–23; DuBois 1995: 18–23; Lippus 1995). Both traditions further resemble the epic texts preserved by medieval hands in Iceland, England, Ireland, and Wales and in content echo masterpieces of prose narrative—the Irish and Scandinavian sagas—produced during the same or somewhat later period. Often, while focusing on mythological events or the exploits of great leaders or heroes, such texts incorporate or stand in generic juxtaposition to lyric songs, performances that give human voice and emotion to the narrative moments depicted. When incorporated in some way into epics, such lyric "interludes" embody and ennoble the associated narrative's characters. The narrative in turn supplies the interpretive framework within which to appreciate the broad themes, oblique references, and small details of the lyrics. At once independent of its accompanying narrative and closely bound to it by physical placement and textual reference, the interpolated lyric offers interesting models of interpretation along the situational axis. In this chapter, I examine embedded lyrics in three medieval textual traditions: Old Norse epic and saga, Old English epic, and Irish saga. While many generic and associative factors remain similar from one tradition to the next, interpretations along the situational axis vary. Some traditions tend toward highly narrativized interpretations closely linked to associated composers or subjects of laments. Others favor proverbialized understandings along the situational axis; that is, they gloss a particular lament as reflective of the typical experience of persons in a certain situation. Where Old Norse and Irish cases tie lyric and narrative into a seemingly close narrative unity (albeit one possibly fabricated by the compiler of the manuscript or rendition), the Old English case shows a looser connection, in which lyric serves as a more tangential commentary on a narrative situation. In all three cases, however, the association between the lyric and its surrounding text can be seen as an artistic, idealized representation of the mode of lyric interpretation operative within the community or society that produced and enjoyed the texts, an enunciation of the community's normative lyric hermeneutics.

Lyric songs expressing sorrow at the death of a leader, friend, or kinsman formed an important lyric subgenre during the medieval period, with formal laments and elegies continuing as a tradition in some parts of the region into the twentieth century. Ethnographically, it is possible to divide these songs into two broad varieties: spontaneous improvised laments, often performed by women during the funeral ritual and seldom remembered word-for-word thereafter, and formal laments or elegies, composed after the funeral by male or female poets in remembrance of a deceased figure, sometimes preserved in oral tradition for generations after. In practice, however, the two "varieties" can most aptly be regarded as opposite ends of a single generic continuum, and each depends on the other for part of its rhetorical and emotional weight. The spontaneous lament is seen to echo the high imagery and sentiments of the formal elegy; the formal lament often draws on images of spontaneity and erupting emotions characteristic of its improvised counterpart. In the medieval accounts examined here, the boundary between these extremes is blurred, as medieval authors offer their own idealized representations of mourning for great heroes. Part of the power of these passages, in other words, lies in their more or less fictive portrayal of memorable mourning and of exemplary performances of a highly valued genre. At the same time, their power also derives from interpretive expectations along the generic, associative, and situational axes: the competent audience should expect lamentation at the death of a hero, and the lyrics provided within an epic poem or saga answer this generic need.

MEDIEVAL SCANDINAVIA
Nú em ec svá lítil (Now am I so little)

Among the tenderest of the heroic lays preserved for us by the compiler of the thirteenth-century *Codex Regius* is the one he titled *Guðrúnaqviða* (The Lay of Guðrún), identified by later editors as "The First Lay of Guðrún." Focusing pointedly on the narrative moment immediately after the death of the hero, Sigurðr, the lay recounts his wife, Guðrún's, initial reaction to his murder. Dismayed both at her husband's sudden death and at the treachery of her sister-in-law and brothers who conspired against him, Guðrún sits silent at first. In a stanza that is repeated twice, the poet notes:

> Þeygi Guðrún   gráta mátti;
> svá var hon móðug   at mög dauðan
> oc harðhuguð   um hrer fylkis
>   (*Guðrúnarqviða I* str. 5, 11; Kuhn 1983: 202–3)

––––––––––

> Yet Guðrún   could not weep;
> so distressed was she   beside her dead husband
> and hardhearted   by the corpse of her king.

In an attempt to free her tears, kinswomen recount their own losses of husbands and sons but to no avail: Guðrún remains silent. At last, Guðrún's sister, Gullrönd, takes matters into her own hands. Pulling the shroud off the slain Sigurðr's body, she commands her sister to look upon her husband, kiss his lips, and experience his death concretely. Guðrún breaks down in tears, stoops over her husband's body, and utters a lament:

> Þá hné Guðrún,   höll við bólstri;
> haddr losnaði,   hlýr roðnaði,
> enn regns dropi   rann niðr um kné.

> Þá grét Guðrún,   Giúca dóttir,
> svá at tár flugo   tresc í gognom,
> oc gullo við   gæss í túni,
> mœrir fuglar,   er mær átti. . . .

> "Svá var minn Sigurðr   hiá sonom Giúca
> sem væri geirlaucr   ór grasi vaxinn,
> eða væri biartr steinn   á band dreginn,
> iarcnasteinn   yfir öðlingom.

> Ec þóttac oc   þióðans reccom
> hverri hærri   Herians dísi;

nú em ec svá lítil,   sem lauf sé
opt í iölstrom,   at iöfur dauðan.

Sacna ec í sessi   oc í sæingo
míns málvinar,   valda megir Giúca;
valda megir Giúca   míno bölvi
oc systr sinnar   sárom gráti."
    (*Guðrúnarqviða I* str. 15–16, 18–20; Kuhn 1983: 204–5)

————

Thus sank Guðrún   with grief in the hall
hair loosened,   cheeks reddened,
like drops of rain   tears trailed to her knees.

Thus wept Guðrún,   Gjúki's daughter,
so that tears flowed   through her tresses
and the geese in the farmyard   let up a din,
famous birds   that the mistress owned. . . .

"So was my Sigurðr   when compared to Gjúki's sons:
like a stalk of garlic   growing over blades of grass,
or like a gleaming stone   on a string of beads:
a gemstone   above noblemen.

I was also honored   by the prince's retinue
more than was worshiped   the *dísir* of Óðinn;
now I am as little   as a leaf
upon a willow   now that the king is dead.

I miss the hall   and the bed
of my companion in speech,   taken by Gjúki's sons
Gjúki's sons took him   to cause me grief
and to give their sister   tears of sorrow."

A shift from epic to lyric is, of course, an old and common feature of the
epic genre. Unwilling merely to *tell* of the heroine's sorrow, the poet may choose

to *show* it as well. "Code-switching" between epic and lyric may involve substantial stylistic and musical shifts; it may even violate gender norms, as Dwight
Reynolds (1991) has shown in the case of Egyptian epic. In many epic traditions,
the "quoted" lyric is invoked in an abridged, slightly altered form; nonetheless,
the quotation reproduces at least some key elements of the lyric as it would occur
outside of the epic performance, incorporating its imagery, meaning, and performative power into the unfolding narrative (DuBois 1995: 127 ff.).

It may be noted that this lay of Guðrún is not the only Eddaic poem to
treat this narrative moment in the Volsung story. The same event is recounted,
with some differences, in *Sigurðarqviða in scamma*. There, the dying Sigurðr
enjoins his Guðrún to weep but also to look to present needs, spiriting away
from the court the son who can someday avenge his father's death:

> Grátaðu, Guðrún, svá grimmliga,
> brúðr frumunga, þér brœðr lifa.
>
> Á ec til ungan erfinytia
> kannat hann firraz ór fiándgarði.
> (*Sigurðarqviða in scamma* str. 25–26; Kuhn 1983: 211)

> Weep, Guðrún, so fiercely
> young bride, while your brothers live.
>
> I have still a young heir
> He will have difficulty escaping this enemy hall.

Guðrún's chief expression of sorrow here is to clap her hands with terrific force
(str. 25, 29), an act that disturbs her flock of geese. This detail is repeated in
Guðrúnaqviða I (str. 16, above) and apparently held particular significance in
the tradition:

> Svá sló hon svára sinni hendi,
> at qvaðo við kálcar í vá
> oc gullo við gæss í túni.
> (*Sigurðarqviða in scamma* str. 29; Kuhn 1983: 211)

So she struck her hands   hard together,
so that the cups   clattered on the wall
and the geese in the farmyard   let up a din.

It is an image of clamor, squawking, and frenzy, connoting a total loss of deco-
rum at a moment of exceptional sorrow. Such a din is expected generically: it is
the ideal accompaniment and undisputed raison d'être for the lament.

In another, fragmentary lay included in the *Codex Regius* (*Brot af Sigurðurqviðo*), Guðrún curses her plotting kin, much as in the lines that follow the
above-quoted lament in *Guðrúnaqviða I*. Compare the passages:

Svá ér um lýða   landi eyðit,
sem ér um unnoð   eiða svarða;
mana þu, Gunnarr,   gullz um nióta,
þeir muno þér baugar   at bana verða,
er þú Sigurði   svarðir eiða.
(*Guðrúnarqviða I* str. 21; Kuhn 1983: 205)

———

May all who live here   depart this land
as you discarded   your sworn oaths;
you will obtain, Gunnarr,   no joy from the gold,
those rings will prove   your bane
for you to Sigurðr   swore an oath.

———

Þá qvað þat Guðrún,   Giúca dóttir:
"Mioc mælir þú   miclar firnar;
gramir hafi Gunnar,   götvað Sigurðar!
heiptgiarns hugar   hefnt scal verða."
(*Brot af Sigurðurqviðo* str. 11; Kuhn 1983: 199)

———

Then spoke Guðrún,   Gjúki's daughter:
"You speak   great abominations;

may fiends have Gunnar   for the death of Sigurðr!
a revenge of spiteful cares   it shall be."

In the poetic fragment, however, Guðrún's actual words of lamentation are not
included. Perhaps it is their absence that makes the poem seem fragmentary
to its medieval compiler, who places it on the same folio page as *Guðrúnaqviða*.
A "complete" account of the narrative moment presumably involves both a recounting of events and a rendering of its lyric moments.

In two other lays—*Guðrúnahvöt* and *Guðrúnaqviða II* (Kuhn 1983: 264–68,
224–31)—Guðrún's voice is heard again, although her "laments" here are largely
narrative paraphrases of the events of the Volsung epic rather than explicitly
presented lyric performances. The lament in these has become an artificial device or frame for the rendering of narrative. Yet it remains enunciated nonetheless, as if a moment of heroic death could not possibly pass without lamentation.
The rhetorical uses of the lament genre in these two poems illustrate the lament's centrality as an experiential component and organizing element of the
mourning event.

A comparison of these various interrelated accounts of Guðrún's grief reveals certain commonalities of understanding, along with some fundamentals
regarding the purpose and meaning of laments in medieval Scandinavian tradition. Clearly, it is considered important for a woman to lament her husband,
or in some other way to demonstrate her strong grief. Clapping, weeping, bend-
ing to the ground—all such physical manifestations of sorrow were expected
of the grieving woman. But performance of special verbal genres—the lament
and the curse—were also expected and could only be dispensed in situations in
which other needs took precedence (as, for example, saving one's son for future
vengeance). And the text of a lament—its expressions of frailty or helplessness,
its praise for the character and physique of the lost beloved, and its depiction of
a happier past now lost forever—was considered valuable enough not only to
remember but also to reperform or imaginatively re-create as a lyric response
to a well-known narrative. The lyric as such carries with it not only its textual
images of intense emotion but also a narrative record of the mourner and the
mourned and a historical assertion that mourning occurred.

Although the narrative account of death and the poetic rendering of mourning thus appear linked generically in this material, scholars of Old Norse poetry
have tended to take sides on which comes first. In his examination of the folkloric bases of the poetic *Edda*, Eleazar M. Meletinsky (1998) points to the fun-

damental similarities between Guðrún's lamentations and traditional funerary laments and lyric songs of sorrow ("everyday laments") from Russian tradition. Meletinsky suggests that such lyric material may be the structural basis as well as the thematic impetus behind these heroic lays: that is, Guðrún's lament may have given rise to its explanatory lay rather than the lay calling for an interpolated lyric. Such an amalgamation would have occurred, he posits, in the "archaic folkloric-literary environment" of Iceland, as South Germanic heroic traditions came into contact with older genres of "ritual-lyric" poetry (226).

Other scholars (e.g., Zeller 1939; Heusler 1941; de Vries 1967) have tended to regard the lament materials in these Eddaic lays as signs of later, ballad-derived aesthetics—the products of changing notions both of lamentation and of lyric, arising with the spread of German ballads into Denmark and Norway or from the influence of British Isle traditions. Where the original epics, in other words, showed no tendency to depict or include lyric lamentation, a dramatic sense informed by the ballad led to the gradual inclusion of laments within such poems. Daniel Sävborg (1997) has questioned the assumptions of these scholars, finding the expressions of grief as well as the form and diction of these "elegiac lays" fully as old as the so-called heroic lays with which the compiler of the *Codex Regius* grouped them. In fact, the tendency to regard such lyric moments as potentially unnecessary "asides" probably says more about the narrative biases of early-twentieth-century scholars than about the structural bases of medieval epics. In the texts described above, epic and lyric appear integrally tied.

Significantly, the lament tradition echoed in these poems is not only tied to narrative, but also strongly narrative itself. Because of the narrative details and specific naming of characters, we can hardly mistake the lyric quoted above for a song about any hero other than Sigurðr. In contrast, laments in Russian and Balto-Finnic traditions tend toward stylization, employing recurrent images and a poetic lexicon that varies little from individual to individual (see chap. 3). From this point of view, Guðrún's lament seems to have more in common with the formal laments composed in Scottish and Irish traditions (see below) than with the varieties of lament that Meletinsky describes. It is a lament with a clear narrative basis and referent.

Guðrún's lyric lament depends integrally on both the narrative of its creation and the identity of its referent and purported creator, Sigurðr and Guðrún. The same appears true for the lament known as *Sonatorrek* (Loss of Sons), a text described in detail in one of the closing chapters of *Egils saga*. Although both saga and lament claim to derive from the actual life experiences of a ninth-century Icelandic chieftain, either or both are just as likely the products of the imagination of a thirteenth-century compiler. In any case, they show the continued strong association of narrative accounts of mourning and the performance of powerful laments. The saga recounts the aging poet Egill Skallagríms-son composing a lament in memory of his fallen son. Egill has already lost one heir to accidental death when his second son, Böðvar, is drowned while carrying out some routine tasks. Stricken with grief for a son whose life has ended too early, Egill locks himself in his bedchamber, intending to starve himself to death. His daughter pretends to share his intention and asks him to compose a lament in honor of her brother. While begrudgingly composing the lament, Egill frees his grief and reawakens his will to live. By the time the lament is finished, he has resolved to live after all. His change of heart is, of course, partly humorous, representing a marked contrast between his poetic enunciations of unconsolable sorrow and their resultant consolation of the poet. Such a therapeutic function for the lament, however, is evident in the accounts of Guðrún as well: she, too, gains a will to live following her lament for her fallen lord. The idea that the lament serves a purpose for the living as well as for the dead seems a well-established element of the tradition and one that creates its own explanation for the existence and preservation of lament texts.

Lament and narrative account thus appear integrally bound in *Egils saga,* but many of the surviving manuscripts left to us truncate or excise the lament nearly completely. Often a manuscript will preserve only the first stanza of Egill's poem, leaving the rest to the audience to discover elsewhere or do without. This textual choice implies either the eventual primacy of the narrative account or the very familiarity of the lyric verse to the text's intended audience. Composed in an elaborate skaldic meter known as *kviðuháttr,* the lament—once composed—was potentially a linguistically more stable and enduring work than its prose explication, even if it is supposedly "dependent" on the narrative for its sense. Yet its omission in manuscripts suggests that it was viewed as a more or less expendable element of the overall text, one dominated by narrative concerns.

A second noteworthy aspect of this lament is the fact that it is far less specific in content or narrative referent than the brief lament for Sigurðr quoted above. Consider its opening stanzas:

Mjök erum tregt   tungu at hrœra
eða loptvætt   ljóðpundara;

esa nú vænligt   of Víðurs þýfi
né hógdrœgt   ór hugar fylgsni.

Esa auðþeystr,   þvít ekki veldr
höfugligr,   ór hyggju stað
fagnafundr   Friggjar niðja,
ár borinn   ór Jötunheimum,
lastalauss   es lifnaði
á Nökkvers   nökkva bragi.
Jötuns hals   undir þjóta
Náins niðr   fyr naustdyrum.

Þvít ætt mín   á enda stendr
Hræbarnir   sem hlynir marka;
esa karskr maðr   sás köggla berr
frænda hrørs   af fletjum niðr.
   (Chap. 78; Nordal 1933: 246–56)

———————

Great is the weight   of moving the tongue
or in lifting   the tool of song;
nor is it likely   that I may carry Víður's theft [= poetry] easily
from the caverns of my thoughts.

Deep sobbing   hinders it,
heavily it comes forth   out of my mind,
a joyful meeting,
brought from Frigg's kinsman
of old   from Jötunheim
drenching   the land.
And the lash   of wind and water.
On Nain's   rocks the sea splinters and howls.

My lineage ends,   like the storm—
felled maples   of the forest.
I have buried   the bodies
of too many   of my kin.

Although the text could easily refer to any number of mourning fathers, its accompanying narrative consistently ties it to Egill. What the text lacks in narrative specificity it makes up for in stylistic distinctiveness, for *Sonatorrek* is a masterpiece of skaldic art, a poem whose tightly interlocking images and turns of phrase call attention at every turn to the poet who is said to have composed them for his sons. Like Guðrún's lament, *Sonatorrek* ultimately serves not so much as a detail in the story of Egill's grief as it does a historical record of the mourning that Egill experienced at the death of his sons. It is a monument as purportedy enduring as a runestone or grave. And like the modern tombstone or epitaph, specificity is part of the very essence and purpose of the work.

OLD ENGLISH EPIC
Sorhléoð gæleð án æfter ánum (He utters a song of sorrow, one alone for another)

The Old English epic *Beowulf* presents a different image of laments and their relation to narrative events. In a quiet but pivotal moment in the epic, the Geatish hero and king Beowulf recalls a tragic incident that occurred in his maternal grandfather's court. King Hrethel lost his eldest son and heir apparent, Herebeald, through an accidental arrow shot. Even worse, the slayer was Hrethel's own son Hæthcyn, making it impossible for Hrethel to seek vengeance for his heir's death in a manner consistent with his rank. The king's sorrow and frustration is likened to that of another unhappy father in a lyric that Beowulf then performs:

Swá bið geómorlíc gomelum ceorle
tó gebídanne, þæt his byre ríde
giong on galgan þonne hé gyd wrece
sárigne sang þonne his sunu hangað
hrefne tó hróðre ond hé him helpe ne mæg
eald ond infród ænige gefremman
symble bið gemyndgad morna gehwylce
[page break]
eaforan ellorsíð óðres ne gymeð
tó gebídanne burgum in innan
yrfeweardas, þonne se án hafað
þurh déaðes nýd dæda gefondad
Gesyhð sorhcearig on his suna búre

wínsele wéstne,   windge reste
réóte berofene   rídend swefað
hæleð in hoðman   nis þǽr hearpan swég
gomen in geardum   swylce ðǽr iú wǽron.
xxxv
Gewíteð þonne on sealman,   sorhléoð gæleð
án æfter ánum   þúhte him eall tó rúm
wongas ond wícstede   swá Wedra helm
æfter Herebealde   heortan sorge
weallinde wæg   wihte ne meahte
on ðám feorhbonan   fǽghðe gebétan
nó ðý ǽr hé þone heaðorinc   hatian ne meahte
láðum dǽdum,   þéah him léof ne wæs.
        (2444–67; fol. 184r+v; Zupitza 1959: 114–15; Klaeber 1950: 92–93)

Thus is it mournful   for an aging earl
to endure,   that his son rides
young upon the gallows.   Then he utters a speech,
a sorrowful song,   while his son hangs,
a morsel for the raven.   And he may not gain help for him,
though old and wise,   from any quarter.
Ever is he reminded,   every morning,
[page break]
of his offspring's departure;   he cares not
to wait for   another heir
in the hall   when that one has,
through death's compulsion,   come to an end of his deeds.
He gazes sorrowfully   upon his son's chambers
the wine-hall emptied,   the windy resting place,
of joy bereft.   Riders sleep
heroes in the grave,   there is no sound of the harp,
joy in the court,   as once there was.
xxxv
He withdraws then to his bed,   utters a song of sorrow,
one alone for another.   All seemed too vast to him,

the lands and dwellings. Thus the helm of the Weders,
his heart welling forth with sorrow
for Herebeald. In no way might he
undertake a feud against that slayer
nor might he accost that warrior
with hostile deeds, though he bore him no love.

This lyric interlude—referred to by *Beowulf* scholars as *The Father's Lament*—provides a fascinating glimpse of the role and nature of lamentation in Anglo-Saxon society. It also furnishes us with a concrete example of how a lyric song could relate to the narrative of a surrounding epic in Anglo-Saxon poetry, an inkling of how epic could serve as an interpretive frame for the lyric's details in this tradition.

In terms of content, the passage contains more narrative details than the lyrics examined thus far. We know that the lyric's main figure is an aging earl, and we observe him as he watches his son die on the gallows. A narrator recounts the man's mournful perusal of his son's quarters and summarizes the man's feelings of desolation at the prospects of life without his heir. Nonetheless, we have no knowledge of who the man is or what larger narrative the scene fits into. Rather, the purpose of the text appears to be to depict the feelings of sorrow that might typically attend such a desperate turn of events. In the guise of seeming narrative specificity, we are actually confronted by a work far less definite than those portrayed in Old Norse.

Just as Guðrún's and Egill's laments teach us about Scandinavian lament traditions, so we can can learn much about the nature and function of lyric lament singing in Anglo-Saxon society from this passage. In its lines, we see a man moved to perform a lament for his son by a telling combination of sorrow and helplessness as he watches, powerless, as his son hangs on the gallows and again when he surveys the deserted hall that his son and his retainers had previously enlivened. Presumably unable to take action to save or restore his son, the man chooses to sing instead. Such an image has much in common with the depiction of Egill Skallagrimsson, although his singing appears more extemporaneous than the carefully composed lament stanzas that Egill is said to have fashioned. The depiction also squares well with lines at the end of *Beowulf* in which first a woman sings a lament for her fallen king (3150–55) and then twelve warriors ride around his barrow singing as well. The woman sings of the impending misery and vulnerability of the Geatish people now that their protector has died, images reminiscent of the expressions of vulnerability in Guðrún's lament. The men sing of their sorrow as well but also praise their leader's greatness and heroism, *swá hit gedéfe bið* (as is proper; 3174) at the passing of a king. Lament singing thus has its time and place in Anglo-Saxon society: it marks a moment of singular mournfulness in the surviving community. We can also note that in the above lyric the singing is directly contrasted with the "joy in the hall" imagery embodied in the sound of the harp, a key type-scene in Anglo-Saxon epic (Opland 1976; Niles 1983: 228, 232). The lament thus replaces the warm sounds of cheer and poetic recitation that fill the hall during normal times, even if the expressions of a king's greatness (like the *Beowulf* poem itself) may eventually find their way into the recitations and music of future joy-filled halls.

As illuminating as the passage is from the standpoint of Anglo-Saxon laments, however, it offers us even more insights concerning the relation of lyric interludes and epic poetry in Anglo-Saxon tradition. For here, we find not only a clear example of a lyric embedded in an epic text to match that of *Guðrúnaq-viða I* but also a poetic depiction of how an Anglo-Saxon warrior such as Beowulf might be supposed to use such a lyric to comment on a situation in his own life. By examining the lyric and its surrounding narrative, then, we may glimpse the means by which an Anglo-Saxon singer or audience expected such a song to be interpreted, albeit in an idealized case.

Let us consider the song's surrounding narrative framework in detail. Beowulf has received word of a dragon's attacks on his kingdom and has resolved to confront the threat himself. With a company of twelve men, he has journeyed to the dragon's lair. Before launching into battle, however, he takes stock of his life and career, noting that he has settled every score required of his kingship and honor. This accounting leads him to recall the nagging instance of unavenged death in his family's past, one that Beowulf witnessed in youth as part of Hrethel's court. And that account of Hrethel's dilemma prompts Beowulf to perform the lyric above. Beowulf, we may conclude, does not intend to let events overtake him in the way that led Hrethel—or the lyric's father—to descend into sorrow: rather, he plans to take action to save his kingdom and maintain his heroic status, even if his deeds prove fatal.

What is most noteworthy about this narrative moment, however, is that the lyric Beowulf turns to in order to comment on his familial tragedy is not specific to the tale of Hrethel, Herebeald, and Hæthcyn but proverbialized: it is a depiction of an unnamed father in a narratively less complicated and unrelated situation. In fact, the content of the lyric is not only not specific to Hrethel's case but actually differs from it substantively. Where Hrethel is caught in the double bind of the need for vengeance against a son's slayer and the (unwanted) duty to protect the life of his own son (Hæthcyn), the lyric father's plight is simpler: the early loss of a grown son and the sorrow of finding oneself without an heir. Hrethel, in contrast, has several sons, and his patrimony is not threatened by the tragic death of Herebeald. Indeed, although the death of Herebeald leads to a weakened Geatish state, Hrethel's kingdom and line does not fall in the subsequent generation. Yet his sorrow at the death is likened to—perhaps clarified by—that of the lyric's father: this figure's very comprehensible grief helps an audience to imagine the more unfathomable grief that Hrethel faces in his unforeseen dilemma. Beowulf's lyric aims at contemplating Hrethel's sorrow not by narrative enlargement but by analogy. And thus, we can say in turn, such a lyric could be interpreted not by narrative specificity but by proverbialized comparison.

This choice on the part of the character Beowulf as well as the *Beowulf* poet is noteworthy, since from the standpoint of narrative likelihood, it is certain that a king such as Hrethel would have had poets at his court capable of composing a specific lament in remembrance of his family's sorrow. Such is, after all, what we see in the description of the aftermath of Beowulf's own death at the end of the epic: retainers compose specific songs in praise of a specific king. And it is also likely that Beowulf, Hrethel's dutiful former retainer, might be expected to remember and perform that lament in recalling the event many years later. Perhaps Hrethel or Beowulf could have composed such a lament themselves if they had chosen to, the rules governing Anglo-Saxon verse being far less demanding than those that Egill faced in composing the lament for his own son. Yet, crucially, they do not: rather, Beowulf and the *Beowulf* poet seem to accept a proverbialized lyric as fully satisfactory for the contemplation of a loved one's sorrow.

However surprising this fact may seem when viewed with assumptions born of the Old Norse cases above, it appears quite normal in an Anglo-Saxon context. Proverbialized laments appear to have been common and even normative in Anglo-Saxon tradition. This point is made clear in the studies of C.L. Wrenn (1967) and Patrick L. Henry (1966). Wrenn addresses what he terms the "elegiac tone" of Anglo-Saxon poetry, exploring not only *The Father's Lament* but also *The Wanderer, The Seafarer, The Wife's Lament, The Husband's Message, The Rhyming Poem,* and *The Ruin* (139–54). Each of these addresses a specific

narrative situation only to a small degree, focusing instead on the more generalized ("gnomic") feelings a person in such a situation might be expected to
feel. Each is, according to Wrenn, a "general meditation in solitude of what may
be called universal griefs" (139): the early loss of a son, the loss of one's comrades, the loss or distrust of a husband, the longing for an absent spouse, the
loss of one's honor and reputation, the temporal destruction of human institutions. And although it may be possible with some of these poems to discover
a narrative core (as in the case of *The Father's Lament,* above, or in various attempts related to *The Wife's Lament*) or to reconstruct a specific poetic referent
(e.g., the ruins at Bath as the possible basis for *The Ruin*; see Leslie 1961: 22),
such inferences affect little the workings or force of the poems themselves.
As Henry (1966: 70) terms it in his examination of Welsh and Anglo-Saxon
lyrics, the "personal" grounds and sustains the "gnomic": "And so phenomena
subtly change into universals and description into gnome, and a poem becomes
a subtle mixture of the personal (emotional, lyrical) and the sententious." So
dominant may the gnomic aspect of the poem become, writes Henry, that the
personal story nearly disappears: "It may at times be almost impossible to un-
ravel the thread of the human situation from its gnomic setting; hence the modern impression of almost deliberate obscuration in Early Welsh and Old English poetry" (69).

Illustrative of the nature of such proverbialized lyrics are the two poems
known to scholars as *The Wanderer* and *The Seafarer*. Unlike *The Father's Lament,* these poems occur outside of epic texts, recorded in the compilation of
poems and riddles known as the *Exeter Book*. In *The Wanderer,* a man reflects
on his lonely wandering in search of a court to replace that of his lost king and
comrades. Little narrative plot is included in the work, but we see the speaker
dealing with the bleak sea and surveying abandoned ruins, both visual cues that
prompt the speaker's musings on the transcience of earthly existence. Most of
the poem's lines, and all of its stirring images, address the feelings of a man in
exile, tortured by memories of faded relations and haunted by the grim realities
of a desolate present. *The Seafarer,* similarly, presents only the barest narrative,
recounting in first person how a man of apparently high status came to devote
his life to the endless travels of a pilgrim, anchorite, or outcast. As in *The Wanderer,* the poem speaks in gnomic generalities, as when the speaker states:

For-þon nis þæs mód-wlanc mann ofer eorðan,
né his giefena þæs gód né on geoguðe to þæs hwæt,

né on his dǽ dum to þæs déor   né him his dryhten to þæs hold,
þæt hé á his sǽ-fóre   sorge næbbe,
to hwon hine Dryhten   gedón wille.
   (Pope 1981: 34)

But there is not so   self-possessed a man on earth
So born to greatness,   so bold with his youth
Nor so brave of deeds,   nor so favored of his lord
That he has no distress   at putting out to sea
As to what the Lord   will do with him.

These lines clearly are not meant to delineate a single character, nor do they
rely on the identity of the speaker for their force or sense as do lyrics in Old
Norse. Rather, the generalized experience of setting forth is presented so as to
evoke in the audience associations and feelings that the poet views as universal.
These images and interpretive tendencies match closely those of *The Father's
Lament,* which appears by comparison a somewhat abbreviated rendering of a
kind of lyric familiar in Anglo-Saxon tradition. Needing no more specific plot
or composer for its proper interpretation, such a lyric reveals the appeal, effectiveness, and independence of proverbialized lyrics.

   If we accept the normative nature of such proverbializing interpretation,
then, we can appreciate the ways in which it could be used nonetheless to comment on specific situations. Beowulf uses the more generalized situation in his
lyric to render familiar, and thus to create sympathy for, the decidedly unusual
circumstances that face Hrethel. Whereas Herebeald's death is enough out
of the ordinary that it falls outside Anglo-Saxon legal norms, the father's distress is entirely comprehensible both in Anglo-Saxon law and in contemporary
human experience. As Whitelock (see Wrenn 1953: 220–21) explains, death by
hanging designates the son as guilty of a criminal act, and the father thus has
no recourse to legal action against his son's slayers. Further, his advanced age
makes him unwilling or unable to await the birth and maturation of a new heir,
a crisis that must have faced many men in a era of high childhood mortality
and frequent warfare. This situation creates a common ground upon which an
audience could identify with the feelings of loss or desolation that Hrethel is

said to have felt. The general situation may thus ground the specific, even when the specific is not explicitly commented on in the song.

One sign of this associative process is the subtle elision by which the lyric segues back into the account of Hrethel. Modern editors (e.g., Klaeber 1950; Wrenn 1953) have sought to clearly differentiate lines depicting the father from those devoted to Hrethel by capitalizing and even indenting the half-line beginning with *swá* (so, thus) in line 2462b, making it directly parallel to the opening *swá* of line 2444. The lyric depiction of the father thus runs through the ending of the scribe's fit xxxiv and into the beginning of fit xxxv, with no special emphasis associated with either the beginning of a new fit or the pronounced capitalization of the *g* in the *Gesyhð* (withdraws) of line 2455. The lines' shift back to preterite tense in the verb *þúhte* (seemed) of 2461 is likewise ignored in this editorial scheme in order to emphasize the boundary between the father and Hrethel. Yet it may be argued that the text calls for a more nuanced understanding: one in which the description of a father's broken withdrawal from the world can be seen as equally applying to either the lyric's father character or Hrethel. In essence, by the end of Beowulf's proverbialized lyric, father and Hrethel have become one, united in the common experience of grief.

Such proverbialization seems normative in Anglo-Saxon lyric, and we can appreciate the subtleties by which it creates sympathy for a specific situation. At the same time, it may have had other aesthetic and thematic uses, particularly in a complex epic such as *Beowulf*. Niles (1983: 232), for instance, suggests that *The Father's Lament*, along with the embedded lyrics known as *The Lament of the Last Survivor* (2247–66) and *The Messenger's Prophecy* (3014b–24), advance an overarching theme in *Beowulf* as a whole: the transience of human action, even when glorious, in comparison with the workings and judgments of God. In *The Lament of the Last Survivor*, an unnamed man recalls the passing of his people, mourning the lack of joy in the hall while laying up his inherited treasure in a barrow away from the eyes and use of other men. In *The Messenger's Prophecy*, a warrior predicts the coming downfall of the Geats now that Beowulf has died. The once joyous sounds of the harp will be replaced with the sound of raven and eagle. Together, Niles argues, these lyrics sustain a deeply melancholic tone in the last portion of the epic that foreshadows both Beowulf's death and the eventual destruction of his people, an event lying outside the scope of the narrative. For such a theme to work, of course, the lyrics in question must have universalizing, gnomic, force, something harder to gain from laments addressing specific narrative events. Thus, the grandeur of *Beowulf* as described by scholars since Tolkien (1936)—its capacity not only to address the specifics of one warrior's glorious career but also to offer its audience transcendent and timeless lessons that reach beyond the text and narrative—may arise in part directly from the norms by which elements such as interpolated lyrics were employed and interpreted in Anglo-Saxon tradition. Where Egill can erect an enduring monument to the memory of his sons, the *Beowulf* poet comments on the passing of men in general.

IRISH LAMENT
Caoineadh Dheirdre i ndiaidh Naois (Deirdre's Lament for Naoise)

While the Old Norse and Anglo-Saxon texts discussed above indicate some of the complex and varying relations that may have existed between medieval lyrics and their (possible) epic settings, the case of the Irish *Lament for the Sons of Uisneach* provides the most complete case possible for examining these issues over time, particularly within Irish tradition. Here a medieval lament is surrounded by a prose narrative, both dating to at least the twelfth century and possibly to an era several centuries earlier. There is also textual evidence that allows us to trace both narrative and lyric as they change over centuries of transmission, textual as well as oral. What this evidence demonstrates is not so much the persistence of narrative or lyric per se (for both have undergone drastic changes over time) but rather the persistence of a particular *relation* between the narrative and the lyric, ensuring that each endures through reliance on the other. The narrative glosses the lyric; the lyric encapsulates the narrative. This relation demonstrates a consistent, pervasive hermeneutic norm in Irish lyric tradition: an expectation of complementarity between lyric and narrative that performers and audiences have heeded for at least eight centuries.

The medieval tale of Deirdre, her lover, Naoise, and her jealous husband, Conchobhar, first appears in textual form in the twelfth-century *Book of Leinster*. Titled *Longes mac nUislenn* (The Exile of the Sons of Uisliu), the work recurs in the fourteenth-century *Yellow Book of Lecan* and the sixteenth-century manuscript *British Museum MS Egerton 1782* (Hull 1949: 29–32; Mac Giolla Léith 1993: 9–10). In abridged form (without its lyric contents), the narrative appears also in Geoffrey Keating's seventeenth-century *Foras Feasa ar Éirenn*, one of the most popular manuscript works in Irish Gaelic history (Mac Giolla Léith 1993: 21–22; Bergin 1970: 2–5).

These narratives follow the life and trials of Deirdre from her days in the womb to her suicide as an adult. The tale purports to explain how certain Ulster heroes—especially Fearghus mac Róigh—ended up on Connaught's side during the events of the *Táin Bó Cúailgne* (The Cattle Raid of Cooley) (Mac Giolla Léith 1993: 11; Gantz 1981: 256). In fact, however, the events of the tale relate to those of the *Táin* only tangentially, and in nearly every respect the narrative is independent of the rest of the Ulster Cycle and thoroughly sufficient in and of itself.

In the *Longes* version, King Conchobhar and his men first meet with Deirdre when she cries out from her mother's womb. The druid Cathbhadh prophesies (in verse) that the infant will grow into a beautiful woman who will cause the Ulaid great harm. Conchobhar's men call for immediate destruction, but the king refuses, raising Deirdre instead to become his wife. As she reaches adulthood, however, Deirdre sees and falls in love with the warrior Naoise, whom she browbeats into running away with her, threatening him in fact with satire. Naoise, his brothers, and Deirdre take refuge at various courts throughout Ireland until, hounded by the king, they seek exile in Scotland. After the king there attempts to take Deirdre for himself, the brothers and bride flee to an island until the Ulaid persuade Conchobhar to let them return to Ireland. Conchobhar permits their return but treacherously plans their demise, luring their guarantors, including Fearghus mac Róigh, away to feasts so that Eóghan mac Durthacht can attack and kill the three brothers. Deirdre is forced to return to Conchobhar but mourns Naoise for the entirety of a year. When Conchobhar tries to force her to live with Eóghan mac Durthacht for the following year, she jumps from their chariot, dashes her head against a rock, and dies. Her laments for Naoise and his brothers are recorded in two interpolated poems that contrast the fineries of life at Conchobhar's court with the rustic pleasures Deirdre previously enjoyed with Naoise in Scotland. The laments go on to praise Naoise's face, form, garb, and weapons, bewail Fearghus's seeming betrayal, and detail Deirdre's boundless sorrow for her lost husband and brothers-in-law.

A related but distinct version of the tale survives in a variety of manuscripts dating from the fourteenth and fifteenth centuries (and later) under the title *Oidheadh Chloinne h-Uisneach* (The Violent Death of the Sons of Uisneach; Mac Giolla Léith 1993). This version has manuscript and oral counterparts in both Scotland and Ireland down into the twentieth century and corresponds to the musical notation that Edward Bunting published in 1840, reproduced below (Example 2.1).

EXAMPLE 2.1

Shields (1993: 19–22) compares surviving melodies for the song, and for the Irish *laoi* in general, noting that the regular tempo presented in Bunting's transcription probably misrepresents the more variable rhythms of the tradition itself.

In this narrative version, the story begins with King Conchobhar's announcement that he will welcome the sons of Uisneach back to Ireland. Conchobhar treacherously sends Fearghus to Scotland to convince them to return, a task the honest warrior is able to accomplish despite Deirdre's dreams and prophecies of destruction.

Upon returning to Ireland, Fearghus is detained at a feast while the sons of Uisneach continue toward Conchobhar's court. They are brought to a hall away from Conchobhar where Conchobhar ascertains that Deirdre is still as beautiful as ever. Filled with jealousy, he orders the hall burned and the brothers killed, but the sons of Uisneach and one of Fearghus's sons hold off the attack, causing great loss to Conchobhar's troops. At last, Conchobhar deceives the druid Cathbhadh into enchanting the brothers so that they can be captured. They are put to death by Maine Lámhgharbh with a single stroke of Naoise's own long sword. After securing Maine's death through the vengeance of Cú Chulainn, Deirdre takes her place upon Naoise's body in the grave and dies.

Given the stretch of time that separates these different versions of the Deirdre story and lament, and the fact that they straddle Old, Middle, and Modern Irish, the song ascribed to the sorrowing widow shows a remarkable degree of continuity. In the *Book of Leinster*'s *Longes* version, for instance, Deirdre sums up her anguish with a clear prediction of her impending death:

> Na briss in-diu mo chride
> Mos•ricub mo moch-lige;
> Is tressiu cuma in-dá muir,
> Madda éola a Chonchobuir.
>   (Hull 1949: 51)

> Break no more my heart today—
> I will reach my early grave soon enough.
> Sorrow is stronger than the sea
> If you are wise, Conchubur.
>   (Gantz 1981: 266)

In different words but with the same finality the *Oidheadh* Deirdre makes largely the same pronouncement:

> Is mé Deirdre gan duibhe,
> Is mé air fhuidheall mo bheatha;
> A bheith dá n-éis is misde,
> Ní bhiaidh mise go fada.

I am Deirdre without darkness
And I am at the end of my life;
It is bad to be after them
I will not myself be long.
   (Mac Giolla Léith 1993: 138, 139)

And later versions, largely derived from the *Oidheadh* redaction, contain similar lines. A manuscript version dating from the eighteenth century (*Edinburgh MS 56*; Cameron 1894: 421–63) has Deirdre state:

Do sheachnas aoibhneas Uladh,
Móran churaidh agus charad;
Ar mbeith ionna ndiaigh am aonar,
Mo shaoghal ni ba fada.

———

I have shunned the joy of Ulad,
Many warriors and friends;
Now that I am alone behind them
My days will not be long.
   (Cameron 1894: 456, 457)

In a Scottish Gaelic version collected from Donald Macphie of the island of Barra in 1865, a rather more exulting Deirdre intones:

Theid mise gu aobhach, uallach,
Do 'n triuir uasal a b' annsa,
Mo shaoghal 'n an deigh cha 'n fhada,
'S cha 'n eug fear-abhuilt domhsa.

———

I will go joyfully, proudly,
To the three nobles most beloved,

My time behind them is not long,
Nor coward's death is mine.
    (Carmichael 1914: 130–31)

And in an oral version of the lament collected from Máirtín Ó Conaire of County Meath, Ireland, in 1985, the same steadfast pronouncement recurs, albeit a little more plaintively:

Bíodh a fhios ag gach agaibh
Nach mhairfinnse beo i ndiaidh Naois;
Cluinfidh mise an t-anam
Ach ní mhaireann agam lucht mo chaointe.

————

Let each one of you know this:
That I would not remain alive after Naoise;
I will hear the soul
But no one is left to lament me.
    (Shields 1993: 208, 209)

To be sure, differences also occur. Where the *Longes* manuscripts contain only a single lament, the *Oidheadh* manucripts depict Deirdre singing a great variety of songs from the time of their exile in Scotland through to the final moment of her death. She uses verse to praise the land that gave them asylum and prophesy their deaths if they return to Ireland. In a further poem, she entreats Naoise to delay his journey to Conchobhar's court until Fearghus or a suitable guarantor can be found to accompany them. In several more poems, she argues about their course of action with Naoise. In yet another—which proves popular in the oral tradition that follows—she recalls an instance of Naoise's unfaithfulness to her in Scotland and how he promised to remain true to her thereafter. In a poetic catalog of their epithets and qualities, she describes her lost husband and brothers-in-law. A number of these poems occur apart from the prose account in various manuscripts of the eighteenth and nineteenth centuries, leading to the conclusion that they must have had a performative life at least partially distinct from that of the prose narrative. The great variety and number of lament texts suggests that multiple poets over time turned their talents to depicting Deirdre's feelings in verse, responding to the narrative by creating poems that supplemented the preexisting relation of story and lament.

Shields's interview with Máirtín Ó Conaire provides valuable insights into the relation between such lament texts and the story of Deirdre and Naoise. Ó Conaire's version matches that of *Oidheadh* manuscripts in a number of respects but contains its own unique lines as well. For instance, in preparing to join her beloved in the grave, Ó Conaire's Deirdre details what pieces of her garments will lie on each man:

> Beidh mo léine féin ar Naois
> Mar 's é mo chéile é 's mo chéad ghrá;
> Beidh mo bhrat sróil ar Aill'
> Is mo chóta féin ar Ardán.

> ———

> My closest garment shall be on Naoise
> For he is my spouse and my first love;
> My satin cloak on Aille
> And my coat on Ardan.
> (Shields 1993: 208, 209)

The lines find no parallel in the *Oideadh* manuscripts, although they recall somewhat distantly Deirdre's loving enumeration of Naoise's garments in the *Longes* versions (Hull 1949: 50; Gantz 1981: 266). Although Ó Conaire's song includes relatively few narrative details, the singer knew a good deal of the story related in both *Longes* and *Oidheadh* versions and was able to recount it before his performance (Shields 1993: 210). He knew, for instance, of Deirdre's cries in her mother's womb and of Conchobhar's decision to raise her as his wife. He detailed how Deirdre fell in love with Naoise, their flight to Scotland, and their return to Ireland. In his telling, the sons of Uisneach remain victorious in battle until magic is used against them, blinding them so that they strike each other dead. Then Deirdre sings her lament and dies. Ó Conaire's narrative furnishes an indication of how lyric and accompanying narrative could have been performed more generally in the past—the narrative acting as an explanatory *míniú*, to be performed in addition to the song in cases when an audience was unfamiliar with it or simply wished to hear it told again. Both song and story were subject to change, but the relation between them remained.

In interviewing the Scottish raconteur Alastair Macneill in 1867, on the other hand, Alexander Carmichael (1914: 6–7) notes that Macneill knew the tale of "Deirdire" well, and knew of the existence of a song, but could not perform the latter: "There was a lay on Deirdire, too, but I have not the lay. I never took a lay or song with me." Such evidence indicates that lyric and narrative need not have co-occurred even in the same performer's repertoire in order to be associated with each other in the tradition. A talented singer and tale teller might have active control over both, but one with more limited gifts might know only one or the other to perform. So secure is the relation between lyric and prose narrative that, even when a performer could not relate them both, their linkage remained undisputed, shared by performer and audience in the body of knowledge in which the present performance was to be contextualized. It was a "tradition" in which oral and manuscript versions appear to have closely informed each other over the course of centuries, and one that balanced innovation with a fidelity to past models.

The laments of Guðrún, Egill, Beowulf, and Deirdre together illustrate both the commonalities and the distinctions that occur in using the situational axis to relate a lament to a particular historical or narrative moment in these northern European traditions. In all cases, generic expectations stipulate that the death of a great hero, or of a hero's great love, should call forth a lament, to mark the moment of mourning and console the deceased's survivors. The resulting lyric became associated with its referent and often also with its composer. Yet the specifics of how that lyric relates to its situational referent vary markedly. In the Old Norse examples, the lament is so narratively specific as to be applicable to virtually no other being or moment than the ones for which it was composed. In contrast, the Old English laments bear an analogical relation to the narratives they are associated with, so that the lyric itself could easily refer to another being or time than the one in which it is textually embedded. Its use is proverbial, in that the epic character who performs the lament sees it as representative of a certain situation in general rather than of one historical event in particular. In such cases, the lyric hardly appears subordinated to the narrative; in fact, narrative seems to set the stage for the weightier existential musings encapsulated in the lament. Finally, in the laments of Deirdre for her Naoise and his brothers, we see the extent to which lament and narrative explanation could prove independent of each other performatively, even while depending on each other completely for interpretive sense. Both narrative and lyric undergo continual and sometimes drastic change in oral and manuscript traditions over the centuries, with the single commonality lying in their mutual association. As long as lyric and narrative are understood as interrelated, they can be used to interpret each other, even when not performed together.

Through the juxtaposition of these different medieval and postmedieval cases, we see that lyric interpretation cannot be taken for granted, even in a genre like the lament that shows great formal and contextual commonalities over space and time. Interpretations along the situational axis must be carefully discovered through examination of narrative contexts, commentary, and interpretive evidence. It varies by culture and period, and requires the same careful study that is required to discern the textual meaning of the lyrics themselves.

In Ritual and Wit

The Hermeneutics of the Invocational Lyric

> While the community sits here and relaxes, they make conversa-
> tion, and as this nectar of life begins to affect their senses, the
> conversation grows more lively, more cheerful, more affectionate;
> the prose ceases and one begins to converse in song.
>
> Petrus Laestadius, quoted in Rolf Kjellström,
> Gunnar Ternhag, and Håkan Rydving, *Om jojk* (1988)

The lyric tendency referred to in this study as invocation lies at the intersec-
tion of the generic, associative, and situational axes. It is generic in that lyrics
may make use of second-person address in an unambiguously stylized and
predictable manner, for example, by calling out to the deceased in a lament that
foregrounds its distinctiveness from an ordinary utterance in every way. It is associative in that it powerfully underscores both an inscribed speaker and an inscribed recipient, be it a lover, an absent friend, or a powerful supernatural entity.
It is situational in that the stylized communication embodied in the lyric carries
with it signs of its own "natural" environment, for example, a narrative moment
in which the utterance purportedly first occurred, or more proverbially, a typical situation in which the utterance would prove particularly apt. Yet lyrics are
not the only expressive genre to make use of invocation, leading to the need of
traditional audiences to recognize such lyrics for what they are and to distinguish
them from other varieties of communication. In this chapter, I explore the workings of invocational lyrics in a number of northern European traditions, examining their associated mechanisms of interpretation and their relation to other
genres that typically make use of second-person address.

In the stylized narrative world of the medieval epic, time stands still for the lyric. As friend and foe alike stand by, the epic's mourning Guðrún, Egill, Beowulf, or Deirdre sing of feelings, giving voice to personal or proverbial sensations through texts that may include dozens of lines and a diction challenging to even an expert poet. No narrative action occurs until the singing is over, and at that point, it is as if no time at all has passed. This one of the generic artifices of the epic, one without which the long lyrics discussed in the previous chapter probably could not have been preserved.

Yet in the "natural" world of lived interactions, lyric often occurs in situations in which it is more intimately and significantly tied to conversation, context, and control. Illocutionary in intent, it seeks to remind, to instruct, to persuade, to compel. It may be deployed amid the ebb and flow of ordinary communication by singers intent on influencing their situation in some way. Or it may occur in a ritual context, be it in the heightened moment of a key life cycle event (a healing, wedding, or funeral) or in those subtler ritual moments that pervade the everyday: the pause over coffee or evening at the pub.

It is these "naturally occurring" lyrics that I examine here, though not so as to draw a distinction between "real" lyrics and the ones discussed in chapter 2. Both are "real" in every sense, and both found or find active performance in living culture. Yet here I hope to indicate how certain varieties of lyric become integral parts of intimate human interaction, even while their form and content distinguish them for "ordinary" speech. Often shorter, and sometimes harder to place within the boundaries of the lyric genre, these invocational lyrics possess their norms of interpretation, ones that allow an audience to recognize and appraise them both as aesthetic experiences and, perhaps more important, as tools by which communication occurs. These are norms based on a mystical understanding of song and its relation to referent, recipient, and ritual.

THE SÁMI *JOIK*

In the epigraph above, the nineteenth-century Sámi missionary Petrus Laestadius describes the ways in which his friends and neighbors used the musical genre called *luohti, vuolle,* or *joik* in daily life. An adjunct to conversation, the *joik* came to the fore when the talk grew "more lively," "more affectionate," more intimate. In his description of the *joik* genre for a non-Sámi audience, the native Sámi scholar and writer Johan Turi calls *joik* a way of remembering:

> Tat læ okta muitim konsta nubit olpmoit: muhtomat muitet vašis ja muitet rakisvuoðain, ja muhtomat muitet moraštemin, ja atnojit tat laulot muhtom ætnamin ja ælibin, naudes ja bocos, kodis. (1911: 91)

> ———

> This is a way of recalling other folk; some are remembered with hate, some with love, and some with sorrow. And often these songs concern certain places, or animals: the wolf, and the reindeer, and the wild reindeer. (1931: 202)

"Recalling" in this sense is a powerfully creative act: the *joik*'s referent is summoned forth through some combination of verbal and musical description in a manner that underscores the referent's identity, frailties, or strengths. It is a portrait of the referent, rendered by a singer for other community members to decode and appreciate. Yet the *joik* is also denotative: it represents the referent but also shares in that referent's identity. Thus, the *joik* is said to belong to its referent rather than to its creator. It is also said to make the potentially absent referent present to the community of listeners for the duration of the performance (Gaski 2000: 193). In this sense, it is an integrally invocational genre, one addressing the referent directly, even if it does so in the third person. Tellingly, Sámi custom frowned on the performance of one's own *joik:* such, in a sense, would be talking of, or to, oneself.

Turi described this complex use and understanding of the *joik* through examples. Thus, in the text that became his chapter on *joik,*[1] Turi tells of the courtship of a Nilas and Ele and of the other young men and women who vie for their affections. Nilas is a handsome and very desirable young man. In gauging their chances of winning his affection, and sizing up their competition from other women of the locale, the women in Turi's account challenge each other to *joik* Nilas. Turi writes:

> Voia voia nana nana
> stuora haga, stuora kæmpa,
> stuora fauru, stuora læmbada

voia voia nana nana
ko dat juo vehkali
te manai tego lodi
voia voia nana nana.
  (1911: 91)

———————

Voia voia nana nana,
very vigorous, very bright
very beautiful, very fit
voia voia nana nana
when he ran off on two feet
he went like a bird
voia voia nana nana.
  (1931: 202)[2]

Much of the song's message was no doubt contained in its musical performance, in how the singer used her voice to express Nilas's vigorous character or quick step. Through vocal artistry and sometimes also gestures or pantomime, Sámi joikers can depict their referents as plodding or quick, lumbering or spry, tired or lively (Jones-Bamman 1993: 129–30). An audience knowing Nilas could presumably perceive his qualities in the performance of his *joik*, whether flattering (as in the above case) or otherwise. The words of the song also carry meaning: the vocables *voia* and *nana* can be regarded as simply implements for conveying a melody, although some scholars have suggested that they may also encode the singer's attitude toward the content or character of the *joik* (e.g., Szomjas-Schiffert 1996: 75). The other words in the text express an estimation of Nilas in artful and economic manner. As Gaski (2000: 205) has shown in his study of *joik* poetry, adjectives such as the ones in Nilas's *joik* carry deep resonances and wit, and linking human referents metaphorically to certain animals was a common means of characterization used in the genre. Describing humans in this way allowed the singer or composer of the *joik* to draw on the rich store of terms and associations that Sámi shared concerning certain kinds of reindeer, birds, or other wild animals. The adjectives included here connote physical vitality and desirability and are repeated in the *joik* that Nilas sings of Ele (Turi 1911: 91) as well as that which Nilas's rival Mahte sings of her (96). The bird image in the text seems to connote Nilas's freedom of movement but also, on a more metaphorical level, his ability to play the field. In describing the *joiking* that goes on between drunken revelers after Mahte and Marja's wedding, Turi has the women use the same metaphor in largely the same manner as their suitors: "stuora faurot ja stuora haga . . . mana ᷠekie teko kirdi lodi" (very beautiful, and very vigorous . . . they go like a bird flies, 97). Turi closes that scene of revelry laconically: "Ja æi si nohkan tan ija" (And they got no sleep that night, 97). On the other hand, when Nilas and Ele have their wedding, revelers tease Nilas that he has finally broken his leg (99).

As Turi's account goes on, this initial encapsulation of Nilas's character seems to ring true. He is portrayed as affable, well-liked, and lucky but also quick-tempered, occasionally drunk, and sometimes destructively foolish. Are the words of his *joik,* like those directed at him by the revelers, meant to be derisive, to imply *too much* freedom of movement? Or does the derision arise only from the contrast between what Nilas usually is and what, in his bad moments, he could be? Whatever the case, it is clear from Turi's account that this complex constellation of personal characteristics—balanced against the ongoing realities of Nilas's life and experiences—are somehow summed up and expressed in the *joik* with which he is associated.

Similarly evocative and meaningful *joiks* existed for animals, seasons, places, and situations—in short, the whole array of beings and sensations with which Sámi people shared their world. Jonas Eriksson Steggo (1873–1957) of Arjeplog, Sweden, gave an account of his life in words and *joik* in interviews with Harald Grundström and A. O. Väisänen in 1946 (Grundström and Väisänen 1958). His account, recorded phonographically, shifts midsentence between *joik* and regular speech, as he relates places where he has lived and herded reindeer, people who have played important roles in his life, and animals with which he has had dealings. When describing his seasonal migrations to a mountainous area in Norway, for instance, Steggo reminisces about the places and paths the migration passed over, breaking into a *joik* when mentioning the mountain Rávdurte:

EXAMPLE 3.1

Ja de judiimeh nåv de vuostale Rávdur'tái.
  [Sings:] *vai de budiimeha Rávdurte guov'delii*
  ja de lei vai vaija dov gula
  Rávdurte le gula valla val guov'delii
Men čuoikah val ja bálgoh mudiin šid'din (Grundström and Väisänen
1958: 12–13)

────────

And then we moved first to Rávdurte.
  [Sings:] *Well, we came into Rávdurte's center*
  And that it was vai vaija that, oh!
  Rávdurte it was, oh, valla val, into its center
but sometimes there were a lot of gnats and terrible heat there.

In recalling *joiks* for the bear, Steggo performs a song from the area of Tjidtjak
and then another from north of the Pite River. Performing the latter leads him
into an account of a menacing bear that he managed to scare away from the
vicinity of his herd once in his youth:

EXAMPLE 3.2

[Sings:] *a vaija daveav alla valla*
davev allav alla vav alla dav gul allav alla
bierdnav allav allaa aval allav allav allatj
sáno bierdnav alla va

ik'ti läv mån de bierdnav, ja guokte bale laved viesodiin mån bierdnav tyd-
ligen uʒʒum čilmiin vuoi'dnet, ja vil bär guoraʒin. (Grundström and Väisänen 1958: 42)

————

[Sings:] *A vaija this alla valla*
this allav alla vav alla this, oh, allav alla
bear allav alla aval allav allav alla and
formidable bear alla va
Once, twice in my life have I laid eye on a bear clearly, and that quite near
at hand.

As these passages suggest, Steggo uses his *joiks* to pause, emphasize, and characterize musically figures that arise in his memories or narration. The mountain
that he would not have seen for years due to the border closing of World War II,
the bear that tested his mettle as a defender of his herd—these beings are spot-
lighted through *joik*. The *joiks* themselves are lyric: they describe their referents
in static, atemporal terms, giving way then to prose narrative that attaches the
referent described to moments or events in the singer's life. In Turi's terms, the
joiks help to "recall" these referents, drawing them forth for the singer and audience to survey as the related—but ultimately independent—narrative un-
folds. This highly productive, seemingly nearly automatic use of *joik* reflects a
deeply sacral understanding of the songs, a sense that in some way they have the
power to encompass and express.

In his account of *joik* singing, Turi writes of other uses of *joik* as well. The
jilted Matte insults Elle through a *joik* about her trousers. In a threatening *joik*,
Matte announces his intention to kill all of Nilas's draft reindeer, making use of
a verbally abusive form that Krister Stoor (2003: track 3) discusses and illustrates
in a CD recording. *Joik* is also used in Turi's rendering to express the joy of riding by reindeer sleigh and to wish the newly married couple well. The spirits of
the mountain are thanked by performing a *joik* when traveling over dangerous
ground. Covert boasts of success in reindeer theft or allegations of wrongdoing
are performed as *joiks* as well. As Turi closes his account, he writes:

Juoigamus læ dakar, ko læ rievtes čæpes juoigi, de læ nu hauski kulat kosi
čirosat botet kultalækĭðe; muhto ko dagar juoigit læt, kuðet karoðit ja

banit kasket [j]a uhkỉðit kodit bocoit ja vela isỉðanai, ja te tat læt ahkedat kulat. (1911: 102)

———————

Joiking, if it is really clever, is so wonderful to hear that the listener almost has tears in his eyes, but when it is a *joiker* who swears and grinds his teeth and threatens to kill reindeer and their owners too, then it is horrible to listen to. (1931: 225)

Joik is both descriptive and effectual as an implement in human relations.

In certain respects, the *joik* is unique to Sámi people. At the same time, we can explore the degree to which a comparable sacrality or function obtains in other lyric traditions of northern Europe. Perhaps the best place to start such an examination is in those genres of music or speech that share the *joik*'s invocational character. In shepherds' calls there exists the same ability of a musical utterance to encapsulate a complex message but a far more restricted range of possibilities for either the interpretation or the use of such calls. In charms, there exists a similar concept of the inherent power of words but with a far more manipulative rather than descriptive intent. Wedding and funerary laments, for their part, couch their addresses in the framework of rituals, where their meanings are both specific and gnomic at once. Finally, in Scottish *piobaireachd,* there exists a comparable degree of descriptive and interpretive latitude as in the *joiks* described above, achieved through the agency of traditionality and, interestingly, linked more often to a narrativizing than a proverbializing hermeneutics.

SHEPHERDS' CALLS AND CHARMS

In approaching the complexities of the *joik* in form and in use, we find a simpler, more rudimentary counterpart in shepherd's signals. Just as the telephone's ring lets us know that we have a phone call, or the staccato beeping of a truck warns us that it is backing up, so North European agrarian cultures developed signals for conveying essential messages and identity over considerable space. These signals were most elaborate in contexts where conversation was least possible, e.g., across the large spaces of the herding landscape or wilderness. Teppo (or Feoder, as it is given in his baptismal papers) Repo, an Ingrian immigrant to Finland, remembered the signals that he had used in his youth as a shepherd in rural Ingria. His call to wake up farmwives furnishes an apt example of such signals. It is presented in Example 3.3, as transcribed by Jukka Louhivuori and Rauno Nieminen (1987: 46).

EXAMPLE 3.3

The first line of the example portrays a rooster waking the shepherd; the remainder consists of the shepherd's call to the sleeping women (Louhivuori and Nieminen 1987: 46). Here, where words would prove a strain, the shepherd used his pipe to send out a nuanced and effective message. Repo's tune conveys the fact that he is approaching the farm. His call, at its most practical, would allow the farmwife to prepare the provisions or instructions that she would have for him on his arrival. It may also have allowed him to rouse farmwives playfully, to awaken women whose lives were significantly more luxurious than that of a shepherd and who could sleep later in the mornings. In any case, as with the *joik,* this tune was seen as Repo's own. It expressed his identity, not necessarily through description (although the tune does seem to capture its creator's verve and wit), but through customary association. It was the tune by which he was known. Repo knew tunes for other aspects of his herding life and composed tunes for places and occasions in which he found himself later in life. After becoming literate musically as a military musician, Repo wrote down his repertoire, giving his pieces titles like "The Rooster Awakens the Shepherd," "Sorrow," and "The Forest Bee."

In her *Sing the Cows Home* (1985), Kerstin Brorson explores the musical world of the *fäbod,* a wilderness area that peasants in Dalarna, Sweden, used in common during the summer months. Across this rugged area of forest, field, and mountain, women tended their farms' cattle, sending messages to each other in times of need or boredom. Using a birchbark pipe, a flute fashioned from an animal's horn, or a form of vocal performance known as *kulning*, women in *fäbod* culture were able to call and command their cows so as to move the herd, begin milking, or provide other care. They were also able to call for help, even if the nearest person was engaged in similar duties miles away. Brorson writes:

> If a cow were lost during the day, a *vallkula* [cowherd] would climb a knoll and blow her message, the "my cow is lost" melody, to the east and wait for an answer. If they answered with the "we have not seen her" melody, she would repeat the procedure in the other directions. If a cow belonging to someone else came and joined a *vallkula*'s herd, she blew the "search no more, your cow is here" melody. Everyone knew these melodies, and there were also melodies for "my cow is stuck in the bog," "a wolf or bear is nearby," "I'm sick," "My cow is sick," and so on. There were also happy messages, invitations to a cup of coffee, "come over to my noon resting place," or "come to an evening by the fireplace." (1985: 94–95)

Gunnar Turesson (1960) discusses similar musical signaling in the rural tracts of Värmland, Sweden. When two people wanted to communicate over long distances, be it across a lake, through a forest, or from one field to another, they employed a combination of shouts and melody. A message was standardly prefaced by a melodic phrase, sung with the vocables *la-la* or *lo-lo*. Then the singer performed the message in short musical phrases, occasionally punctuated by the nonsense vocables. A final musical formula ended the message. Turesson collected one such message from Ester Jönsson, who had learned the mode of communication from her mother. It is reproduced below in Example 3.4 as transcribed by Turesson (1960: 85).

EXAMPLE 3.4

La-le la-le la; lôle lej! Lo-lo-lo-lo-lo! Ô-le dej!
Här växer dä môlter, här växer dä bär!
Här växer dä alla slags krydder.
A-le dej! A-le dej! O! A! Alle dä gör di, a-le dej!
(Turesson 1960: 85)

La-le la-le la; lôle lej! Lo-lo-lo-lo-lo! Ô-le you!
There's mulberries growing here, there's berries growing here!
There's all sorts of herbs growing here.
A-le dej! A-le dej! O! A! That's what they're doing a-le you!

This system is akin to the English *yoo-hoo* call, although a good deal more complex in detail. Turesson (94) notes a similar device in Shakespeare's representation of shepherd's calls in *The Winter's Tale*:

Shepherd: I'll tarry till my son come;
He hallooed but even now. Whoa, ho, hoa!
Enter Clown.
Clown: Hilloa, loa!
Shepherd: What, art so near?
(III: 3, 78–81; Craig 1961: 1231)

Turesson (1960: 86) also reports vocable singing intended to appease trolls while frightening away wolves and bears. Performances of this nature occurred especially on the first day of releasing cattle to the forest after their long winter stay in the barn. No text was used in the singing besides the vocables *li-li*, which were sung melismatically in a high, clear voice. Here, at least, melody is seen to communicate by itself, with or without verbal accompaniment. Brorson (1985: 95) notes that, as in Turi's examples, *fäbod* music also could be used in courting: "When the boys were walking up to the *fäbod* on Saturday nights, they often played an instrument or sang, so that they would be heard long before they were seen. The *vallkula* could then blow a 'welcome' melody on her horn."

How do these shepherds' calls and signals compare with Sámi *joik*? In some respects, there is substantial overlap, for instance, in a signal such as "a bear or wolf is near" and any of the numerous Sámi *joiks* referring to the bear or the wolf. Both cases seem to possess a strong interactional level, a function for music as part of what might otherwise be spoken conversation. Yet differences emerge as well. The *vallkula* plays her melody with the intent of notifying others of danger or of calling for assistance when faced by the threat of a dangerous predator. In contrast, the Sámi *joik* for a bear carries with it no instructions but rather a portrait of the essence of its referent. That portrait can then be used in conversation or musing as the performer sees fit: to comment on a bear's presence, to pay respects to a powerful animal, or merely to meditate on its nature. Brorson records an account of a young girl playing a *vallkula* tune out of context: a neighbor responded to the call by making the long hike to the *fäbod* camp only to learn that the call was not made in earnest. His displeasure at the imposition distinguishes the *vallkula*'s call from the *joik*: whereas the *joik* could be used expressively, the call could not. Its meaning was purely denotative, even if *fäbod* workers remembered calls and calling long after in a nostalgic and appreciative manner. Regardless of whether we view this difference as a mark of varying degrees of "lyricality" in the *joik* versus the shepherd's call or as a defining generic difference separating the call from true lyrics, it remains clear that function and context-dependence can run counter to the purely descriptive, contemplative, and context-free qualities observed in the lyrics discussed in the first two chapters. The various highly functional and context-dependent genres discussed below help us to explore this question further.

CHARMS

Just as shepherd's calls obscure the boundary between song and signal, so, too, charms obscure the line between ritual song and speech. In many respects it is difficult to draw a firm line between the charms available to us in medieval or modern sources and the kinds of efficacious songs described above. Through description, characterization, imitation, the singer can gain access to the very essence of a being, using that access as a means of control.

Collectors of folklore have recorded a wide array of charms or incantations from agrarian communities throughout northern Europe. Performed as need arose in daily life, charms helped people to accomplish difficult tasks, ward off evil fortune, or gain assistance from supernatural sources, especially in times of crisis, such as sickness or calamity. Where a prayer can be seen as an *entreaty* for supernatural help, a charm is generally seen as a *command:* in most cases, users believed that, provided it was performed correctly (with absolute fidelity to its wording or ritual accompaniment) and provided no countermagic had been invoked, the charm would accomplish its task. Typical is the commanding charm to ward off a bear attack, collected in Värmland, Sweden, during the 1880s:

Du är björn och jag är människa,
du är inte döpt i samma dopskål som jag.
Du skall springa i skogen
och bita i träden
men inte in mig!
(af Klintberg 1965: 99)

You are bear and I am a person,
you are not baptized in the same font as I.
You shall run in the forest
and bite trees
but you won't bite me!

As is typical of such formulas in general, this charm combines direct address and description with a kernel narrative. The bear is spoken to, told of its inferiority to the human speaker in a key aspect (Christianity), and then instructed in what it will do henceforth. The bear, hearing the incantation, will be expected to turn and bite a tree rather than the speaker.

A more cajoling tone is used in the following Finnish charm for trapping squirrels, recorded from Uhtua, Karelia, in 1888.

Oravainen, värtäjäinen,
metsän valkie vasanen,
puun puria puhtahainen,
korven kirjo lähtemäinen,
ojennaite oksaselle,
levitäite lehväselle.
Lapsimies on ampumassa,

pentukoira haukkumassa,
pärejouset, puikkonuolet,
ei ne tietä kannattane.
  (Virtanen and DuBois 2001: 182)

———————

Little squirrel, little jokester,
little white calf of the forest,
clean biter of wood,
calf with mottled ear,
you stretch upon this little branch,
extend yourself upon this leafy twig.
A young man is shooting,
a whelp is biting,
shingle bows, pin shafts,
may not carry you far.

Here, the speaker provides elaborate and loving epithets for the squirrel, disparaging himself as a mere *lapsimies* (teenager, young man,) or *pentukoira* (whelp). Ultimately, however, the charm employs the same approach used in the Swedish charm: it suggests a sequence of narrative events that will end in the speaker's victory over the squirrel.

The strongly narrative character of these charms is underscored by the incantation that the Norwegian healer Pål Jostugun (b. 1826) of Gudbrandsdalen recorded in his own book of magic at the end of the nineteenth century:

Jesus og St: Peder gik sig veien frem. Der møtte de en død mand. "Hvad skader dig?" sagde Jesus. "En slange har stungen mig." Jesus sagde "Stat op! Du skal faa bod i same stund. I 3:N: og Fader vor. (Espeland 1974: 60)

———————

Jesus and St. Peter were walking along. They met a dead man. "What harmed you?" said Jesus. "A snake stung me." Jesus said, "Stand up. You shall be healed at once." In the name of the Father, the Son, and the Holy Spirit, and an "Our Father."

Like many other Scandinavian and Finnish charms, the Christian content of this text is evident. At the same time, the text is no mere retelling of a biblical passage: the narrative and address, although reminiscent of accounts of Christ's healing, are unique to the charm itself.

Charms could also be addressed to ailments or diseases. An Anglo-Saxon charm for wens cajoles the cyst to leave by telling it that it has no home in its present site:

> Wenne, wenne, wenchichenne,
> hér ne scealt þú timbrien, ne nenne tún habben
> ac þú scealt north eonene tó þan nihgan berhge
> þér þú hauest ermig énne bróþer.
> Hé þé sceal legge léaf et héafde
> under fót wolues, under ueþer earnes,
> under earnes cléa, á þú geweornie.
> Clinge þú alswá col on heorþe.
> Scring þú alswá scearn áwáge,
> and weorne alswá weter on ambre.
> Swá lítel þú gewurþe alswá línsétcorn,
> and miccli lésse alswá ánes handwurmes hupebán,
> and alswá lítel þú gewurþe þet þú náwiht gewurþe.

> Here you shall not build, nor any dwelling have,
> But forth you must, even to the near-by hill,
> Where a poor wretch, a brother you have;
> He shall lay you a leaf at your head.
> Under the wolf's foot, under the eagle's wing,
> Under the eagle's claw—ever may you wither!
> Shrivel as the coal upon the hearth!
> Shrink as the muck in the stream,
> And dwindle even as water in a pail!
> May you become as little as a linseed grain,
> And much smaller, likewise, than a hand-worm's hip-bone!
> And even so small may you become, that you become as nought.
> (Grendon 1909: 166–67)

Here, the fact that the speaker is addressing a cyst rather than an animal seems of little consequence to the structure or mechanics of the charm. We find the same authoritative pronouncement of a coming narrative event, one that the speaker imposes on the wen with little sympathy or patience. Indeed, the speaker seems to revel in detailing the miseries of the wen in its coming predicament.

In a Scottish Gaelic charm, the speaker exerts similar authority over neighbors as well as the overall prosperity of their farms, creating an either or narrative in which others can comply with the speaker's will or suffer supernatural consequences:

Cuirim sian a bheatha bhuan,
Mu'r crodh luath, leathann, lan,
An creagan air an laigh an spreidh,
Gun eirich iad beo slan.

A nuas le buaidh 's le beannachd,
A suas le luaths 's le leannachd,
Jun ghnu, gun tnu, gun fharmad,
Gun suil bhig, gun suil mhoir,
Gun suil choig an dearmaid.

Sughaid mise seo, sughadh feith farmaid
Air ceannard an tighe 's air teaghlaich a bhaile,
Gun eirich gach droch-bhuil, 's gach droch-bhuaidh
Bu dhualta dhuibh-se dhaibh-san.

Ma mhallaich teanga duibh,
Bheannaich cridhe duibh;
Ma ghonaich suil duibh,
Shonaich run duibh.

Tionndanam is teanndanam,
Culionn cruaidh is creanndagaich
Air an caoire boirionn 's air an laoighe firionn,
Fad nan naodh 's nan naodh fichead bliadhna.

———

I will place the charm of the lasting life,
Upon your cattle active, broad, and full,
The knoll upon which the herds shall lie down,
That they may rise from it whole and well.

Down with success, and with blessing,
Up with activity and following,
Without envy, without malice, without ill-will,
Without small eye, without large eye,
Without the five eyes of neglect.

I will suck this, the sucking of envious vein
On the head of the house, and the townland families,
That every evil trait, and every evil tendency
Inherent in you shall cleave to them.

If tongue cursed you,
A heart blessed you;
If eye blighted you,
A wish prospered you.

A hurly-burlying, a topsy-turvying,
A hard hollying and a wan withering
To their female sheep and to their male calves,
For the nine and the nine score years.
   (Carmichael 1928: vol. 2, 32–33)

Here again, the impression given by the speaker is that the narrative is set—dictated by the interests and power of the speaker on behalf of a client (possibly oneself).

In most cases, such incantations were recited or read in a speaking tone, often with the accompaniment of ritual actions (e.g., blowing, sucking, spitting; application of medicinal herbs, salve, ashes, or holy water). There is evidence, however, that the charms commonly may have been sung in the past.

Anglo-Saxon texts call for the user to "sing" (e.g., Grendon 1909: vol. 2, 162, 171), and Anna-Leena Siikala (1992: 70–71) finds similar evidence for a singing tradition in Finnish epic accounts of healing rituals. The Karelian Petri Shemeikka performed his fire charm as a song when recorded in 1905 (Virtanen and DuBois 2001: 183–84). In his analysis of singing in Old Norse accounts of *seiðr* rituals, Jón Hnefill Aðalsteinsson (2001) calls attention to the reported musicality of the incantations used in these ceremonies, suggesting that such practices may have been influenced by the chanting characteristic of medieval Christian mass. In the medieval accounts that Aðalsteinsson examines, the sound of the magician's song is credited with the power to transfix, inspire, and even kill the listener (for further discussion of *seiðr*, see DuBois 1999: 121–38). I return to the topic of Christian song in the next chapter, but from the evidence left to us from pre-Christian Scandinavia, it appears unlikely that ritual song would have been wholly absent from Nordic cultures prior to the arrival of the Christian faith. Ultimately, however, the available evidence indicates that the line between "song" and "speech" in the charm genre was murky, suggesting a broader concept of performed word than that encompassed by the modern notions of melodic versus oratory delivery.

In certain respects, the charm as we find it in northern European traditions is reminiscent of the kind of lyric epitomized by the *joik*. Like *joik*, it relies on the mystical act of invocation, the notion that beings that share our cosmos will hear and heed our words. It also relies firmly on the notion of words as effectual, apparently because they share in the essence of their referents. Rather than act as "arbitrary signs" (as Saussurean linguistics would put it), words are seen, confidently, as links to the beings they identify, handles by which we can grasp, and ultimately control, the things around us.

On the other hand, in key respects, the charm as presented here differs strikingly from the *joik*, and perhaps from lyric more generally. For rather than exist to describe or to contemplate, the charm exists solely to control. This may be seen as a question of mere emphasis, as charms do on occasion present elaborate descriptions and lyrics (such as the wedding and funerary laments below) occasionally seek to control their audience. Yet the difference is qualitative as well as quantitative, for in nearly every case in which the charm tradition lives as a viable genre in northern Europe, its use outside of instances of real infirmity or need is explicitly taboo. Like the shepherd's call, the charm is bound by its function to the point that performance outside of that situation could be seen as injurious to the performer or to its potency.

A further defining difference between joik and charm appears to lie in the area of narrative. While the *joik* may be understood through reference to a narrative or, as in the case of *piobaireachd*, as a commemoration of a specific narrative event, the charm itself presents a narrative in the making. It is a script, which, through the compelling power of words, a listening entity will be forced to obey. Without the existence of this presumptive narrative, the charm would have no purpose: its very existence is predicated on the desire to effect a certain narrative outcome in the near or immediate future.

Laments in Funerals and Weddings

What can the rich tradition of wedding and funerary laments found in various parts of northern Europe tell us about this opposition of lyric descriptiveness and contemplation, on the one hand, and the strongly context-dependent, functional nature of other invocational genres, on the other? Are we dealing with an issue of degree, or of a key defining difference? As we shall see, the lament traditions examined here manage to bridge this divide through relying on the entirety of the generic axis discussed in chapter 1. While constituting context-dependent and highly functional addresses aimed at accomplishing certain ends in the listening community, they also make use of content that is readily recognized as traditional. This act allows the performance to become more than merely a present illocutionary act and to take on the contemplative and atemporal aspects that obtain from viewing the present moment within a framework of established tradition.

As discussed in chapter 2, funeral laments represent an ancient and once widespread component of northern European funerary practices. The highly formal, often first-person laments put into words a speaker's grief at the passing of a loved one. Such songs may have their moment of origin in an accompanying narrative, but they could also be performed later, as moving entertainment in ordinary singing occasions. Rachel Macdonald's eighteenth-century *Cumha na Canaraig*, which contemplates the sorrows arising from the early loss of an able fisherman and his crew, provides an apt example. An excerpt from the song illustrates its tone and content:

Do ghulan a Sheumais, bha leirsinneach, eireachdail,
Bu dumhail do dhurachd 's bu chaomhail do dheoin;

Bi faileas do chuimhne ri filbheas gu mareann domh,
Cha 'n fuaraich am flam domh am blaths bha 'nad pheig;
Bu chubhraidh ar run ann am buillsgean ar leannanachd,
Cha soradh domh bhi luaidh mu d'chagar am chluais;
Bha siubhlachd na inntinn cho riomhach'nad ghealladh domh,
Cho aoibhneach ri ban-dia mi, le millseachd do bheoil;
Bu tu gallan uraidh, a ruin, righ nam fearaibh thu,
'S iom' aite air am b'eol thu ri seoladh na stoirm;
An Arcamh, an Ile, an Eirionn 's am Mannain thu,
'S is glan a ghearradh fuaradh air Sruth na Fear Gorm.

––––––––––

Your conduct, my James, was discerning, distinguished,
Intense was your loving and kind was your wish;
The shad of your memory keeps you alive for me,
Death can never freeze up the warmth of your kiss;
Our love still was fragrant and secret our rendezvous,
'Twas sweet of you to whisper loving words in my ear,
The light of your mind was so brilliant in vows to me,
Then happy as a goddess and inspired by your talk;
Strong as a sapling were you, my love, king of men were you,
And many places knew you when riding the storm;
In Orkney, in Islay, in Ireland and Isle of Man
And safely sailing to windward the Stream of Blue Men.
    (Fergusson 1978: 46–47)

Rachel Macdonald composed the elegy soon after her husband's ship was lost. Strongly narrative in some of its verses, it also focuses directly on characterization of the dead fishermen and the sorrow their loss evokes among their survivors. As discussed in chapter 2, laments of this sort provide historical testimony to particular occasions of death and mourning in the community that produced the song. Tomás Ó Canainn (1978: 50) notes that such local memories could last for long periods in Ireland as well, sustained over the generations by the existence of a song.

    In contrast, a far more context-dependent tradition of lamentation— perhaps better termed "keening" or "dirge singing"—existed in funerary rituals throughout the region. Medieval accounts such as that in the final lines of the epic *Beowulf* indicate that the tradition of women crying for the dead reaches far back into the region's history and suffers a decline only because of strong clerical disapproval during the High Middle Ages (Honko 1963: 86–87). In this keening tradition, a lamenter (almost invariably a woman, although some men also occasionally performed as well [Honko 1963: 99], united sobbing with the chanting of highly stereotyped, improvised poetic lines (Honko 1963, 1974; Nenola 1981, 1982; Utriainen 1998). Meter, alliteration, and other marks of formal poetry occurred with frequency but usually not with the regularity characteristic of formal poetry or other lyric songs in these same cultures. Crucially, the keening tended to be directed at the deceased, and, at least in the case of Balto-Finnic laments, was regarded as a key (perhaps the only) means of communication left open between the living community and its deceased former member.

As with the charm, prohibitions usually prevented the keener from performing her songs outside of their sanctioned context. When Elias Lönnrot attempted to collect laments from women in Viena Karelia during the first half of the nineteenth century, he found them willing to dictate their compositions but disinclined to actually perform them. At last, one of the younger women consented to the collector's request that she perform as if in an actual funeral, despite the strong dissuasion of the other women present (Utriainen 1998: 186). Similar experiences marked fieldwork expeditions throughout the Balto-Finnic song region, and find a parallel in Ireland (Cowell 1957: 11). That the supernatural banshee and the mortal keening woman merge in Irish folk legendry is probably a sign of the degree to which the sound of the keening itself became an object of dread or foreboding among the living (Lysaght 1986: 64–86). On the other hand, a variety of lament existed outside of the funeral and wedding rituals and could be performed in more ordinary contexts. These "occasional laments" merge strongly with other types of lyric songs of sorrow (Nenola 1982: 205–34).

In its proper context, the funerary lament was regarded as a desirable, even essential element of the community's leave-taking of a loved one. Women avidly participated in the ritual, often communally, and the custom survived well in a number of places in the Balto-Finnic region, despite the official disapproval of Soviet authorities and a more generalized decline in folk song traditions in the same area (Nenola 1982: 250–51; Honko 1993: 571). Scholars of the Balto-Finnic lament tradition have examined the degree to which such lamentation expressed communal understandings of the afterlife, as well as ways in which the performance gave voice to personal relations ruptured by death (Honko 1963; Apo 1981; Nenola 1982; Honko, Timonen, and Branch 1993; Utriainen 1998). Directed at the deceased, the laments of keening women were regarded as efficacious communications, ensuring the peace of the deceased's soul and its passage into the next life, provided they were performed properly and without excess (Utriainen 1998: 188). At the same time, the lament had functions among the living: it marked key steps in the unfolding ritual procedure (e.g., washing the corpse, carrying it to the cemetery, burying and commemorating it) and underscored the efficacy of the ongoing ritual to handle and heal the rupture in the community that death had created (Honko, Timonen, and Branch 1993: 572–73). Thus, the audience for the lament was also to be found among the living, who saw in it both a paragon of mourning behavior and the assurance that proper custom was being performed. In this sense, the keening lament underscored the event's traditionality, enveloping the present experience in the reassuring web of past tradition. This fact allows the lament to rise above the present in crucial ways: it permits its performer and audience to view their situation in an atemporal, traditionalized manner, to find consolation in the sharing of grief with past generations.

Stereotyped expressions and nomenclature underscore this connection with tradition and the past. Typically, the deceased is referred to with names and images that derive from the locale's own lament tradition, one that may be, in the case of Balto-Finnic laments, quite specific (Nenola 1981: 46–48; 1982: 57–78). By referring to the deceased along these highly stereotyped lines, the personal experience and communication of sorrow is merged with the collective experience of past generations. The character of such lamentation is illustrated by the following Karelian lament.

Tulgua valgiet syndyset
valgieta armastani valgein
tuohustulien kera vastualemah.
Tulgua olevat spuassaset orheiarmastani
oigeis käydysis ottelemah.

Kui tulou tuntemattomih muahusih.
Availgua Abraman aiguhiset ruajun veriähyöt.

Viisiltoista vintoil verijät vibuveriähyöt avualgua.
Kui vakkimuahusil tulou,
pitkien matkasien peril.

Vietelgiä valgiet syndyset
vihandoi nurmizie myöte.
Viekoitelgua polvisyndyiset juamaset
kuldaisel armaiselleni kublaksendella.

Annelgua valgiel armahaiselleni näiksi
aigasiksi omat valgiet valdaset.
Kui jo lähti ennen käymättömil
da toitshi tuntemattomil goroasil.

Ylen suuret igäväiset jättelit
sulih syndysih mendyö.
        (Impilahti, Karelia; Virtanen and DuBois 2001: 156–57)

————

Come shining spirits
To receive my shining beloved one
Amid the shining waxen candles.
Come blessed saints to take my noble beloved
By the right hand.

When my love comes to those unknown worlds,
Open the gates of Paradise as old as Abraham.
Open the snare gates that turn on fifteen screws,
When my love comes to the strange doors,
To the destination of long journeys.

Take my love, shining spirits,
Along the verdant meadows.
Mark out, spirits of love,
Post roads for my dear beloved to walk.

Give to my shining beloved
Shining freedom for these times.
Since my love has already left
To those untrammeled and unknown pathways.

You left a great longing behind
When you left for the eternal fortress.

Epithets for the deceased, and for saints and other helping spirits, recur plentifully throughout the lament, announcing at once the text's addressees as well as its traditionality. The commands directed at the supernatural audience, often repeated with nearly synonymous alternate lines, underscore the historical continuity of the death experience: the deceased will pass along the same pathways that have always been used, reaching the gates of paradise as old as Abraham. The speaker's own emotions are also traditionalized, summed up in phrases like "great longing" or in stereotypical descriptions of the speaker's dilemma. In these ways, the ritual moment and the actual experience become static—reflections of a set of experiences that members of the community have passed through for ages. This traditionality gives the lament a sense of descriptiveness, of stasis, that moves it beyond the solely illocutionary act and into one of lyric contemplation.

In the Balto-Finnic cultural area, weddings, too, attracted their share of invocational songs, both laments and more fixed-text "wedding songs." In the wedding, two individuals are joined as one, but two families and two communities are also profoundly altered by the event. Given the collective nature of this experience, and its importance for the survival of the community as a whole, it is not surprising that community members would use their culture's lament and song traditions as a means to comment on and influence the marital couple. Elaborate wedding lyrics, performed over the multiple days of the wedding ritual by participants, kin, or semiprofessional wedding singers, were a common and highly valued part of the wedding ritual (Virtanen and DuBois 2001: 152–55).

During the Ingrian betrothal and wedding, the bride was expected to sing traditional laments to her father, godfather, godmother, aunts, brothers, sisters, uncles, and other relations, each growing in intensity until the address to the mother. In the following betrothal lament, the song encodes the very lines by which the bride is to confront her mother and express remorse for their coming separation.

Suloinen sukijaiseni
kallis kantajaiseni
helle helmoin-tuojaiseni!

Olisit tukehuttanut, tuutijaiseni
olisit oikaissut olkiloin päälle ottajaiseni
kattanut kankaan alle, kasvattelijaiseni
käsilläsi olisi liikuttanut liivat, leikuttelijaiseni
sormillasi poiminut someret, suorittelijaiseni!
Olisit pannut liivoihin lämpimiin, lämmittelijäiseni
someriin suojiin soritellut, sorittajaiseni!

Mie olisin makaellut, maalle tuojaiseni,
liivojen lämpymässä, lämmiteltyiseni
somerien suojassa, sorittelijaiseni.

Olisit silloin siekin ollut huoletta,
huolittelijaiseni,
murehitta muijoiseni, tuojaiseni,
miun perästä pesettelijäiseni.
      (Virtanen and DuBois 2001: 154)

———————

Beloved woman who carried me
Treasured one who bore me
Shining one who brings my hems!

You should have suffocated me, you who
Crooned to me, you should have struck me
On straw, you who carried me,
Dunked me in the marsh, you who reared me,
With your hand you should have moved sand,
You who soothed me, with your finger
Plucked gravel, you who readied me.

You should have put me into warmer sand,
You who gave me warmth, pressed me into
Gravelly swamps, you who soothed me.

I would have lain, you who brought me to earth,
Warm in my sand, you who gave me warmth,
In the protection of gravel, you who soothed me.

Then you, too, would have been untroubled
You who cared for me,
Unpained by my familiar form, you who bore me,
You who washed me after my birth.

Here, addressing her mother with a string of epithets characteristic of wedding laments, the bride tells her mother that she would have preferred death as an infant to having to leave their home now as a bride. Her words are meant as catharsis: to release the emotions inherent in this parting of the ways for mother and daughter, scripting in the process a set of convictions that each person is assumed or asserted to have at the moment. There is no room here for an expression of sincerity. The song is simply assumed to represent the feelings of the bride—or of brides in general—at the moment of leaving home. This lament phase of the wedding continued as the bride prepared for her new life by assuming the headdress, clothing, and status of a married woman. It was considered vital to induce a bride to cry, for, as an Ingrian song put it, "kun et itke männessäisi, itket siellä ollessaisi" (If you don't weep when you go you will weep when you are there) (Honko, Timonen, and Branch 1993: 463).

Once the groom arrived on the scene, the "song" portion of the wedding began. In Karelian weddings, songs welcomed and saw the bride off to the groom's home. Once there, other songs sought to compel the new couple to act properly in their new life together. Singing for an audience in the here and now, the speaker nonetheless fit audience and performer into traditionalized images and roles. In thoroughly familiar local tradition, the bridegroom was described as a swooping eagle, snatching the farm's prize daughter for his own. The bride was described as heroically diligent, weaving with such industriousness that the village could hardly find peace at night. And the singer herself could express a call for drink, protesting that she would not continue on a parched throat. What is striking is that all of these roles are stereotyped, bearing only

occasional resemblance to the actual bride, groom, or singer. Further, such traditionality was abundantly evident to all participants in the wedding ceremony,
since the same songs had been heard numerous times before. So it is with songs
that describe the bride or the couple's new home, advise the groom to treat
his bride gently (beating her only behind closed doors), or admonish the new
daughter-in-law to carry out her duties earnestly, rising before sunrise and taking upon herself every possible task (see DuBois 1995: 253–55; Virtanen and
DuBois 2001: 150–51). Lest a participant take the performances too seriously,
however, another song was sung to reassure all involved.

> Laulust ei lakkii käyvä
> Pie ei virsestä vihhaa
> Ei pie suuttuu suusanoista;
> Ei oo virret teistä tehty
> Teistä tehty, meistä tehty
> Virret viitta, kuutta vaste
> Ei o virret eklen tehty
> Teht on toissa torstakinna.

> Don't take the song to heart
> One shouldn't be angered by the verse
> One shouldn't anger at the words
> The verses were not made about you
> Made about you, made about us,
> Five verses, just six
> The verses were not made yesterday
> They were made another Thursday.
>   (DuBois 1995: 256)

What illocutionary force these songs contained, in other words, was veiled behind assurances of traditionality: one should not take the songs *personally,* since
they were composed on "another Thursday." Yet that traditionality had its own
power of compulsion, leading the listeners to comply with the advice not because of its specificity but because of its gnomic force: it was advice that *always*
made for a good marriage. And as the participants lost their specific wedding

into the framing songs of tradition, so their understanding of such songs could become more static, more descriptive, more lyrical.

PIOBAIREACHD

Context dependence and illocutionary function compete with the stasis and descriptiveness of the invocational lyric. When a song's function and place in a given ritual are foregrounded, in other words, it can become difficult to view the song as somehow independent of that function and context. The generic axis offers a community a means of interpreting such songs as more than solely present directives. Instead, they can view them as signs of a continuity of culture and experience that began in the past and that encompasses the present. This same powerful notion of traditionality helps to raise the Scottish *piobaireachd* to the same level of resonance that the *joik* enjoys.

The elaborate Scottish bagpipe performances known as *piobaireachd* were originally intended "to assemble men for battle, to excite them on the battlefield, and to express appropriate feelings at births, weddings, funerals, and other solemn occasions" (Cannon 2002: 95). These functions became known as classes of *piobaireachd*, so that we can speak of "the Battle-tune," "The Gathering," "The Salute," and "The Lament" (Collinson 1966: 175). Composed of a base melody (an *urlar*, "ground"), along with a set progression of changes in musical ornamentation, the *piobaireachd* piece expresses or elicits the essence of a particular emotion.

Like the *joik*, *piobaireachd* achieves its evocative effects through a series of stereotyped and collectively recognized musical techniques, familiar to players and audiences alike. These consist chiefly of a sequence of regularly applied grace note ornaments, which interrupt the melodic flow and alter the emotional charge of the piece. After an initial, comparatively unadorned run through the *urlar*, the player repeats the piece over and over, adding progressively more complex sequences of grace notes, which serve initially to increase but eventually to decrease the tempo, causing player and audience to dwell on particular notes or phrases. At its most elaborate, the *piobaireachd* rendition may consist of eight such movements, beginning and ending with the *urlar* and including runs with single interspersed grace notes and then series of three to seven such notes played in conjunction with every major note of the air. The entire rendition may take some five to twenty minutes to complete and acquires a transfixing, nearly hypnotic quality (Collinson 1966: 185). It is a solo performance genre, one highlighting the virtuoso skills of the player but also the singular emotions of its content or implied speaker.

Whereas *joik* tends toward the atemporal and the proverbial, *piobaireachd*, like much of Scottish and Irish lyric music, tends toward the attributive and the narrativizing. The technique itself, as well as a number of its major airs, is attributed to the MacCrimmon family, hereditary pipers to the MacLeods of Skye (Collinson 1966: 186). Most modern sources for this attribution derive from a single work—Angus MacKay's 1839 *Collection of Ancient Piobaireachd or Highland Pipe Music*—but it is likely that MacKay obtained his information from local oral tradition as well as the testimony of living pipers, some of whom may have belonged to the MacCrimmon family (Cannon 2002: 97). According to this tradition, the sixteenth-century Iain Odhar ("dun") MacCrimmon taught the technique to his sons, one of whom, Donald Mór ("great") MacCrimmon, is said to have composed some of the *urlars* that are known today, thus dating them to the early seventeenth century. These pieces span the typical thematic repertoire of *piobaireachd:* a lament (*Donald Dughal Mackay's Lament*), a salute (*The MacDonald's Salute*), and a march (*The Earl of Ross's March*). Also credited to Donald Mór is a topical song, whose very title, *MacLeod's Controversy,* implies a narrativized hermeneutics (Collinson 1966: 187). Later members of the family are also credited with composing various pieces. Donald Ban MacCrimmon is credited with the piece *Cha Till mi Tuille* (MacCrimmon Will Never Return), which he is said to have composed after a premonition of his death in a battle during the 1745 Rising (Collinson 1966: 196). Another gloss explains the existence of the *piobaireachd Fuoris Póóge i spoge i Rhí* (I Got a Kiss of the King's Hand), which is said to have been composed in 1651 by either John McGyurmen or Patrick MacCrimmon in response to King Charles II's offer to allow the piper to kiss his hand (Cannon 2002: 52–52). That accounts differ not on the detail of the kiss but as to whom the kiss was awarded reflects the workings of such oral tradition, and the vying that might go on in attributing songs to certain players. As with all attributive lore, we cannot say for certain at this point that any of the *urlars* were composed by the figures they are credited to in oral tradition.

Along with composer attribution came narratives concerning the situations and circumstances in which the *urlar* was composed. Roderick D. Cannon (2002: 97) suggests that such stories may have arisen out of the experience of performing a vocal song (perhaps a ballad) in instrumental rendition: "There was a song, and the prose legend we have is a *précis* of the song, while the pibroch is a pipe version of the air." Collinson (1966: 64) provides a possible example in the lament *Tog orm mo phìob*, attributed to Patrick Mór MacCrimmon, the words of which still exist as a separate song. The narrative, then, would compensate for the loss of words in the musical performance. This theory does not account, however, for all the narratives we have left to us, nor does it acknowledge the strong tradition of narrativized hermeneutics that surrounds lyrics in general in Scottish and Irish tradition.

Samuel Johnson records one such narrative in connection with the tune *Glengarry's March* (also known as *Cill Chriosd*) in his *Journey to the Western Islands of Scotland* (1775). After complaining about poor accommodations at Glenelg, Johnson turns positive in praising the home, manners, and ash trees of Sir Alexander Macdonald of Skye. In detailing their dinner at his estate, Johnson writes:

> As we sat at Sir Alexander's table, we were entertained, according to the ancient usage of the North, with the melody of the bagpipe. Everything in those countries has its history. As the bagpiper was playing, an elderly Gentleman informed us, that in some remote time, the Macdonalds of Glengary having been injured, or offended by the inhabitants of Culloden, and resolving to have justice or vengeance, came to Culloden on a Sunday, where finding their enemies at worship, they shut them up in the church, which they set on fire; and this, said he, is the tune that the piper played while they were burning. ([1775] 1924: 44)

Johnson, far from a friend of the notion of oral tradition, nonetheless finds the information provided by the "elderly Gentleman" of sufficient interest to include in his travelogue. In defense of his editorial choice, he writes, "Narrations like this, however uncertain, deserve the notice of the traveller, because they are the only records of a nation that has no historians, and afford the most genuine representation of the life and character of the ancient Highlanders" (44). In fact, it could be argued that the Scots and the Irish have had more than their fair share of historians, leading to the kind of elaborate, historicizing, narrativized hermeneutics in connection with even a piece of what was, for Johnson and his dinner companions, merely background music. The *urlar* associated with this violent tale was published as sheet music during the nineteenth century and has been reproduced on a piping website.[3] Example 3.5 is a simplified rendering of that transcription.

EXAMPLE 3.5

James Logan records another example of a *piobaireachd* narrative in his 1845 *Clans of the Scottish Highlands*. In describing highland festivities, he writes:

> About sixty years ago there was a banquet given in the highlands on some joyful occasion, and during the evening there was a call for the bards to be brought to the upper end of the room, on which Mac Nicail of Scoirebreac exclaimed, "the bards are extinct." "No," quickly replied Alasdair bui' Mac I'vor, "they are not extinct; but those who delighted to patronise them are gone!" This genuine highlander felt keenly the decadence of those ancient, social manners, which characterised his ancestors. (1845: 45)

It should be noted that this narrative has no direct link with either the moment of composition or the composer of the piece. Yet, because it sums up effectively the emotional quality of the *piobaireachd*, it is remembered in connection with it. The piece itself was transcribed by the piper Duncan Campbell in 1853, in a manuscript of pipe tunes that Campbell produced at the height of his career as piper to the duke of Atholl. The tune appears on a piping website[4] and is reproduced in Example 3.6 in simplified form.

EXAMPLE 3.6

Narrative glosses were not always as widespread as the tunes themselves, however. In the case of the *piobaireachd* known as *A' Bhoilich* (The Vaunting), Angus MacKay, one of the earliest writers and collectors of Scottish *piobaireachd*, was able to find no narrative explanation for it in preparing his 1839 collection of highland tunes. He noted simply that the piece was composed by Raonnull Mac Ailean oig, a piper of the MacDonald family of Morar. The later scholar Ian MacKay (2002), however, records an explanatory legend for the same song, from which we can infer either that he was a better researcher on such topics (a difficult assertion) or that a narrativized explanation had developed in the century intervening between the two investigations. The narrative itself—in which a young piper revives from a severe illness on hearing the beauty of the lament his teacher had composed for him—could easily have developed much later. Indeed, the tale seems intended to explain the piece's unusual title, which is said to have come from the fact that the piece could no longer be termed a lament, since its referent was again among the living. And because any song that served to revive its referent from his deathbed could surely be viewed as the cause of a boast, the title for the piece followed naturally.

Such cases reveal that the nearly mystical force of the invocational lyric— so evident in the *joik* and evident in ritual genres such as charms and laments— can exist in conjunction with a largely narrative hermeneutics as well: the rendition brings forth to performer and audience a past event and character, which are made present for the time of the performance and which potentially comment in their essence on a present situation. Like the *joik*, *piobaireachd* works by encapsulating an essence and attitude, associating them with a particular piece of music that can then be used to evoke those qualities at the performer's choice.

With each of the varieties of musical performance discussed above, an illocutionary function competes with the purely descriptive apparatus of lyric song. Performers sing particular pieces in order to effect certain behaviors in their immediate environment. The *joik* singer recalls an absent being through song, making that entity present in the assembled community of singer and listeners. The characterization that entity receives in the *joik* can prove a powerful means of social control. In contrast, the shepherd's call expresses a concrete directive, with only an incidental descriptive or aesthetic component, even if performers sometimes experience it aesthetically and may perform other songs that are more aesthetically oriented as well. The charm singer uses a set progression of words and actions to compel an entity to behave in a certain manner for the benefit of the singer and/or client. The performer of funeral or wedding laments seeks to situate a present reality in the context of past events, urging listeners to heed the call and the comfort of tradition. The performer of *piobai-reachd* seeks to evoke a particular emotion from an audience, shaping the audience's attitude to a present situation through a rendition of stereotyped aural images.

Crucial to each of these genres is invocation: the direct address of an actual or purported listening entity. Invocation is not simply a stylistic choice; on a fundamental level, it shapes the views of singer and audience alike regarding the likely efficacy of the performance and its place in managing the behaviors and events of the immediate environment. It pulls the performance away from the stasis and calm of aesthetic description toward the dynamic pole of an illocutionary agenda. In so doing, it underscores the communicative nature of lyric in general, tying its potentially timeless images of emotion and attitude to a concrete world close at hand. It is a world that individuals not only experience but also seek to shape through their songs.

CHAPTER 4

Conversing with God

Medieval Religious Lyric and Its Interpretation

[S]ed implemini Spiritu,
loquentes vobismet ipsis in psalmis et hymnis et canticis
spiritalibus cantantes et psallentes in cordibus vestris Domino.

———

Be filled with the Spirit,
speaking to one another in psalms and hymns and spiritual songs,
singing and making melody in your hearts to the Lord.

Ephesians 5:18–19

Chapters 2 and 3 examined modes by which lyrics and related genres were interpreted within northern European song traditions, both medieval and more recent. In the survey of lyric interludes within poetic or prose epic texts, we noted the existence of both narrativized and proverbialized hermeneutics and explored how medieval scribes encoded or reflected interpretive norms through their deployment of lyrics within narrative entities. Here I examine how these frameworks become adapted and expanded in the assimilation of the religious hymn tradition that arrives with Christianity. Northern Europeans used their existing lyric traditions to produce hymns of their own, gradually developing a highly personalized, contemplative hymnody that had native roots and also showed the influence of mystical thinkers from central, southern, and, eventually, northern Europe. As the coming chapters show, this new tradition exerted strong influence on secular lyrics as well, and a tension between secular and spiritual lyrics became pronounced, with much competition and cross-fertilization. To understand the influence of this new type of lyric on interpretive practices in medieval Europe, I survey the evolution of hymnody in northern Europe from the early medieval period to the eve of the Reformation.

It should be noted at the outset that the topic of medieval religious lyric has, happily, received a great deal of attention, particularly in English-language scholarship. Peter Dronke's classic, *The Medieval Lyric* ([1968] 1996), contains a fine survey of the development of the genre on the Continent, and a number of other works have surveyed the genre in England (e.g., Greenberg 1961; Davies 1963; Stevick [1964] 1994; Silverstein 1971; Luria and Hoffman 1974; Gray [1975] 1992). The following discussion draws on this foundation but focuses on issues of interpretation, which are only tangentially treated in most previous works. In tracing the development of a highly emotive religious lyric tradition during the twelfth and thirteenth centuries, I suggest that such lyrics provided models for interpretive practices that eventually became normative in the genre as a whole. Of particular importance is the expectation of emotional identification with the speaker of the song, a practice that plays a central role in later lyrics.

THE LITURGICAL ROOTS OF HYMNODY

Three occasions of hymn singing in the Christian New Testament map the logic and justification for the liturgical and personal use of sacred song. In the first instance (Lk 2:10–14), at the birth of the Savior, angels sing his praises on high, performing the first of what would eventually become thousands of Christmas carols. In the second instance (Mt 26:30, Mk 14:26), Jesus prepares for the Passion by singing a hymn with his apostles, thereby gaining strength and resolve for the difficult events that follow. In the third instance, in the infancy of the new faith, Saint Paul and his disciple Silas keep up their spirits in prison by singing hymns deep into the night (Acts 16:25). These moments inform hymn use in northern Europe from the early medieval period onward. Performed to proclaim publicly a shared understanding of the cosmos and the sacred, hymns can also serve as sources of personal comfort or reassurance in times of trial. In either case, they accomplish the same task: they place words in the singers' mouths that are meant to express each singer's love for God and, significantly, to shape that singer's personal views and practices into an expression deemed most pleasing to God.

While such scriptural references provide a textual justification of hymnody, liturgical practices inherited from Judaism gave the singing of spiritual songs its real foundation in Christian worship. The liturgical music and song of early Christianity derived almost entirely from the Hebrew and Greek Scriptures, the Book of Psalms in particular. As in Jewish practice, the presider over the choir or bishop was authorized to select a psalm for performance in the daily liturgy. The selection often rested on thematic emphases of the emerging liturgical year: for example, a psalm of joy on days associated with celebration (Easter, Pentecost); psalms of sorrow associated with moments of sorrow (Good Friday). Even today, the psalms hold a central place in most Christian liturgies, one seldom truly displaced by later Christian hymns.

In monastic practice, however, the performance of the psalms took on still greater significance, and many orders sought to perform all of the psalms over the course of every day. The monastic rules of the early Middle Ages—in particular, that of Saint Benedict (ca. 480–547)—distributed this performance over the course of the week and localized singing to certain temporal moments, corresponding to the solar divisions of the Roman day. By meeting nine times per day, monks were able to cover the Book of Psalms over the course of the week. In addition, codification of the liturgy in the various breviaries of the church from the fourth century onward continued to specify one psalm for performance in each day's mass. In this way, the religious lyric came to play a prominent role in the worship of Christian communities.

Although the psalms held a prime place in Christian prayer and song, other texts from the Hebrew Scriptures and the New Testament enjoyed prominence as well. The interpolated song in praise of God in the third chapter of the Book of Daniel for instance (Dn 3:52–90) became a familiar hymn under the title *Benedicite* and was regularly performed as part of the church Office from an early period onward. Its familiarity in the earliest Christian communities of northern Europe is evidenced by the text of the Anglo-Saxon poems *Daniel* and *Azarias* (Farrell 1974). The lyric anthology known as the Song of Songs, attributed to King Solomon but interpreted in medieval Christianity as a dialogue between God and his church (Gordis 1974), also enjoyed tremendous popularity throughout the medieval period and contributed a variety of important images to later religious as well as secular lyrics. From the New Testament, Mary's lyric song of praise for God (Lk 1:46–55) became familiar to Christians as the *Magnificat*—the voice, text, and beauty of which proved decisive in the development of later Latin and vernacular hymns composed in the voice and manner of the Virgin. The text itself echoes the Old Testament song of Hannah, recounted at the outset of the Book of Samuel (1 Sm 2:1–10) and suggests in this

non horruisti Virginis uterum.
Tu, devicto mortis aculeo,
aperuisti credentibus regna caelorum.
Tu ad dexteram Dei sedes,
in gloria Patris.
Iudex crederis
esse venturus.
Te ergo quaesumus, tuis famulis subveni:
quos pretioso sanguine redemisti.
Aeterna fac cum sanctis tuis
in gloria numerari.
Salvum fac populum tuum, Domine,
et benedic hereditati tuae.
Et rege eos, et extolle illos
usque in aeternum.
Per singulos dies
benedicimus te;
Et laudamus nomen tuum in saeculum,
et in saeculum saeculi.
Dignare, Domine, die isto
sine peccato nos custodire.
Miserere nostri, Domine,
miserere nostri.
Fiat misericordia tua, Domine, super nos,
quemadmodum speravimus in te.
In te, Domine, speravi:
non confundar in aeternum.
      (Cabrol 1929: 419–21)

———————

O God, we praise you and acknowledge you as Lord.
You, eternal Father, the entire earth reveres you—
All the Angels, the heavens and powers of the universe,
Cherubim and Seraphim, in unceasing voice proclaim:
Holy, Holy, Holy, Lord God of Hosts!
Heaven and earth are full of the Majesty of your glory.

The glorious chorus of the Apostles,
The wonderful company of Prophets,
The host of martyrs, clothed in white sing praise.
Throughout the universe, the holy Church acknowledges you:
Oh Father of infinite majesty;
your adorable, true and only Son;
Also the Holy Spirit, the Consoler.
You King of glory, Christ!
Thou art the eternal Son of the Father.
When you took it upon yourself to liberate us,
you did not disdain the Virgin's womb.
Having overcome the sting of death, you opened for the faithful
the Kingdom of Heaven.
You sit at the right hand of God in the glory of the Father.
We believe that you will judge us one day.
We therefore implore you to help your servants
whom your precious blood has redeemed.
Let them be numbered with Thy Saints in everlasting glory.
Save your people, Lord, and bless your inheritance.
Guide them and raise them up for eternity.
Day by day we bless you.
And we praise your name through the centuries and from age to age.
Grant us, O Lord, that this day we may live without sin.
Have pity on us, O Lord, have pity on us.
Let your mercy be upon us, O Lord, as we have placed our hope in you.
I place my hope in you, O Lord: I will not be confounded ever.

When we regard a lyric like the *Te Deum*, rich in allusion to both the *Magnificat* and the *Benedicite* but more emphatically Christian in its theology, we are confronted not so much by an extrapolated speaker through whose eyes we view the world for a moment but rather by an emphatic inscription of a timeless conversation, one that pulls the singer forcefully into the inclusive *We* of the church, the universe, the angels and saints, dictating through its descriptions the singer's own feelings and perceptions of God. Out of the forty-three lines in the Latin text, about 30 percent begin with some form of the second-person pronoun *Tu*, lending the hymn an unmistakably vocative and beseeching tone: God is our interlocutor, our *Tu*, with whom the *We* of the hymn is on respectful but self-assured terms, confident of God's listening presence and openness to entreaty. As the hymn details, the suppliant *We* includes not simply all present or living Christians but all who have gone before or will come hereafter, along with the entirety of God's creation, united in universal praise for the king. The lyric allows an *I* to emerge only in its final verb *speravi* (I have placed my trust), creating punctuation through expressing a personal voice at the end of a corporate address. It is through this tiny final *I* that the individual is allowed to make a timorous personal petition to God while finding support and even protection in the triumphant adoring *We* of the hymn as a whole. The religious lyric in this sense is far more corporate and didactic than the secular, causing the singer's potentially unruly constellation of perceptions and desires to conform to the clear and accepted theology of the faith. In a very concrete sense, the religious lyric puts words in our mouths.

We may note also that the *Te Deum* conforms to the rhetorical frameworks for praise poetry that Georges Dumézil (1943: 82) identifies in his comparative study of Indo-European worldview. The broad formulas *laudo ut des* (I praise so that you will give) and *dedisti, laudavi, da* (You gave, I have praised, now give)—typical of ancient panegyrics from Rome to India—become embodied in Christian hymns from Ambrose onward, continuing a role for the genre of praise poetry that is rooted in the ancient practices of Indo-European court poets in general (see also McKenna 1991: 5). The poet praises so as to underscore the social and economic relations that bind lord and follower; the lord receives praise and requites it generously to show his acknowledgment of the responsibilities of his office. Requests are made through reminding the lord of his past good deeds and asking for a continuation of the exemplary behavior already displayed. In this sense, the praise poem-turned-prayer not only puts words in our mouths but prescribes actions for God as well. As we shall see, cultural variations in the expression of these ancient rhetorical norms gradually became harmonized through the growing dominance of a particular variety of Christian hymnody during the course of the Middle Ages.

SAINTS' HYMNS AND NARRATIVES

The Latin hymnody pioneered by Saint Ambrose evolved during the next two centuries. Hymns composed in honor of specific saints began to appear, filling in new liturgical gaps created by the development of the cult of the saints (Brown

1981). The spread of Christianity had led to the spread of sainthood beyond the confines of the Mediterranean world, and because saints and their shrines were now to be found throughout the reaches of Christendom, it made sense that new Latin hymns in honor of these saints would find authors throughout the Christian world. Such hymns found place in the Breviary as it expanded beyond its original core Psalter to incorporate a Proper of the Season, a Proper of the Saints, the Common, and the special Offices. Accompanying hymnody received new impetus and inspiration through the efforts of Pope Gregory the Great (ca. 540–604), whose own hymns enriched the Breviary and whose musical interests are reflected in the term for liturgical plainsong—Gregorian chant. Subsequent medieval popes returned repeatedly to the task of revising or expanding the church's store of sacred hymns.

Although Latin hymnody rose up around various saints, hymns and prayers addressing the Virgin Mary enjoyed prominence. Such works were primarily clerical in composition and liturgical in performance, but evidence in the medieval texts points toward a strong popular embrace of hymns and their efficacy in daily life. In a twelfth-century compendium of legends of the Virgin (Crane 1925), many of them ascribed to British or northern European locales, the Virgin frequently indicates her pleasure at hearing herself praised in song. In one such legend, the Virgin appears to a priest to teach him how to chant her Complines correctly (no. 29); in another, she restores the authority of a priest who has been removed from office for his ignorance of all Masses but that of the Virgin (no. 9). A legend of Saint Dunstan recounts how the Virgin herself led Dunstan to her chapel at the cathedral of Canterbury so that he could hear the choir sing a particular hymn in her honor (no. 25). A cleric who had made a habit of singing the "Five Gaudes" in praise of the Virgin is visited by her at his deathbed, where she assures him of rich reward in the hereafter (no. 4). In other legends, Mary rewards singing of her praise with miraculous help. A prior who had regularly sung hours to the Virgin was rescued from torment after death by an approving Mary (no. 12). In a storm at sea, an abbot convinces his traveling companions to invoke the Virgin and chant a Latin response in her honor: as a result, a light appears above the mast and the storm abates (no. 28). The thirteenth-century Saint Birgitta of Sweden was widely said to have seen in a vision that she and her followers would be protected from angry Romans if they recited the lyric of praise *Maria Stella Maris*. Such accounts, extant in both Latin and vernacular, were matched by official incentives for the repetition of certain lyrics in praise of Mary, Jesus, or others. These incentives—indulgences—

guaranteed a shortening of time in purgatory if the person praying repeated the lyric with sincerity and faith. Numerous Marian lyrics were awarded indulgences, including the *Magnificat,* the rosary, and Bernard of Clairvaux's majestic *Salve Regina* (Canal 1963). Such accounts and customs clearly increased the performance of religious lyrics, leading some to be repeated numerous times in a single day. Combined with the compelling calls for assistance in the lyrics themselves, such works appealed to the faithful on a fundamental and emotive level. It probably reflects not only liturgical but also folk practice that the character of Mary in the fifteenth-century N. Town Mary Play states of the *Magnificat*:

> This psalme of prophesye seyd betwen vs tweyn,
> In hefne it is wretyn with aungellys hond;
> Evyr to be songe and also to be seyn,
> Euery day amonge us at oure evesong.
>   (Meredith 1997: 82)

From Latin to Vernacular Hymns

It was during the first real flowering of Latin hymnody that Christianity reached northern Europe, first in the Roman settlements of Britain and soon finding fruitful ground in Ireland. After the sixth-century Anglo-Saxon invasion of England, a combination of Roman and Irish missionaries reconverted the island, and monks from the resulting society played a prominent role in the conversion of most of the rest of northern Europe. Latin learning may have seemed an exotic and aloof intellectual tradition for these early converts, but it also served as a direct line into the heart of European art and philosophy. Without the unifying force of Latin, native geniuses like the Venerable Saint Bede and Charlemagne's adviser Alcuin could not had gained the continental education they acquired in England, nor would they have attained the broader European prominence and respect that their works enjoyed both during their lifetimes and after.

From nearly the beginning, however, the Christian communities of northern Europe proved not simply recipients of this Latin heritage but also active contributors to its treasures. By the sixth century, Irish monks were composing hymns in Latin, creating their own innovative and startlingly complex combinations of metaphor, syllabic verse, rhyme, and alliteration. Indeed, the liturgical practice of invoking the names of saints in long litanies has been traced to the Irish church and was actively promoted by Irish missionaries elsewhere in the British Isles (McKenna 1991: 59). It is difficult to miss the connection of the earliest Hiberno-Latin works with native Irish lyrics as we know them from medieval epics and from the kinds of invocations discussed in chapter 3. Illustrative of such works is the hymn *Noli Pater,* attributed to Saint Columba (Columcille, ca. 521–97) and preserved in the eleventh-century Irish *Liber Hymnorum.*

> Noli pater indulgere tonitrua cum fulgore
> ac frangamur formidine huius atque uridine
>
> Te timemus terribilem nullum credentes similem
> te cuncta canunt carmina angelorum per agmina
>
> Teque exultent culmina cæli uagi per fulmina
> o Iesu amantissime o rex regum rectissime
>
> Benedictus in sæcula recta regens regimina
> Iohannes coram domino adhuc matris in utero
>
> Repletus dei gratia pro uino atque siccera
>
> Elizabeth et Zacharias uirum magnum genuit
> Iohannem baptizam precursorem domini
>
> Manet in meo corde dei amoris flamma
> ut in argenti uase auri ponitur gemma.
> (Bernard and Atkinson 1898: vol. 1, 88; trans. of preface, vol. 2, 28)

> Give not full power, O Father, to the thunder and lightning,
> Lest we be overwhelmed by the fearful might and blazing fires.
> We fear Thee, the Terrible One, believing that there is none like Thee:
> All the songs throughout the ranks of the angels praise Thee;
> And the heights of the wide Heaven by the thunderbolts extol Thee.
> O most loving Jesus, O most righteous King of kings,

Thou Regent of righteous hosts, blessed art Thou forever.
Elizabeth and Zacharias were the parents of a Mighty Man,
John the Baptist, the Forerunner of the Lord.
John at the Presence of the Lord, while still in his Mother's womb,
Instead of wine and strong drink, was filled with the Grace of God.
The flame of Love of God abides in my heart
Like a jewel of gold set in a vessel of silver.
   (MacGregor 1897: 81)

The text of this hymn is striking for its fusion of Latin hymnody with native modes of invocation. Certain of its lines echo unmistakably the *Benedicite* and the *Te Deum*, especially in their praise for the power of God and the earthly and angelic hosts arrayed in praise. Other lines, however, display the commanding tone and confidence typical of the traditional charm. The ritual utterance or performance of the hymn would ensure supernatural protection while its words expressed the feelings of a lyric speaker toward God and the saints. A narrative kernel is included in the references to John the Baptist, whose acts during life are seen to relate somehow to the acts or intentions of the present performer. Evocations of thunder and fire recur as well.

In a manner typical of Irish lyric hermeneutics in general, the hymn appears in the *Liber Hymnorum* with an extensive set of narrativized explanations. In a mixture of Latin and Irish, the scribe relates that Saint Columba composed the hymn at the door of the hermitage of Daire Calcaig, where Mobi, king of Derry, offered him hospitality. The hermitage caught fire, and Columba composed the hymn to protect the nearby oak grove. The preface continues with yet more explanations:

No is lathe bratha dorat di-a aire, no tene feile Eoin, ocus canair fri cech tenid ocus fri cech torann o-shein ille; ocus cip e gabas fo lige ocus fo érge no/n/again ar thenid nhgellan, ocus angid in nonbur is ail di(-a) mu(intir).
(Bernard and Atkinson 1898: vol. 1, 87)

———

Or it was the Day of Judgment that he had in mind, or the fire of John's Feast, and it is sung against every fire and every thunder from that time to this; and whosoever recites it at lying down and at rising up, it protects him against lightning flash, and it protects the nine persons of his household whom he chooses. (Bernard and Atkinson 1898: vol. 2, 28)

A functional, invocational use of the hymn has grown here to equal, if not exceed, its purely contemplative use. Ethnographically, we know that the hymn was a regular part of Midsummer or St. John's Night bonfire celebrations, common throughout northern Europe. The use of prayers or charms to ensure health or protection from harmful forces such as lightning is also well attested for the region down to the recent past. At least by the eleventh century, then, Latin hymnody had become enmeshed in the narrative and functional interpretations of preexisting Irish lyric: in a sense, the genre had become naturalized to native interpretive modes.

While the narrativizing explication of Saint Columba's hymn bears a strong resemblance to the kinds of narratives attached to secular lyrics, other recorded hymns multiply narrative explanations in what seems a fit of pious excess. The Irish hymn to Saint Brigid, included in the eleventh-century Irish *Liber Hymnorum* is an example.

HYMNUS S. ULTANI IN LAUDEM
S. BRIGIDAE
Brigit be bith-maith
breo orda oiblech,
do•n•fe do'n bith-laith
in grian tind taidlech.

Ro•n•soera Brigit
sech drungu demna,
ro•roena reunn
catha cach thedma.

Do•rodba innunn
ar colla císu
in chroeb co mblathaib
in mathair Ísu

Ind [f]ir-óg inmain
co n-orddain adbail,

biam soer cech inbaid
la'm nóeb do Laignib

Leth-cholba flatha
la Patraic prímda;
in tlacht uas lig[d]aib
ind rigan ríg[d]a.

Robbet iar sinit
ar cuirp hic-cilicc;
di-a rath ro•n•broena,
ro•n•soera Brigit.
Brigit bé.
    (Bernard and Atkinson 1898: vol. 1, 110–11)

————

Brigid, ever-good woman,
flame golden, sparkling,
may she bear us to the eternal kingdom,
(she), the sun fiery, radiant!

May Brigid free us
past crowds of demons!
may she win for us
battles over every disease!

May she extirpate in us
the vices of our flesh,
she, the branch with blossoms,
the mother of Jesus!

The true-virgin, dear,
with vast pre-eminence,
may we be free, at all times,
along with my Saint of Leinster-folk!
One (of the two) pillars of the Kingdom,

along with Patrick the pre-eminent (as the other pillar);
the vestment beyond (even) splendid (vestments),
the royal Queen!

May they lie, after old age,
our bodies, in sackcloth;
(but) with her grace may she bedew us,
may she free us, Brigid!
Brigid ever.
   (Bernard and Atkinson 1898: vol. 2, 39)

Brigid is invoked in the third person here, incorporated in a prayer that also invokes Mary and Saint Patrick. In its elaborate epithets and exhortations, the hymn shows far more exuberance than many of its Latin counterparts, and it is hard to read the text's final lines without a sense of the profound supernatural power that the speaker attaches to the very name of the saint. While the text may be read along lines suggested from Latin hymnody—for example, noting the inclusive *We* of the text and the invocation of Brigid as an intercessor for present needs—the manuscript's preface to the hymn again provides a chain of narrativizing and attributive explanations quite similar to those discussed in chapters 1 and 2. According to the preface, the song may have been composed by Saint Columcille when he was beset by a great sea storm. He is said to have uttered this prayer invoking Saint Brigid. Or, the scribe tells us, the hymn may have been composed by a shadowy poet "Broccan the Squinter," who was also known to have composed another hymn to Brigid. A further source of the hymn, the text relates, may lie in the adventures of three members of Brigid's household during a pilgrimage to Rome. When they seek hospitality at a certain house in Blasantia, their unwilling host tries to poison their drink. But by invoking Brigid with this hymn, they are not only able to drink the host's poison without harm but are also seen to have a young woman in their company. Unable to explain who the young woman is, they are imprisoned until they are able to demonstrate that the maiden in question is an apparition of Saint Brigid, called forth by their performance of the hymn. Still another source of the hymn may lie in the words of a sea monster who, when confronted by Saint Brendan on the sea, declares that Saint Brigid is the greatest of all saints. Saint Brendan later seeks out Saint Brigid and finds her just as laudable as the beast had asserted. Or, finally, the hymn could have been composed by Ultan of Ardbreccan, a kinsman of Brigid on her mother's side who lived in the days of the two sons of Aed Slane. That the learned cleric can make no judgment about which attribution or narrative hits closest to home is evident from his text, which dutifully records all explanations for the hymn. His preface gives evidence of an already thriving narrativizing and attributive interpretive system surrounding lyric songs of all kinds in Irish oral tradition, one that ties the text's details to heroes and narratives of the greatest renown on the island.

The elaborate and ornate Latin hymnody of Ireland spread to Anglo-Saxon England through the poetry of Saint Aldhelm (ca. 640–709), who was also said to have composed songs in the vernacular, performing them outdoors with a harp accompaniment for the edification of the masses (Wrenn 1967: 60). By the time of the Venerable Saint Bede (673–735), however, a more continental Latin had come to prevail in England, governed by tracts such as Bede's own *De Arte Metrica*, a handbook on Latin verse forms. Knowledge of Latin metrics led composers to reembrace older syllabic meters, and it was thus in the Frankish Carolingian Renaissance advanced by the English monk Alcuin (ca. 735–804) that the first real challenges to the rhythmic hymns of the preceding centuries occurred.

While the learned Christians of the British Isles thus appear to have excelled in the Latin of the church, the vast masses of the laity in these tracts required religious instruction in the vernacular. In England, the poets Cædmon and Cynewulf continued the work initiated by Saint Aldhelm, adapting the native epic and lyric traditions to sacred Christian content. In his *Historia Ecclesiastica Gentis Anglorum* (731), Bede provides a striking account of Caedmon's poetic debut. Cædmon, a poor herdsman employed by a Northumbrian monastery, is depicted first as musically inept. During evening drinking and singing sessions, Cædmon would leave the hall before the harp was passed to him. Bede's passing description of such entertainment, along with its Anglo-Saxon glosses by later scribes, provides a valuable glimpse of one of the earliest contexts for folk song in general in northern Europe and one with strong continuities in the song traditions of northern peoples ever after. One evening, after Cædmon has absented himself from such entertainment and gone to bed, he hears a voice in a dream commanding him to sing. When Cædmon timidly asks what he should sing about, the voice commands him to sing of the Creation. The peasant then produces a hymn of grace and beauty, the Anglo-Saxon version of which is recorded as follows:

Nú sculun herigean   heofonrícaes Weard,
Meotodes meahte ond his módgeþanc
weorc Wuldorfæder,   suá hé uundra gihwæs,
éce Drihten, ór onstealde.
Hé ǽrest sceóp   eorðan bearnum
heofon tó hrófe,   hálig Scyppend.
Þá middangeard   moncynnæs Weard,
éce Drihten,   æfter téode
fírum foldan,   Fréa ælmihtig.
   (*Tanner Manuscript*; Whitelock 1967: 46–47)

———————

Now should we praise   the Guardian of the heavenly realm,
God's might   and his conception
the work of the glorious Father: how in the beginning
He created every wonder,   eternal Lord.
He first created   for the children of men
the heavens as a roof,   holy Creator.
And then the earth   Guardian of mankind,
eternal Lord,   after that time
almighty Lord   the world for men.

In the morning, Cædmon is able to perform the song for his farm master and
eventually for the monastery's abbess. With the abbess's support and encour-
agement, Bede tells us, Cædmon learns many more stories from the Bible and
composes hymns about them. He eventually becomes a monk himself and lives
out his days continuing his compositions in the service of his faith.

It is probable that Cædmon's hymn—and perhaps also the narrative regarding its origin—became part of Anglo-Saxon oral tradition. The manuscript
versions of the hymn show variations greater than that to be expected of a purely
manuscript transmission process (Wrenn 1967: 95), and the ninth-century translation of Bede's account into Anglo-Saxon reflects a view of the hymn and narrative as valuable to a more general audience. If this is the case, then we may
see the song as strong evidence of the early transferral of the interpretive traditions of Latin hymnody to native religious songs. Here there is the same clear
reliance on attribution and narrative to place the song in the mind and life of

a single saintly individual and a simultaneous assertion that the hymn can prove proverbially salutatory to believers in the here and now. As in Saint Ambrose's *Te Deum*, Cædmon's *Creation* pulls us into an inclusive *We*, whose attitude toward God is carefully managed and stipulated in the text. Precisely the same mechanics of interpretation underlie the similarly brief hymn known as *Bede's Death Song*, the composition of which manuscripts ascribe to either Bede himself or one of his attending disciples at his deathbed:

> Fore thém neidfaerae náénig uuiurthit
> thoncsnottura than him tharf síe,
> tó ymbhycggannae, áér his hiniongae,
> huaet his gástae gódaes aeththa yflaes
> aefter déothdaege dóémid uueorthae.
>
>   (Whitelock 1967: 183)

> Before that necessary journey no one will be
> wiser than he need be
> to consider, before his departing
> what good or evil his soul
> will be judged of after his death.

In its terse gnomic contemplation of life and mortality, this lyric encapsulates the proper Christian attitude toward life's final accounting. At the same time, in its apparent reception, it relies on its narrative association with Bede and his death for much of its interpretive significance.

But for all this apparent interpretive continuity between Latin hymnody and Anglo-Saxon adaptation, it is important to note how nonlyrical (i.e., narrative) works such as Cædmon's *Creation* actually are. When we remove the half-lines that supply epithets for God (of which the poem contains fully eight), we are left in fact with a barebones narrative account of God's creative acts on the second and third days of Creation (Gn 1:6–10). We find no focus on feelings or a speaker, none of the aspects that normally characterize lyric in general. Nor are we placed into a dialogue with the Creator as in the *Te Deum*. And if we credit Bede's account of Cædmon's subsequent compositions with some degree of accuracy, then it appears that few of them were lyric in any real sense either.

The monk is said to have composed works on other events in Genesis and the Old Testament as well as the Incarnation, Passion, Resurrection, Ascension, and Pentecost. The poet's possibly lyric compositions are fewer in number and include contemplations of heaven and hell, blessings, judgments, and exhortations to piety (Whitelock 1967: 48).

A similar preference for narrative poetry is evinced by Cynewulf, the ninth-century poet behind the great Anglo-Saxon accounts of the life of Saint Helena (*Elene*), Christ's Ascension (*Christ II*), and other largely biblical or hagiographic poems. Most of the Anglo-Saxon religious poetry from the ninth and tenth centuries, in fact, shows this same narrative preponderance, so that even in the rendering of Psalm 50 (51) into the vernacular, the Anglo-Saxon poet expands the Vulgate's two short verses on the origin of the song (50:1–2) into a detailed thirty-line narrative account of David's meeting with Nathan and sin with Bathsheba (Whitelock 1967: 208–14). Similarly, the Advent "lyrics" of Cynewulf's *Christ I* make frequent use of narration, turning constantly from a lyric address or contemplation to the relating of events in sacred history. Consider, for instance, the beautiful but highly narrative hymn to Mary:

Éala þú mǽra   middangeardes,
séo clǽneste   cwén ofer eorþan
þára þe gewurde   tó wídan féore,
hú þec mid ryhte   ealle reordberend
hátað ond secgað,   hæleð geond foldan,
blíðe móde,   þæt þú brýd síe
þæs sélestan   swegles Bryttan.
Swylce þá hýhstan   on heofonum éac
Crístes þegnas   cweþað ond singað
þæt þú síe hlǽfdige   hálgum meahtum
wuldorweorudes,   ond worldcundra
háda under heofonum,   ond helwara;
forþon þú þæt,   ána   ealra monna,
geþóhtest þrymlíce,   þrísthycgende,
þæt þú þínne mægðhád   Meotude bróhtes,
sealdes bútan synnum.   Nán swylc ne cwóm
ǽnig óþer   ofer ealle men,
brýd béaga hroden,   þe þá beorhtan lác
tó heofonháme   hlútre móde

siþþan sende. Forðon heht sigores Fruma
his héahbodan   hider gefléogan
of his mægenþrymme,   ond þé meahta spéd
snúde cýðan,   þæt þú Sunu Dryhtnes
þurh clǽne gebyrd   cennan sceolde,
monnum tó miltse,   ond þé, María, forð
efne unwemme   á gehealdan.

    (*Christ I*, ll. 275–300; Cook 1909: 11–12)

———————

Hail, you glory   of this middle-earth,
Purest woman   of all the earth,
Of those created   from time immemorial,
How rightly you are proclaimed   by all endowed
With the power of speech!   All mortal beings throughout the earth
Declare, glad of heart,   that you are the bride
Of the one   that rules the firmament.
So, too,   in the highest heavens above,
The thanes of Christ   proclaim and sing,
That you through your holiness   are queen
Of the hosts   of heaven and earth,
Of those beneath the heavens   and those within hell,
For you alone   of all humankind
Nobly decided,   most honorably,
To bring your virginity   before the Lord,
Your soul without sin.   None like you have ever come,
No other   of all humankind,
A bride adorned with rings,   to send
Heavenward   in spirit
Such a glowing gift.   In response, the Lord of victories
Bade his herald   fly here
From his glorious   presence unto you,
To demonstrate his power,   that you should bear
The Son of God   in a state of purity,
For the mercy of humankind,   and yet you, Mary,
Should remain   pure forever.

At best in such early vernacular hymns, lyric sentiment plays a supplementary role to the dominant narrative force and function of narrative. The audience is called to identify itself in the collective image of grateful humankind repeatedly mentioned in the text, but it is hardly possible here for a listener to identify with Mary herself, or to associate any of the images or lines of the hymn with one's personal circumstances or situation. Rather, the hymn seems intent on enunciating the concept of Mary's willing acceptance of the virgin birth, underscoring the importance of her act within the divine plan. It is a catechetical tract rather than a lyric meditation.

The earliest extant religious poem in Welsh dates from the ninth or tenth century. On the first page of a manuscript containing Latin paraphrases of the Gospels by Juvencus, an unknown writer carefully wrote nine *englynion,* verses in praise of God. Beginning in Latin, the verses soon shift to Welsh to offer us a glimpse of vernacular piety at the very dawn of Welsh literature:

> Omnipotens auctor tidicones
> Adiam .r...

> Nit arcup betid hicouid canlou
> cet treidin guel haguid
> t..e—rdutou ti guird . . .

> Dicones pater harimed presen
> isabruid icinimer
> nisacup nis arcup leder.

> Dicones ihesu dielimlu pbetid
> aguirdou pan dibu
> guotiapaur oimer didu

> Gur dicones remedau[t]t elbid
> anguorit anguoraut
> ni guor gnim molim trintaut.

> It cluis [it] dibán iciman guorsed
> ceinmicun ucnou• ran
> ueatiutaut beantrident.

It cluis it humil inhared celmed
rit pucsaun mi ditrintaut
gurd meint icomoid imolaut.

Rit ercis d..raut inadaut presen
piouboi· int groisauc
inungueid guoled trintaut.

Un hamed hapuil haper
uuc nem isnem intcouer
nitguorgnim molim map meir.

————————

Almighty Creator,
You have made . . .

The world cannot express in song bright and melodious,
Even though the grass and the trees should sing,
All your glories (miracles, riches), O true Lord!

The Father has wrought [such a multitude] of wonders in this world
That it is difficult to find an equal number.
Letters cannot contain it, letters cannot express it.

Jesus wrought on behalf of the hosts of Christendom
[such a multitude] of miracles when he came
(like grass in the number of them)

He who made the wonder of the world
Will save us, has saved us.
It is not too great toil to praise the Trinity.

Purely, without blemish,
In the great assembly,
Let us extol . . .

Purely, humbly, in skillful verse
I should love to give praise to the Trinity
According to the greatness of his power.

He has required of the host in this world that belong to him
That they should at all times
All together, fear the Trinity.

The one who has both wisdom and dominion above heaven,
Below heaven, completely,
It is not too great toil to praise the Son of Mary.
    (Williams 1972: 101–2)

The poet praises God with joy and exuberance, both in response to God's acts of creation and in obedience to God's demand. While asserting that letters cannot contain all the wonders wrought by the Lord, the speaker nonetheless sets out to offer praise for these through poetry. While the sixth *englyn* exhorts a collective assembly to extol, the seventh focuses on a specific lyric speaker, one skilled in verse and eager to praise God in poetry. Here we glimpse the empowered sense of individuality and authorial identity that was to persist in Welsh poetry ever after, leading to the rich tradition of lyric attribution discussed in chapter 6. In this poem, however, poised on the threshold of a vernacular embrace of Latin hymnody, there is a carefully managed openness that allows the audience to identify with the prayer and its universal sentiments. When the speaker declares in the fifth and ninth *englynion* that it "is not too great toil to praise" the Trinity or Christ, his listeners are led to assent, even if the skill to compose such praise far exceeded their own abilities. The speaker of this hymn speaks on behalf of the assembly but not in any sense that would hide or diminish his own identity and skills. His is the confidence of a bard commissioned to give praise to a great lord, a singer whose work is simultaneously communal and individual.

Several centuries later, this same self-consciousness remained in Welsh religious poems, despite a long and complete embrace of the Christian worldview. The court poet of the twelfth and thirteenth centuries remained true not only to the strictures of Christian hymnody but also to the norms of bardic praise poetry, with its characteristic focus on specific performers and addressees. In the Laws of Hywel Dda, named for a tenth-century king but first appearing in manuscripts from the early thirteenth century, the chief royal poet (*pencerdd*) is said to be responsible for reciting two poems before the king in any royal entertainment: one referring to kings, the other to God (McKenna 1991: 8). As this pairing implies, the religious poems produced (*awdlau i Dduw*, "odes to God") often strongly resemble those addressed to kings. God is described with terms such as *gwledig* (ruler), *modrydaf* (chieftain), *modur* (lord), or *cedwallaw* (dispenser of gifts), while Christ's acts are portrayed as a warrior's heroism or a chieftain's generosity. The deity is expected to rejoice in the bard's words of praise and to reward these with favors, while the poet often calls attention to his own skill and experiences through ostentatious turns of phrase or even overt self-identification (McKenna 1991: 24–25). The death song of Cynddelw Brydydd Mawr, composed in the early thirteenth century, illustrates these tendencies. Describing God in royal terms, Cynddelw declares that his gift of praise for God will be graciously rewarded:

Mi wyf fardd digardd y'm digoned
Ar helw gy nghreawdr, llywiawdr lliwed;
Mi Gynddelw geiniad, rhad a'm rhodded:
Mihangel, a'm gŵyr, a'm gwrthfynned.
 (McKenna 1991: 166, 168)

—————

I am a poet who was made flawless
Under the protection of my creator, the host's leader;
I am Cynddelw the singer, grace has been given me:
Let Michael, who knows me, welcome me.
 (McKenna 1991: 167, 169)

It is difficult in a poem such as this for an audience to lose itself in an identification with an inscribed *I* or *We*. Instead, the poem highlights the identity of its composer, an act that has made it possible for scholars to talk about the poet Cynddelw seven centuries after his death. In the eyes of professional bards, the native genre of panegyric—so important to the careers of bards and kings alike—needed to be extended to the King of all. The resulting praise poetry combined native tradition with an imported creed and genre.

At times, the early vernacular hymns of northern Europe become nearly exclusive of all lyric sentiments. A good example is a tenth-century Latin hymn in honor of Norway's Saint Sunniva. Composed, in all likelihood, on the island of Selja, where Sunniva's shrine and church stood from the late tenth century, the hymn consists of a series of distinct narrative stanzas, each relating the details of a miracle credited to the saint. The following is typical of the hymn as a whole.

> In Sunnivæ basilica
> pernoctans cæca nata,
> gaudens luce mirifica
> virgo redit sanata.
> (Storm 1880: 152)

———

> A woman born blind, spending the night,
> In Sunniva's basilica, to her delight,
> Saw at once a miraculous light
> And headed home, cured, with her sight.

The hymn appears designed explicitly to chronicle and extol the saint's growing cult among the laity. Sunniva, an immigrant from the British Isles, had lived on Selja as an anchorite along with a company of followers before arousing the distrust of her still-pagan neighbors. Her sanctity as a martyr was revealed when King Oláfr Tryggvason had her grave opened in 995 to discover her remains uncorrupted. The king ordered a church built in her honor, and it became an important pilgrimage site until the translation of Sunniva's relics to Bergen in 1170. The *Breviarium Nidrosiense* of Trondheim includes additional hymns for use on her feast (July 8). Gustav Storm (1880: xxxiv) conjectures, however, that the present hymn, with its specific references to a basilica of Sunniva, dates from the era prior to the translation, when the local Benedictine monastery would have used such songs to recall and celebrate her local miracles.

The strongly narrative tone of such hymns to Sunniva is paralleled by poems in honor of King Oláfr (995–1030), another of the principal saints of the Nordic region. Snorri Sturluson includes a vernacular hymn to Oláfr in his *Oláfs saga helga.*

Nú hefr sér
til sess hagat
þjóðkonungr
í Þrándheimi.
Þar vill ae
ævi sína
bauga brjótr
byggðum ráða—

þars Óleifr
áðan byggði,
áðr hann hvarf
til himinríkis
ok þar varð,
sem vitu allir,
kykvasettr
ór konungmanni.

Hafði sér
Harðla ráðit
Haralds sonr
til himinríkis,
áðr seimbrjótr
at setti varð.

Þar svát hreinn
með heilu liggr
lofsæll gramr
líki sínu,
ok þar kná
sem kvikum manni

hár ok negl
hönum vaxa.
   (Aðalbjarnarson 1962: vol. 2, 406–7)

———————

Now the king of the people
Has acquired
A seat for himself
In Trondheim.
There he will
Preside in power
His whole life long
Over his realm.

There, where Ólafr
held his lands
before he left
for heaven.
And there he,
As all people know,
Was alive
As a monarch.

Scarcely had
Harald's son
Received a place in heaven
When he became
A powerful intercessor.

There he lies in state,
Whole and pure,
The renowned king,
And his hair and nails
Grow on him
As on a living person.
   (Monsen 1990: 469)

Like the hymn to Sunniva, this lyric consists largely of narrative kernels associated with the saint: the location of his shrine, the miraculous continued growth of his nails and hair after death, the miracles witnessed at his side, and so on. It also combines these with terms, forms, and images typical of skaldic poetry, a task easily accomplished in that Ólafr is himself a king. The poem merges a royal encomium with a favorite skaldic genre of static description, in which the poet artfully describes a scene or object before him, in this case, King Saint Ólafr lying in state. Such hymns of description and praise can hardly be called lyric contemplations, even if they sometimes contain moving, emotive images. Yet they reflect the naturalization of Christianity into the aesthetic and cultural norms of northern Europe.

We can begin to see artistic room opening up for lyric sentiments more reminiscent of southern Europe over the course of subsequent centuries. Illustrative of this process is the final section of the Anglo-Saxon *Dream of the Rood*, in which a speaker reflects on his miraculous vision of the Holy Cross and longs for an end to his tiring life:

> and ic wéne mé
> daga gehwylce   hwænne mé Dryhtnes ród
> þe ic hér on eorðan   ǽr scéawode
> on þysson lǽnan   lífe gefetige
> and mé þonne gebringe   þǽr is blis mycel
> dréam   on heofonum
>   (Whitelock 1979: 135b-140a; 159)

> And I wait
> each day   for when the Lord's Cross
> which I once saw   here on earth
> will take me   from this fleeting life
> and bring me to where   there is great joy,
> fellowship   in heaven

Whereas the bulk of the poem is epic, centering on the Cross's narration of the Crucifixion, Harrowing of Hell, and Resurrection, this final portion gives voice to the lyric sentiments of the human speaker. This accords well with the use and appearance of lyric passages in Anglo-Saxon epic poetry in general, as discussed in chapter 2. A new, more overtly emotive and meditative form of religious lyric was about to develop in the region, however.

THE ARRIVAL OF CONTEMPLATION

According to Patrick L. Henry (1966), a strong tradition of penitential poetry—replete with images of outcasts and sorrow—developed in the British Isles in the ninth and tenth centuries. Native genres like the epic-lyric elegy of Anglo-Saxon poetry or the formal laments or regret poems of Welsh and Irish court poets became vehicles for broader, often allegorical explorations of Christian themes. Two masterpieces of Old English poetry—*The Wanderer* and *The Seafarer*—illustrate this trend. Characters bewail a life of exile or banishment, in which the former mirth and friendship of the hall are gone forever, plaguing the speaker in lingering memories of once-easy joy. The poems have been seen as meditations on the spiritual state of the estranged sinner, longing for reconciliation with God. At the close of *The Wanderer*, a narrator comes forth to offer a Christian interpretation of the speaker's Job-like lament:

> Swá cwæð snottor on móde,   gesæt him sundor æt rúne.
> Til biþ sé þe his tréowe gehealdeþ,   ne sceal næfre his torn tó rycene
> beorn of his bréostum ácýþan,   nemþe hé ær þá bóte cunne,
> eorl mid elne gefremman.   Wel bið þam him áre séceð,
> frófre tó Fæder on heofonum,   þær ús eal séo fæstnung stondeð.
>   (Whitelock 1967: 164)

> So spoke the wise man in his heart,   sitting alone in contemplation.
> It is good to hold fast to one's faith   and not let one's grief break forth
> Too quickly from one's breast,   until one knows of a remedy
> And seeks valiantly to bring it about.   It is good to seek honor
> And comfort from the Father in heaven: there our fortress stands.

A native fusion of epic and lyric is thus transformed into a Christian allegory, with little formal change in the genre itself. Similarly, as Catherine A.

McKenna (1991: 33 ff.) shows, the Welsh Gogynfeirdd poets of the twelfth and thirteenth centuries adapted the poem of reconciliation, the *dadolwch*, to encompass the relation of sinner and God. In the *dadolwch*, a speaker bemoans his estrangement from his lord and asks for a return to easy relations. In the early-twelfth-century Meilyr Brydydd's deathbed poem, the poet-speaker beseeches:

Rex regum, rhebydd rhwydd Ei foli,
I'm arglwydd uchaf archaf weddi:
Gwledig gwlad orfod goruchel wenrod,
Gwrda, gwna gymod rhyngod a mi.
Adfrau adfant cof Dy rygoddi
Erof ac edifar ei ddigoni.
Digonais gerydd yng ngŵydd Duw Ddofydd,
Fy iawn grefydd heb ei weini;
Gweinifif hagen i'm rhëen rhi
Cyn bwyf deyerin diwenynni.

———————

King of kings, leader easy to praise,
Of my supreme lord I ask a petition:
Real-mastering ruler of the most high holy orb,
Noble sire, make peace between You and me.
Frail, insubstantial the mind, having offended You
For my own sake, and penitent for doing it.
I have committed sin in the presence of the Lord God,
Failing to attend to my due devotion;
Yet I will serve my Lord King
Before I am earthbound, powerless.
    (McKenna 1991: 154–55)

The poem's opening Latin epithet reflects the poet's familiarity with continental hymnody, while the bulk of the poem follows the norms of the courtly *dadolwch*. And, in keeping with the tradition's emphasis on authorship and attribution, Meilyr later identifies himself by name in the same poem:

Amdlawd fy nhafawd ar fy nhewi.
Mi Feilyr Brydydd, bererin i Bedr,
Porthawr a gymedr gymes deithi.

—————

Poverty stricken is my tongue upon my falling silent.
I am Meilyr the Poet, pilgrim to Peter,
Door ward who assesses appropriate virtues.
   (McKenna 1991: 154–55)

While lamenting his sins, Meilyr remains confident of the central role of the court poet in assessing the actions and praising the achievements of his Lord.

In Christianity as a whole, a widespread and popular embrace of lyric contemplation occurred during the thirteenth and fourteenth centuries. At that point, under the guidance of the new and revolutionary mendicant orders— the Franciscans (founded 1209) and the Dominicans (founded 1216)—the elaborate contemplative practices of the monastery came to be shared at last with the wider lay public, proselytized by friars whose message and aim can aptly be characterized as a "monasticization of the laity" (Vauchez 1993: 72). The abrupt rise of this movement built on the earlier devotionalism of the Cistercian Saint Bernard (1090–1153) and took Bernard's ideas of the emotional comprehension of God to new lengths. The new mendicant orders turned their energies to the edification of the general populace of Europe, a vast mass of peasants and townspeople who were Christian in name but often ignorant of Christian theology. With papal approval, the orders spread rapidly throughout the Continent, establishing a system of provinces that paralleled and in some cases competed with established diocesan divisions. Under their aegis, devices for personal devotionalism began to appear, such as the rosary, a simplified regimen of prayer and meditation on the joys, sorrows, and glories of Christ's life and the Virgin's experiences. Dominican and Franciscan confraternities, lay institutions associated with the priories, became widespread, particularly in towns and cities (Vauchez 1993). And in art as well as theology, Saint Bernard's emphasis on the human side of Christ and his followers led to works that evoke and explore human emotions—love, joy, fear, pain, loss, and sorrow—as keys to spiritual understanding. It became important to evoke these feelings in the faithful so that they might *feel* the full reality of the Christian story and recognize its applicability to their own lives. More abstract understandings of God were to be based on this basic human foundation. And given this new emphasis in terms of preaching, praise, and prayer, the mendicant orders took ample advantage of the religious lyric.

This new embrace of emotive lyric, and its use as the basis of deeper contemplation on God's truths, can be sensed as well in a Welsh lyric recorded in the mid-thirteenth-century Black Book of Carmarthen:

Kintevin keinhaw amsser.
Dyar adar glas callet.
Ereidir in rich. ich iguet.
Guirt mor brithottor tiret.

Ban ganhont cogev ar blaen guit guiw
Handid muy. vy llauuridet
Tost muc amluc anhunet.
kan ethint uy kereint in attwet.

Ym brin in tyno. in inysset mor
Impop fort itelher.
Rac Crist guin nid oes inialet.

Oet in chuant in car in trosset
Treitau ty tir dy alltudet
Seith seint a seithugeint a seithcant
A want in un orsset.
Y gid a Crist guin ny forthint-ve vygilet.

Rec a archaw-e nim naccer.
Y rof a duv. dagnouet.
Ambo forth.y porth riet.
Crist ny buv-e trist y'th orsset.

———————

Maytime, fairest season,
Loud the birds, trees are green,

Ploughs in the furrow, the ox in the yoke,
Green is the sea, dappled the fields.

When cuckoos sing on the top of fine trees
My sadness grows;
Smoke stings, (my) grief is revealed,
For my kinsmen have passed away.

In hill, in dale, in islands of the sea,
Wherever one may go,
There is no refuge from the White Christ.

It was our desire, our Friend, our merit,
To cross over to the land of thine exile.
Seven saints and seven score and seven hundred
Went to one throne,
With the White Christ they were unafraid.
A gift I ask; let me not be refused:
Peace between me and God.
May there be for me a way to the noble gate!
Christ, may I not be sad before Thy Throne!
    (Henry 1966: 67–68)

Here we see the same petition for peace between the speaker-poet and his Lord
that occurs in Meilyr Brydydd's adaptation of the *dadolwch* form. Yet now the
speaker is anonymous, an open figure with whom an audience is called to identify, one who declares the sorrow of estrangement that faces all sinners. God,
likewise, is depicted here, as in earlier Welsh poems, as a powerful lord seated on
a throne and potentially revengeful against sinners: "There is no refuge from the
White Christ." Yet the poem also couches its sentiments in the speaker's obser-
vation of the world in May, redolent with life and contrasting all the more with
the bitterness of the sinner's sorrow and loneliness. Reminiscent of the Anglo-
Saxon *Seafarer* and *Wanderer*, with which it is often compared (e.g., Henry 1966;
Davies 1996: 39–42), the poem's images are not, however, allegorical but rather
vividly descriptive of the feelings of a contrite sinner. This speaker's conscious
feelings toward God are enunciated in first person in the poem, and the audi-

ence is invited to identify with the speaker's compunction and hopes. The text's profoundly emotive images and declarations reflect the new themes that had arrived in Christian spirituality.

This fundamental shift in theological and artistic emphasis is reflected also in the dramatic rise of Passion lyrics at this time (Brown 1924; Woolf 1968; Jeffrey 1975). Although earlier religious poems, such as the *Dream of the Rood,* certainly focused on the narrative details of the Passion, the new devotionalism of the thirteenth century placed the Christian meditator at the very side of Christ's cross to experience the human pain and suffering of Jesus and his mother. An English adaptation of the Latin hymn *Respice in faciem Christe* illustrates this new function for the lyric:

> Quanne hic se on rode
> Ihesu mi lemman;
> An besiden him stonden
> Marie an Iohan,
> And his rig isuongen
> And his side istungen
> For the luue of man;
> Wel ou hic to wepen
> And sinnes forleten
> Yif hic of luue kan,
> Yif hic of luue kan,
> Yif hic of luue kan.

> When I see upon the Cross
> Jesus my beloved;
> And beside him standing
> Mary and John
> And his back beaten
> And his side pierced
> For the love of mankind;
> Well ought I weep
> And sins forsake

If I know anything of love,
If I know anything of love,
If I know anything of love.
(Silverstein 1971: 32)

Here, as in earlier hymns such as the *Te Deum*, the prayerful Christian is furnished with words and ideas fit for communication with God. But now the *I* is no longer a timid addendum to the triumphant *We* of the hymn but a unique and personified speaker, who not only imagines the Crucifixion but sees it. And further, this speaker is able to combine the visual experience with personal knowledge of pain and love for a full comprehension of the poignant moment of Christ's death.

Within this movement, the church's long-standing devotion to the Virgin Mary took new turns as well. Now Christ's mother could be seen not simply as the empowered Queen of heaven and earth, interceding with might and readiness on behalf of her son's followers (Crane 1925) but also as a human mother, someone who had experienced the joys and sorrows of a woman's life. This new, very human image of Mary is encapsulated in the thirteenth-century Franciscan hymn *Stabat Mater dolorosa*, traditionally attributed to the Italian Franciscan friar Jacopone da Todi (d. 1306). In lines that encapsulate the very essence of the new spirituality, the hymn's speaker asks:

Quis est homo qui non fleret,
Matrem Christi si vidéret
In tanto supplício?

Quis non posset contristári
Christi Matrem contemplári
Doléntem cum Fílio?
(Cabrol 1929: 328)

———

Who is human but would not cry
At seeing the Mother of Christ
In such distress?

Who could not feel sorrowful
When contemplating the Mother of Christ
Suffering with her Son?

Intent on making the suffering of Mary vivid to the audience, the speaker describes Mary's vision: the torments suffered by her son, his abandonment by the majority of his followers, the anguish and exhaustion of the Passion. And then the speaker asks to be allowed to take up vigil beside Mary at the foot of the Cross, obliterating the passage of chronological time through the power of meditation:

Juxta Crucem tecum stare,
Et me tibi sociáre
In planctu desídero.

Virgo vírginum praeclára,
Mihi jam non sis amára,
Fac me tecum plángere.

Fac, ut portem Christi mortem,
Passiónis fac consórtem,
Et plagas recólere.

Fac me plagis vulnerári
Fac me cruce inebriári,
Et cruóre Fílii.
   (Cabrol 1929: 329)

———

I desire to stand with you by the Holy Cross
To keep you company
In lamentation.

Oh Virgin, noble among virgins,
Do not reject my plea,
Let me weep with you.

Let me experience Christ's death
His Passion let me share,
And his pains relive.

Let me suffer the injuries
Let me be overwhelmed by the Cross
And the blood of the Son.

Here the humanity of Mary is stressed, and the speaker asks to share in the physical pain and sorrow of both Christ and his Mother. This intense physical and emotional experience of the Passion had culminated in Saint Francis's receipt of the stigmata (the five hand, foot, and side wounds of Christ on the Cross) and a similar experience of invisible stigmata in the case of the Dominican tertiary Saint Catherine of Siena (1347–80). Crucially, lyric hymns become a prime means of furthering such devotionalism among the laity, particularly, it appears, among women (Bynum 1982; Vauchez 1993).

In northern Europe, many such religious lyrics take on dramatic form, anticipating the dramatic structure of the ballad and fitting into the emerging tradition of the Mystery plays (Woolf 1968). The Latin *Stabat Mater dolorosa* can be compared to the thirteenth-century English lyric *Stand wel, moder, vnder rode,* which similarly provides a vivid witnessing of the scene at Calvary. The lyric opens with Mary and Jesus arguing about whether Mary should be sorrowful or glad, given the suffering Christ must undergo to redeem all humankind:

"Stand wel, moder, vnder rode,
Bihold thi child wyth glade mode;
Blythe, moder, mittu ben."
"Svne, quu may y blithe stonden?
Hi se thin feet, hi se thin honden
nayled to the harde tre."

"Moder, do wey thi wepinge;
Hi thole this ded for mannes thinge;
For owen gilte tholi non."
"Svne, hi fele the dede stunde;
The swerd is at min herte grunde
That me byhytte Symeon."

"Moder, reu vpon thi bern;
Thu wasse awey tho blodi teren,
It don me werse than mi ded."
"Sune, hu mitti teres wernen?
Hy se tho blodi flodes hernen
Huth of thin herte to min fet."

"Moder, nu y may the seyn
Better is that ic one deye
Than al mankyn to helle go."
"Sune, y se thi bodi swngen,
Thi brest, thin hond, thi fot thurstungen;
No selli thou me be wo."
     (Silverstein 1971: 12–14)

———————

"Stand well, Mother, beneath the Cross,
Behold your son with glad spirit;
Blithe, Mother, may you be."
"Son, how may I stand blithely?
I see your feet, I see your hands
Nailed to the hard tree."

"Mother, away with your weeping;
I suffer this death for man's sake;
For guilt of my own I suffer nought."
"Son, I feel this moment of death;
The sword is at the base of my heart
Which Simeon bequeathed me."

"Mother, have pity upon your son;
Wash you away those bloody tears,
They do me worse than my death."
"Son, how may I hold back my tears?
I see your bloody river flow
Out of your heart and to my feet."

> "Mother, now may I say to you
> That it is better that I alone die
> That that all mankind go to Hell."
> "Son, I see your body beaten,
> Your breast, your hand, your foot pierced;
> What wonder, then, is my woe?"

Here is the same attention to the physical and emotional experience of the Passion, now, however, further dramatized through the imaginative dialogue of Christ and his mother. The blood and horror of the savior's death is amplified through its description by his own mother, who looks on in helplessness and consternation. As Christ prepares to die, he enjoins his mother to identify henceforth with the suffering of all women and to serve in this way as an ideal intercessor for them:

> "Moder reu of wymanes kare
> Nu thu wost of moder fare,
> Thou thu be clene mayden man."

> "Sune, help alle at nede,
> All tho that to me greden,
> Mayden, wyf and fol wyman."
>   (Silverstein 1971: 12–14)

> "Mother, have mercy on women's cares
> Now that you were in a mother's situation.
> Though you be a pure maiden."

> "Son, help all in need,
> All who cry out to me,
> Maiden, wife, and harlot."

Mary's suffering is thus merged with that of all women, and the female audience member in particular is led to regard her own suffering in light of Mary's experience. This emotive union between saint and present suppliant, grounded in physical and emotional experience but rendered sacred through Christ's redemptive act, becomes a prime theme in the religious lyrics of the late Middle Ages. And Mary's exhortation to her dying son assures the living listener that the Virgin will indeed plead with Christ, regardless of the sins or status of the petitioner. Similar adaptations of the hymn into German began to appear on the Continent by the fifteenth century, reflecting the increasingly international and standardized nature of the emotive religious lyric (Krass 1998: 188).

As mystics and composers sought to reach the soul through the flesh, so they often looked upon the secular lyric as a resource in their work. Often religious lyrics of the era imitate or co-opt secular themes—songs of human love, longing, or passion becoming vehicles for depicting the emotions of Jesus or his mother, or of the human penitent before the Lord. Typical is the fifteenth-century English lyric *I Sing of a Maiden*, in which the Virgin is depicted as the object of the singer's love:

I sing of a maiden
That is makeles:
King of alle kinges
To here sone her ches.

He cam also stille
Ther his moder was
As dew in Aprille
That falleth on the grass.

He cam also stille
To his moderes bowr
As dew in Aprille
That falleth on the flowr.

He cam also stille
There his moder lay
As dew in Aprille
That falleth on the spray.

Moder and maiden
Was never non but she:

Well may swich a lady
Godes moder be.
   (Davies 1963: 155)

———————

I sing of a maiden
Without a match:
The king of all kings
She chose for her son.

He came as quietly
To where his mother was,
As dew comes in April
That falls on the grass.

He came as quietly
To his mother's bower
As dew comes in April
That falls on the flower.

He came as quietly
To where his mother lay
As dew comes in April
That falls on the spray.

Both mother and maiden
Was never one but she:
Well may such a lady
God's mother be.

The song's images parody the lyric in praise of a maiden as well as the lyric account of a lovers' tryst and use these as devices to contemplate the miracle of the
Incarnation. The poet's device is clear throughout the poem, but the artistry of
the work is in how close to a secular lyric the text can come while still focusing
purely and piously on the religious theme.

In a different way, Richard de Ladrede, the fourteenth-century Franciscan bishop of the Norman Irish diocese of Ossory, used secular lyrics as the basis for his religious works. Irritated by the popularity and themes of the secular songs he heard even his clergy singing in his locale, Ladrede composed Latin hymns to be sung to the same melodies. His attempt at supplanting the secular with the sacred was apparently less effective than the strategy of co-option illustrated above. His work's chief interest to modern folk song scholars lies in its hints regarding the secular lyrics he sought to displace. Titles and first lines included in the manuscript to acquaint the reader with the correct melody for each hymn reconstruct the popular music of the locale during Ladrede's lifetime. Lines such as "Alas, hou shold I syng?" indicate that lovers' complaints and other secular subgenres were commonly performed in the era (Shields 1993: 41–42). They also indicate a sometimes acute tension between religious lyrics (like the *planctus*, a complaint by Christ or Mary), its secular counterparts, and the performative choices of clergy and laity alike.

In medieval religious lyric, then, there was a gradual evolution from a predominantly narrativized and attributional system of interpretation (an outgrowth of biblical sources and native epic and panegyric traditions) toward a more intensely emotive, proverbialized interpretive system, one that soon began to spread to secular song. This new interpretive norm still relied on the master narratives of Christianity—the events of the Bible as well as those of the various saints' lives—but it came to focus more centrally on common emotions and to use these as the basis for spiritual comprehension of the Christian message. The invocational form remained operative in these lyrics, transforming the discrete words of another into the living words of a praying singer or community. In the invocation, the temporal and spatial limitations of the world disappear: the singer-speaker is placed at the very site of sacred events, allowed to share in their core human emotions and to benefit from sacral miracles that reoccur there. With the Reformation, hymnody became itself a theological issue, rejected by Calvin as an art of human making and embraced by Luther as a device for creating social unity. Through the subsequent centuries, it endured or reemerged as a key device for molding personal, congregational, and even national orientations toward God. At the same time, its effects on lyric interpretation became central to the genre as a whole.

Confronting Convention

Reading Reception in Shakespeare's Use of Lyric Song

That strain again! It had a dying fall

Twelfth Night I: 1, 4–8

This chapter focuses on the generic axis of interpretation, that constellation of formal and contextual features that permit a knowledgeable audience member to recognize, categorize, and appreciate a lyric performance as an exemplar of a tradition. Although lyric songs can at times appear startlingly original in their imagery, structure, or lexical or musical presentation, this novelty often can prove quite illusory when a certain song is compared to others from the same tradition. What I explore here is the degree to which this predictability can represent a pleasing and complex artistic achievement, one that carries with it a wealth of meaning for audience and performer alike. Communities may possess elaborate norms by which such generic understandings are managed and applied to given performances. In the lyric tradition of Elizabethan England, the responsibility of the audience to appraise such songs was weighty indeed, even while the songs themselves could and did appear utterly predictable. In large measure, this responsibility consisted of allowing the generic to awaken sensations of the personal: that is, to let the song hit home on an emotional and imaginative level.

Scholars of the English lyric have long acknowledged—and lamented—the tendency of the genre toward the conventional. Employing familiar, commonplace details and forms that recur in lyric after lyric from the Middle English through the Elizabethan period and after, such songs often seem intent on failing an aesthetic evaluation that hinges on "freshness," "originality," or "unique vision." Typical of such works is the early Middle English song *Svmer is icumen in,* which appears in a thirteenth-century manuscript just before an antiphon in praise of Saint Thomas à Becket, a conjunction that is reminiscent of the opening *Prologue* of Chaucer's *Canterbury Tales.* The song, in modernized notation, is presented below as in William Chappell's classic *Popular Music of the Olden Time* ([1859] 1965: 24).

EXAMPLE 5.1

Sing cuckoo now, sing cuckoo!
Sing cuckoo, sing cuckoo nu!

Springtime has arrived
Loudly sing cuckoo!
Seeds grow, the meadow blooms
and the wood springs anew
Sing cuckoo!

The ewe bleats for her lamb,
The cow lows for her calf,
The bulluck starts, the buck farts
Merrily sing cuckoo!
Cuckoo, cuckoo
How well you sing cuckoo
Never cease you now!

The above melody is combined with a foot, or burden, for two voices, made up of the line "Sing cuccu nu, sing cuccu!" (Sing cuckoo now, sing cuckoo!) that lends the song an ebullient and vigorous character. One of the earliest evidences of part singing in European music, the song conforms musically to the strictures of a medieval genre of round known as the *rota*. Verbally, it belongs to the French-derived poetic genre of the *reverdie*, a spring song filled with imagery of the bloom and abundance of the season and depicted in familiar agricultural details, juxtaposed in lively and jubilant manner. Its only departure from that norm is the absence of an erotic theme, what A. K. Moore (1951: 50) terms "the gaudy description and love interest of the songs of greeting to the spring in the *Carmina Burana* and the nature introductions of Old French poetry." Chappell ([1859] 1965: 25) notes two other thirteenth-century songs beginning with the line "Svmer is comen," and given the relative paucity of musical texts surviving from the era, this recurrence can be seen as strong evidence that the theme was a commonplace in the lyric song of its day. The images of springtime and cuckoos recur also in a song that closes Shakespeare's *Love's Labour's Lost* some three centuries later. Duffin (2004: 442–43) conjectures that this song may have been sung to the tune of the very popular *Packington's Pound*, but the actual melody has not survived. Shakespeare's text, as it appears in Hardin Craig's edition (1961), is as follows:

When daisies pied and violets blue
    And lady-smocks all silver-white

And cuckoo-buds of yellow hue
  Do paint the meadows with delight,
The cuckoo then, on every tree,
Mocks married men; for thus sings he,
  Cuckoo;
Cuckoo, cuckoo: O word of fear,
Unpleasing to a married ear!

When shepherds pipe on oaten straws
  And merry larks are ploughmen's clocks,
When turtles tread, and rooks, and daws,
  And maidens bleach their summer smocks,
The cuckoo then, on every tree,
Mocks married men; for thus sings he,
  Cuckoo;
Cuckoo, cuckoo: O word of fear,
Unpleasing to a married ear!
  (*Love's Labour's Lost* V: 2, 904–21)

Although here the meaning of the cuckoo has shifted from its association with spring to its association with cuckoldry, the musical and thematic linkage of these songs is evident. In both, the cheerful voice of the calling bird becomes one—unproblematically or ironically—with the persona of the human speaker, whose seemingly fresh perceptions, as Dronke ([1968] 1996) so aptly shows in his now-classic study of the medieval lyric, recur with startling regularity throughout Latin and vernacular lyrics from England across Holland, France, and Germany to Andalusian Spain and southern Italy.

What can be said of such lyrics, whose very form announces not originality but familiarity; not surprise but recognition? Literary scholars writing on the medieval lyric have tended, by and large, to acknowledge the genre's conventionality while trying to rescue at least a few songs as remarkable for their "creative" or "original" handling of familiar *données*. In his introduction to a critical anthology of medieval English lyrics, for instance, R. T. Davies (1963: 20) notes the "avowedly conventional" nature of the lyric genre while asserting: "The ridiculous or tedious consequences of this at the hand of a mechanical or uncreative poet can be compared with those where, at the hand of the true artist, the same conventions have come to life." Such a critical approach retains a modern sensibility of what makes a lyric "good," holding up one song or "artist" as exemplary and denigrating in the process the majority of other creators who employed conventions in ways deemed more "stock," "hackneyed," "clichéd," or "derivative." Modern scholars have thus succeeded in naming themselves the arbiters of taste and quality for communities centuries removed from them, yet they have done little to delineate in any real manner the ways in which conventions appealed to the actual audiences that enjoyed, employed, or engendered such songs in their own time. For that work, the scholar must attend not simply to the compositional use of convention but to its reception as well. I argue here that we can glimpse this reception, at least as it existed in the Elizabethan era, by looking at the uses that Shakespeare makes of lyric songs in his plays. Although these instances present at various points an idealized picture of the workings of lyric reception in Elizabethan culture, they nonetheless capture, I believe, a means of accepting and appreciating the very conventions that literary scholars have found so vexing.

Valorizing Convention from the Compositional Side

Scholars of literature have labored, for the most part unsuccessfully, to discover in oral-derived English lyrics an adherence to modern literary aesthetics. In recent years a number of folklorists have offered theories to account for convention on terms derived from the study of oral genres themselves. Flemming G. Andersen (1985), in a work aptly titled *Commonplace and Creativity,* suggests that the commonplace elements of the ballad genre in fact hold considerable meaning for the singer and listener conversant in the song tradition (see also Bradbury 1998). Drawing on oral formulaic theory, Andersen suggests that such conventions occur in ballads not simply as a byproduct of the ways in which songs are memorized, classified, and retrieved in an oral tradition (i.e., as a product of a process of stereotypification) but also as an integral element of the songs' aesthetic and narratological workings. A singer, in fact, might actively—creatively—choose to incorporate a familiar image or formula into a song in order to achieve a kind of resonance with other ballads. An entirely novel image, although valued by a modern editor, would fail to offer this same resonance to a contemporary audience, and would thus prove less desirable in performance.

John Miles Foley (1990; 1991) makes similar observations of formulas (commonplaces) as they occur in various epic traditions. Drawing on the vast and important body of literature initiated by the publication of Albert B. Lord's *The Singer of Tales* (1960), Foley shows how a familiar turn of phrase, for example, an epithet for a particular hero, or a familiar situation in a story line, can be seen to act metonymically, evoking in the mind of the conversant audience member a host of other prior images or moments that he knows from the tradition. Foley argues that the resonance of such associations creates in the audience's experience of the performance not the disdainful recognition of a cliché but the appreciative response to a pregnant image, economically and effectively conveyed through the device of metonymy. This weightiness or press of convention is what Foley describes as *immanence,* or *word power,* and the process by which it functions in the aesthetic transaction of the performance as *traditional referentiality.* In fact, such referential weight conveys upon the utterance a sense of "nontextual permanence" (1991: 56) that can be regarded as an apt substitute for (or even superior alternative to) the weight that utterances accrue through writing in a literate society.

Such a characterization of the function of "the conventional" offers a valuable counter to the aesthetic hand-wringing of earlier literary scholars as well as the mechanistic theories of stereotypification proposed by earlier folklorists (e.g., Gummere 1901, 1907; Nygard 1958; Jones 1961). In these studies, commonplaces were discussed as "stock" devices, familiar textual or music elements that performers incorporated into their songs in lieu of doing the harder intellectual work of creating something original. Idiosyncratic or original elements that did appear in songs, scholars theorized, were liable to become replaced over time with more conventional ones due to the faulty memories or lack of imagination of subsequent performers, so that performances would grow more and more stereotypical (and less and less artful) with each passing generation.

Conventions were thus regarded as a sign of the homogenizing effects of oral tradition rather than as a medium through which the individual and the tradition become creatively entwined. With the concept of traditional referentiality, however, we can conceptualize these observations in ways that appreciate the complexities that obtain in the use of predictable elements. Commonplace elements—the signposts of the generic axis—can help to establish the conceptual space in which the real work of lyric interpretation occurs for the Elizabethan audience: that is, in the appraisal of the generic from the vantage point of one's own emotional experiences. It is the interplay of the generic and the personal, I contend, that makes even the most familiar lyric powerful to Elizabethan listeners, at least as Shakespeare portrays them.

In this light, the examination of Shakespeare's plays offers a valuable source of evidence. For here we see—both in the ways in which Shakespeare's characters interpret or respond to lyric songs and in the ways in which Shakespeare seems to expect his contemporary audience to respond—clear indications of what was *expected* of a competent audience member. We can glimpse, in other words, the workings of lyric reception as Shakespeare understood (and idealized) it during the Elizabethan era. Looking at the lyric songs in Shakespeare's plays from this perspective opens up a rich and productive source of insights both on the functions of lyric conventions in general and on their workings in Shakespeare's plays themselves (Fox-Good 1998).

EXPECTATIONS OF THE OUTSIDE AUDIENCE

But release me from my bands
With the help of your good hands:
Gentle breath of yours my sails
Must fill, or else my project fails,
Which was to please.
                    Tempest, Epilogue 9–12

Shakespeare's plays were written to be performed, and in an economic situation in which acting companies vied with each other for popularity and patronage, they were meant to entertain. Shakespeare's mode of creation was literate, but his works were received (at least in his day) in a wholly oral context, performed on a stage that catered to both the high and the low of Elizabethan society. In this context, we could expect the playwright to make use of every means available to him to concisely and effectively convey his story, be it in terms of plot, characterization, or imagery. If the kind of word power that Foley describes existed in Shakespeare's day, in other words, we should expect Shakespeare to make use of it.

And indeed, the plays show ample evidence of precisely the kinds of resonance that Foley's theory predicts. In fact, not only does Shakespeare rely on audience knowledge of lyric song conventions in general at various points in his plays, he also displays considerable, sometimes even daunting, expectations concerning specific songs then in circulation and an array of metageneric discourse concerning musical and thematic features of the lyric song tradition. I illustrate each of these varieties of expectation below. Together, they seem to reflect precisely the kind of operative traditional referentiality that makes the conventional in English lyric not a source of embarrassment but a sign of vitality.

When the quick-witted and cynical Benedick wishes to tease his lovesick friend Claudio about his pining for Hero in *Much Ado about Nothing,* he does so by invoking a lyric commonplace.

> Benedick: Come will you go with me?
> Claudio: Whither?
> Benedick: Even to the next willow, about your own business, county. What fashion will you wear the garland of? about your neck, like a usurer's chain? Or under your arm, like a lieutenant's scarf? You must wear it one way, for the prince hath got your Hero. (II: 1, 193–99)

Benedick's remarks, although perhaps cryptic to a modern reader, would have made good sense to the audience of Shakespeare's day. For the willow, and the weaving of garlands under it, was a recurrent lyric image for the longing—and usually unfortunate—lover. As Benedick himself later explains his jest, "I offered him my company to a willow tree, either to make him a garland, as being forsaken, or to bind him up a rod, as being worthy to be whipped" (II: 1, 224–27). But Benedick's humor falls flat, because Claudio is already convinced (wrongly) that his friend the prince Don Pedro has stolen his true love's heart. Thus, Claudio interprets Benedick's mention of the willow not as a jest concerning all love but as a taunt regarding his loss to a social superior.

That this invocation of the willow would have been comprehensible to an Elizabethan audience is made clear by several further uses of the commonplace in other Shakespeare plays. As Desdemona nears her unhappy end in the tragedy *Othello,* she continues to hold out hope for a reconciliation with her jealous and now-obsessed husband. Nonetheless, she finds herself drawn to the song of a former servant, which she eventually performs as her present servant, Emilia, dresses her for bed. The song survives in a collection of vocal songs with lute accompaniment dated to the early seventeenth century, modernized by Chappell ([1859] 1965: 207) as follows:

EXAMPLE 5.2

Shakespeare intersperses lines from the song with instructions that Desdemona gives to her servant:

> Desdemona [singing]: The poor soul sat sighing by a sycamore tree,
>   Sing all a green willow;
>   Her hand on her bosom, her head on her knee,
>   Sing willow, willow, willow:
>   The fresh streams ran by her, and murmur'd her moans;
>   Sing willow, willow, willow;
>   Her salt tears fell from her, and soften'd the stone;—
> Lay by these:—
>   Sing willow, willow, willow;
> Prithee, hie thee, he'll come anon:—
>   Sing all a green willow must be my garland.
>   Let nobody blame him; his scorn I approve,—
> Nay, that's not next.—Hark! Who is't that knocks?
> Emilia: It's the wind.
> Desdemona: I call'd my love false love; but what said he then?
>   Sing willow, willow, willow:
>   If I court moe women, you'll couch with moe men.
>   (*Othello* IV: 3, 41–56)

Chappell ([1859] 1965: 206) notes that "Willow, willow" was a favorite burden in lyrics of the sixteenth century, citing several other surviving songs and plays that make use of it. The words of the willow song here, combined with the dressing of Desdemona, powerfully recalls the lyric commonplace and transforms the scene into a foreshadowing of Desdemona's fate, a fate that is in sharp contrast to the deluded optimism that the heroine shows. This foreshadowing effect is underscored at the end of the play, when a dying Emilia, lamenting her mistress's murder, repeats the willow image:

> What did thy song bode, lady?
> Hark! Canst thou hear me? I will play the swan,
> And die in music, Willow, willow, willow.
>   (*Othello* V: 2, 146–48)

Invoking in the bargain the commonplace of the swan song, Emilia reminds the audience of Desdemona's lyric performance, in which she not only recalled the typical willow song but also *embodied* it before the knowing audience, a technique that Shakespeare uses frequently (Fox-Good 1998). Shakespeare uses the same device in the description of Ophelia's death in *Hamlet,* as the queen relates the unhappy maiden's final weaving of garlands while sitting in a willow tree:

> There is a willow grows aslant a brook
> That shows his hoar leaves in the glassy stream;
> There with fantastic garlands did she make
> Of crow-flowers, nettles, daisies, and long purples
> That liberal shepherds give a grosser name,
> But our cold maids do dead men's fingers call them:
> There on pendent boughs her coronet weeds
> Clambering to hand, an envious sliver broke;
> When down her weedy trophies and herself
> Fell in the weeping brook.
>   (*Hamlet* IV: 7, 167–76)

Here again, the metonymic force of the willow is used to suggest that Ophelia's fatal insanity is a product not only of her father's violent death but also of the sudden rejection she has suffered from the seething Hamlet. Ophelia and Desdemona personify the figures alluded to in the songs, embodying the very melancholy and distress that the image of the willow would awaken in the audience's minds. In a sense, both Desdemona and Ophelia enact a "willow song."

Similarly, but even more strikingly, Shakespeare marks the fleeting moment of marital bliss in the marriage of Romeo and Juliet by having the lovers enact the situation and dialogue of an *alba,* a dawn song in which surreptitious lovers take leave of each other at the break of day (*Romeo and Juliet* III: 5, 1–35). The young lovers' argument over whether they hear a nightingale or a lark is not, of course, a quarrel over ornithology but the evocation of a familiar lyric image found in countless medieval *alba* texts (Dronke [1968] 1996: 168–69). Shakespeare uses the metaphoric weight of the *alba* to characterize the newly formed and soon to be tested love of his hero and heroine. Through their embodiment of the *alba,* we, the audience, are led to see them as the very ideal of love that poets have praised from ages past. Shakespeare's scene does not "steal" the dawn song argument but rather employs it artfully to create resonance and weight for his image of lovers' parting. His technique relies on audience familiarity with the conventions of lyric song and an ability to interpret the case at hand in comparison with a broader norm that the songs and narratives engage.

Whereas the above instances point to the existence of a system of traditional referentiality operative in Elizabethan lyric—one based squarely on the predictable commonplaces of the genre—other passages in Shakespeare's plays indicate that the playwright expected his audiences to also recognize specific popular songs. An example occurs, for instance, in *Two Gentlemen of Verona*, in which the young heroine, Julia, pretends to have no interest in the love letter her servant Lucetta has brought her:

> Julia: Some love of yours hath writ to you in rhyme.
> Lucetta: That I might sing it madam, to a tune.
> Give me a note: your ladyship can set.
> Julia: As little by such toys as possible.
> Best sing it to the tune of 'Light o' love.'
> Lucetta: It is too heavy for so light a tune.
> (I: 2, 79–84)

Here, Julia and Lucetta quibble on the meaning of "setting" a tune, a technical term for part singing, in which the leader of a chorus establishes the pitch that will set the voices of all the other singers. Julia then suggests that the letter be sung to the tune of *Light o' love*. Of course, the meaning of the phrase, and the next line's rejoinder, "It is too heavy for so light a tune," depend directly on the audience's familiarity with the piece, which eventually appeared in print and is thus available to us today (Elson [1900] 1970: 97–100). Shakespeare refers to the same song again in *Much Ado about Nothing* when he puts its title into the mouth of the lady-in-waiting Margaret as she teases the newly lovestruck Beatrice:

> Margaret: Clap's into 'Light o' love'; that goes without a burden:
> Do you sing it, and I'll dance it.
> Beatrice: Ye light o' love, with your heels! Then, if your husband
> have stables enough, you'll have no lack of barns.
> (III: 4, 44–47)

Beatrice's reply plays on the near-homonyms *barns* and *bairns* and implies in characteristically ribald manner that such dancing has certain inevitable outcomes. The weight and humor of the wordplay relies, of course, precisely on the audience's knowledge of the song, without which it is impossible to gauge the full humor or irony of the characters' words. Fortunately, since the melody has survived (see Elson [1900] 1970: 100), we can note that, although it was probably performed slowly, its regular alternation of syncopated and un-syncopated eighth-note triplets lends it a very danceable rhythm. It is presented below as modernized in Elson's text.

EXAMPLE 5.3

Shakespeare's references seem to play on the piece's association with a jocund, dancing atmosphere, one suitable to those already intoxicated by love but not effective for those still holding back, as in the case of Julia or the would-be spin-ster Beatrice. The kind of woman who goes in for *Light o' Love,* Shakespeare seems to suggest, is more of the forward, serving-class variety than the refined, elegant heroines at the center of his plays.

The same expected familiarity with a popular song underlies the hilari-ous parody of the song *Corydon's Farewell to Phyllis* in *Twelfth Night* (II: 3, 110 ff.). Here, the song's title, as it is known from Robert Jones's 1601 *First Booke of Ayres* (Elson [1900] 1970: 216), is not mentioned at all. Rather, a drunken

Sir Toby simply begins to quote its lines in response to the servant Malvolio's self-important warnings regarding the displeasure of Sir Toby's niece, the Lady Olivia:

> Malvolio: . . . If you can separate yourself and your misdemeanours, you are welcome to the house; if not, an it would please you to take leave of her, she is very willing to bid you farewell.
> Sir Toby: Farewell, dear heart, since I must needs be gone.
> Maria: Nay, good Sir Toby.
> Clown: His eyes do show his days are almost done.
> Malvolio: Is't even so?
> Sir Toby: But I will never die!
> Clown: Sir Toby, there you lie.
> Malvolio: This is much credit to you.
> Sir Toby: Shall I bid him go?
> Clown: What an if you do?
> Sir Toby: Shall I bid him go, and spare not?
> Clown: O no, no, no, no, you dare not.
> Sir Toby: Out o' tune sir: you lie. Art any more than a stewart? Do thou think, because thou art virtuous, there shall be no more cakes and ale?
> (*Twelfth Night* II: 3, 104–24)

Sir Toby greets Malvolio's ultimatum—shape up or ship out—by reversing the person in the opening line of *Corydon's Farewell*: "Farewell, dear Love, since thou wilt needs be gone" (Elson [1900] 1970: 218). The servant Maria (who also has a soft spot in her heart for Sir Toby) initially takes him at his word, but Feste, an accomplished singer and entertainer at the courts of both the Duke Orsino and the Lady Olivia, immediately picks up on the game, again reversing the person in the song's second line: "Mine eyes do shew, my life is almost done." Sir Toby places himself in the persona of the song's speaker, who is faced with a lover "as fair, as she is cruel-hearted" and who is threatening to leave. The speaker is torn in each stanza between adopting an outwardly cavalier attitude to his love's impending departure or letting his breaking heart plead truthfully. Typical of this waffling is the song's second verse, presented here with Elson's modernization of the 1601 publication.

EXAMPLE 5.4

Farewell, farewell: since this I find is true,
I will not spend more time in wooing you;
But I will seek elsewhere, if I may find love there.
Shall I bid her goe? What an if I doe?
Shall I bid her goe and spare not?
O no, no, no, I dare not.
   (Elson [1900] 1970: 216–19)

Sir Toby positions himself as the torn wooer of this rather overblown Elizabethan song and in his questions, places Malvolio in the role of the cruel-hearted mistress who is withholding her love. The repartee is humorous because Malvolio (who dislikes songs and other frivolities) completely misses the joke. The real power of the reference lies, however, in the parallel situation of the song and the play: in both, it is the one who would seemingly be in power — the gentleman — who has been dealt the ultimatum by his hardhearted interlocutor. Malvolio's improper usurpation of the role of superior, representing himself as speaking for his lady when in fact expresses his own desires, is deftly revealed in Sir Toby's parody, made at last thuddingly apparent by his direct question: "Art thou any more than a steward?" In revealing this fault in Malvolio's character, the scene prepares the audience for the smarting practical joke that will follow in the play, as Maria contrives to convince Malvolio that he is actually the Lady Olivia's chosen true love. Modern scholars (e.g., Astington 1993; Cahill 1996; for more discussion, see DuBois 2000) have at times found it difficult to see the reasons behind Maria's joke, which provides some of the funniest — and cruelest — moments in Shakespeare's comedies. Perhaps the inability of modern readers to see the point behind Maria's plot derives from the fact that, unacquainted with *Cordyon's Farewell,* they miss much of the revelation of Malvolio's character failing as Shakespeare sets it forth in this scene. Without the full resonance of Sir Toby's derisive parody, his side of the argument falls to the bald "Ye lie." Presumably, Shakespeare's contemporary audience would have understood better. We cannot, of course, be certain that audiences recognized the lines that Sir Toby and Feste quote, but at the very least, it is likely that they would have recognized a play on the genre of a lover's complaint, of which *Corydon's Farewell* is a typical exemplar, seeing in the scene an ironic use of traditional referentiality. Shakespeare expected much of his actual audience, and given his popularity during his lifetime, it seems that his expectations were met.

EXPECTATIONS OF THE INSIDE AUDIENCE

Mark the music.
Merchant of Venice V: 1, 88

As illustrative as these examples are for an inkling of the kinds of competence expected of a lyric's audience in the Elizabethan period, Shakespeare's characters prove an even richer source of insight in this arena. For here, Shakespeare actually portrays the performative relation between singers and their audiences, creating images of the interpretive practices of ideal listeners as well as ridiculing the failings of the foolish or defective audience members as they appear within the bounds of his dramatized narratives. Through attention to the ways in which these inscribed audiences meet both songs and performers, we gain a detailed picture of the audience's competence in receiving and interpreting lyric songs. In it, convention plays a central role.

The relations among song, singer, and audience are perhaps simplest when the singer is her own audience, as is the case of Desdemona in the willow song performance. Yet this scene is in fact quite complex, containing a layering of two different performance events, the earlier of which forms the foundation and background for the latter. As Desdemona tells it, her current marital strife had led her to remember a song from the past:

> My mother had a maid call'd Barbara:
> She was in love, and he she loved proved mad
> And did forsake her: she had a song of 'willow;'
> And old thing 'twas, but it express'd her fortune,
> And she died singing it: that song to-night
> Will not go from my mind; I have much to do,
> But to go hang my head all at one side,
> And sing like poor Barbara.
> (*Othello* IV: 3, 26–33)

The earlier Barbara, despondent at the failure of her own relationship, sang the "old" song because it "express'd her fortune." Although, as we are told, her own love forsook her because of madness, nonetheless, she found the willow song, with its highly conventional lyric situation and turns of phrase, expressive of her own feelings. And Desdemona, sensing in her own relation a similar decline into both strife and marital insanity, finds herself likewise compelled to perform the song. As audiences of their own performances, then, both women approach the lyric through a process of empathy.

In psychology as well as philosophy, the concept of empathy is little more than a century old. Robert L. Katz (1963: 2) traces the term to the work of the German psychologist Theodor Lipps, who used its German equivalent *(Einfühlung)* to describe "losing self-awareness on the part of an observer as he confronts a painting or a piece of sculpture that absorbs his attention." The loss is not so much one of self-awareness, however, as one of a sense of distance between self and an Other: for the moment of empathy, the self and its perceptions become one with that of an external being, hence the German term's meaning, "to feel as one." Such an act, as Edith Stein ([1917] 1964) points out, is profoundly moral in nature and helps the self not only to learn to consider others but also to regard oneself as one among others. And although the term may be new, the concept goes far back in Western thought, as the discussion of hymnody in chapter 4 shows. In fact, an empathic response to lyrics was a key aspect of medieval lyric. What Shakespeare depicts for Barbara and Desdemona here is a familiar and presumably normative means of relating to a lyric song, even to one rife with stylized conventions and commonplaces.

Shakespeare's noblest and most feeling characters invariably display such an empathic response to lyric songs. When the Duke Orsino of *Twelfth Night* wishes to find comfort in this fruitless pining for the Lady Olivia, he does so by calling for a lyric song:

> Now good Cesario, but that piece of song,
> That old and antique song we heard last night:
> Methought it did relieve my passion much,
> More than light airs and recollected terms
> Of these most brisk and giddy-paced times:
> Come, but one verse.
>   (II: 4, 2–7)

Here we find further evidence of the empathic role of the lyric audience. The duke desires music that will "relieve ... passion," that is, express feelings like his own, which, he states, cannot be accomplished with a lighter melody or tempo. Lyric music should mirror the audience's emotional state. Like Desdemona, he has found a piece ("an old and antique song") that he finds suitable for this task, and he asks that it be performed for him again. Note that Orsino does not describe the song as "fresh" or "original"; rather, he makes it clear that it is old and conventional in character:

> Mark it, Cesario, it is old and plain:
> The spinsters and the knitters in the sun
> And the free maids that weave their thread with bones
> Do use to chant it: it is silly sooth,
> And dallies with the innocence of love,
> Like the old age.
>   (II: 4, 44–49)

It is, he states, an English equivalent of the French *chanson de toile,* a formal and contextual parallel of the Finnish grinding songs discussed in chapter 1. We are to presume that Orsino, although distinct in class and gender from the song's typical performers and audience, finds it significant because he can empathize with its speaker. Its highly conventional content or frequent performance by ordinary women at work does not diminish the song's effect on a noble duke. In fact, the duke seems to take pleasure in the fact that his feelings mirror the feelings of others, and he counsels Cesario (Viola in disguise) to see in him the epitome of a man in love:

> Come hither, boy: if ever thou shalt love,
> In the sweet pangs of it remember me;
> For such as I am all true lovers are.
>   (II: 4, 14–16)

Orsino calls for the same double association that Desdemona shows in recalling Barbara and the willow song: Cesario/Viola is to remember a particular person (an audience member of the song) enmeshed in a particular emotional state along with a particular lyric that gives voice (in a highly conventional manner) to an analogous emotional state. Viola shows her ability and willingness to accomplish this act of empathy by aptly characterizing the music: "It gives a very echo to the seat / where Love is enthroned" (II: 4, 21–22), a statement so apt that the duke comes to suspect that she has firsthand experience with love. The song is expected to create an "echo" of an emotional state, and a personal recollection is to furnish a concrete example, but it is the audience's ability to empathize with a generic commonplace that makes the process function as it should. Conventions help rather than hinder this process of interpretation.

This empathic responsibility of the audience is repeatedly invoked in Shakespeare's depictions of lyric performances, particularly if they involve characters in love. In *Merchant of Venice* (V: 1, 69), Jessica responds to music emotively: "I am never merry when I hear sweet music." And her lover, Lorenzo, confirms the rightness of her response: "The reason is, your spirits are attentive" (70). According to Lorenzo:

> The man that hath no music in himself
> Nor is not moved with concord of sweet sounds,
> Is fit for treason, stratagems and spoils;
> The motions of his spirit are dull as night
> And his affections dark as Erebus:
> Let no such man be trusted. Mark the music.
>   (*Merchant of Venice* V: 1, 83–88)

In the play that chronicles his downfall, Julius Caesar suspects Cassius of treason for precisely this reason: "He hears no music" (*Julius Caesar* I: 2, 204), a tendency that distinguishes him from the merrier and more trusted Antony.

Only soldiers appear exempt from this expectation, although this lack of empathic capacity is typically depicted as creating problems in their private lives. Hotspur, who is portrayed as a noble rebel with heroic qualities, rails against a maiden's song in Welsh (*Henry IV, Part 1*, III: 1, 214–50) and takes pride in his inability to sing or rhyme:

> I am glad of it with all my heart:
> I had rather be a kitten and cry mew
> Than one of these same metre ballad-mongers:
> I had rather hear a brazen canstick turn'd,
> Or a dry wheel grate on the axle-tree;
> And that would set my teeth nothing on edge,
> Nothing so much as mincing poetry:
> 'Tis like the forced gait of a shuffling nag.
>   (128–35)

Notably, Hotspur is defeated by the young Prince Hal, who combines an appreciation for the good life with a surprising degree of martial prowess. Hotspur's railing becomes a sign of his personal limitations or tragic flaw. Benedick voices similar views before he falls in love. In hearing the instrumental prelude to Balthasar's lyric song, he remarks, "Is it not strange that sheeps' guts should hale souls out of men's bodies? Well, a horn for my money, when all's done" (*Much Ado about Nothing* II: 3, 60–62). Once in love, however, he is depicted fervently composing poetry, which he sings as well (V: 2, 26–41). Othello appears completely uninterested in music, so much so that the Clown dismisses a musical ensemble without their even performing.

> Clown: . . . But masters, here's money for you: and the general so likes your music, that he desires you, for love's sake, to make no more noise with it.
> First Musician: Well, sir, we will not.
> Clown: If you have any music that may not be heard, to 't again: but, as they say, to hear music the general does not greatly care. (*Othello* III: 1, 11–18)

Given that the musicians had been encouraged at the first by Cassio, it is clear that Shakespeare means Othello's disdain for music to convey an aspect of the general's personality. Presumably, Othello's tone-deafness is part of what leads him to believe Iago's absurd rumor and suspect his virtuous wife. In general, then, Shakespeare's tuneless military men point to a weakness of the soldier's life: a limitation of feelings that may have its uses on the battlefield but that proves disastrous at home. A fully rounded man, like women in general, should be able to "hear" music and let their souls be haled out of their bodies, engaging in the empathic experience at the core of lyric song.

The Performer's Role

No pains, sir; I take pleasure in singing, sir.
Twelfth Night II: 4, 70

The audience's role in requesting and receiving lyrics is thus clear. Shakespeare also makes observations regarding the performer's responsibilities to an audience. First and foremost, the performer should help this empathic experience to proceed through proposing a "fitting" song. In introducing the roguish minstrel Autolycus, the Servant in *The Winter's Tale* notes, "He hath song for man or woman, of all sizes; no milliner can so fit his customers with gloves" (IV: 4, 191–92). And although Shakespeare pokes fun at the contents and style of Autolycus's hawking songs and narrative ballads (190–330), the image of fitting songs to an audience appears as a key skill of the successful singer. Feste, for instance, greets Sir Toby's call for a song with a choice of genres: "Would you have a love-song, or a song of good life?" (*Twelfth Night* II: 3, 35–36). When Sir Toby and his companion Sir Andrew choose a love song, Feste performs one that admirably suits their character and mood. The song itself, *O Mistress Mine,* appeared already in Queen Elizabeth's *Virginal Book* and reached print in Morley's *Consort Lessons* of 1599 (Elson [1900] 1970: 209–10). Elson has modernized the song as follows:

EXAMPLE 5.5

Shakespeare's text is as below:

> Clown [sings]: O mistress mine, where are you roaming?
> O, stay and hear; your true love's coming,
> That can sing both high and low:
> Trip no further, pretty sweeting;
> Journeys end in lovers meeting,
> Every wise man's son doth know.
> Sir Andrew: Excellent good, i' faith.
> Sir Toby: Good, good.
> Clown [sings]: What is love? 'Tis not hereafter;
> Present mirth hath present laughter;
> What's to come is still unsure:
> In delay there lies no plenty;
> Then come kiss me, sweet and twenty,
> Youth's a stuff will not endure.
>   (*Twelfth Night* II: 3, 40–53)

The song's impetuous call for giving in to love now rather than hesitating or waiting for some uncertain future fits well with the situation and personalities of the aging and comically waistrel Toby and Andrew, whose own youth is fast ebbing. The song is followed by the singing of a catch (a form of round), a genre that was familiar to Elizabethan audiences as a pastime at taverns and drinking. Feste's skill lies in finding a song that fully suits the evolving mood and situation of his audience, thereby facilitating an empathic response.

Not only must performers select an appropriate song, however, they must also perform it with a convincing show of sincerity. Such a performance again eases the process by which the audience can identify with the lyric's speaker, even though, as Shakespeare repeatedly makes clear, such feigned sincerity was completely conventional and therefore as patently artificial to the audience as any of the textual or musical conventions mentioned above. In *As You Like It*, Jaques quips:

> I have neither the scholar's melancholy, which is emulation, nor the musician's which is fantastical, nor the courtier's, which is proud, nor the soldier's which is ambitious, nor the lawyer's which is politic, nor the lady's, which is nice, nor the lover's, which is all these. (IV: 1, 10–15)

The musician imitates the melancholy of the lover, thus creating a "fantastical"—fictive—show of emotion. In *Twelfth Night*, Feste makes his artifice amply clear as he receives payment from Duke Orsino for performing his song of love:

> Duke: There's for thy pains.
> Feste: No pains, sir; I take pleasure in singing, sir.
>   (II: 4, 69–70)

The "pains" that Feste has performed are pretense, intended to awaken and ease the authentic pains of empathy in the audience's hearts.

Such an act, of course, constantly runs the risk of appearing insincere, particularly given its stylized conventions and the likelihood of repeated performances. At the outset of *Twelfth Night*, Orsino calls for the repetition of a musical strain, only to discover that its emotive capacity diminishes with greater familiarity:

> That strain again! It had a dying fall:
> O, it came o'er my ear like the sweet sound
> That breathes upon a bank of violets,
> Stealing and giving odour! Enough, no more:
> 'Tis not so sweet now as it was before.
>   (I: 1, 4–8)

When asked to repeat a song, the minstrel Balthasar of *Much Ado about Nothing* tries to demure, noting, "O, good my lord, tax not so bad a voice/to slander music any more than once" (II: 3, 46–47). Presumably, as a repeat performance would oblige the singer to repeat his acts of feigned sincerity, his contrivances might become noticeable to the audience, thus ruining their effect.

When Identification Goes Awry

> Which time she chanted snatches of old tunes.
>   *Hamlet* IV: 7, 178

The essential insincerity of the lyric genre, both in terms of its content and in terms of its performance, can make for trouble for its audience as well, however.

In *Measure for Measure,* Mariana's enjoyment of a performed love lyric is curtailed by the arrival of Duke Vincentio in disguise, who warns, "Music oft hath such a charm to make bad good, and good provoke to harm" (IV: 1, 14–15). An angry Egeus attributes his daughter's love of Lysander to the latter's use of music:

> This man hath bewitch'd the bosom of my child:
> Thou, thou, Lysander, thou hast given her rhymes
> And interchanged love tokens with my child:
> Thou has by moonlight at her window sung
> With feigning voices of feigning love.
>   (*Midsummer Night's Dream* I: 1, 27–31)

Similarly, the would-be lover Cloten tries to reach the heart of Imogen by hiring musicians to serenade her, noting pragmatically, "I am advised to give her music o' mornings; they say it will penetrate" (*Cymbeline* II: 3, 12–13). After his hired ensemble performs a dawn song, Cloten dismisses them with words that reveal his own utter insincerity as well as his inability to empathize with a lyric speaker:

> So get you gone. If this penetrate, I will consider your music the better; if it do not, it is a vice in her ears, which horse-hairs and calves'-guts nor the voice of unpaved eunuch to boot, can never amend. (II: 3, 31–35)

Such passages reveal the ambiguities of the Elizabethan lyric as performed: outwardly conventional, performed with utterly pretended sincerity, it nonetheless held the potential to move the hearts of listeners, who, in fact, were enjoined to allow empathy to occur. The genre's contrivances facilitate identification between lyric speaker and audience member, and thus, feigned emotions bring forth real emotions.

And such an act, when practiced upon the innocent, could lead to harm. The emotional thrill and danger of the lyric lay in its potential to overwhelm the perceptions and understandings of the audience member. The empathic response necessarily involves a reseparation of self from other at the end of the performance, a savoring of similarities of situation within a broader recognition of essential differences. The facts of this world must remain, on some basic level, distinct from the fictions of the lyric situation. Yet, as Shakespeare makes clear several times in his plays, reseparation could occasionally fail. The inebriated, such as Sir Toby of *Twelfth Night,* often talk with greater or lesser degrees

of consciousness through quoting lines from lyrics. The distracted Ophelia becomes entirely reliant on lyric lines after her fall from sanity:

> Ophelia: Where is the beauteous majesty of Denmark?
> Queen: How now, Ophelia!
> Ophelia [sings]: How should your true love know
> From another one?
> By his cockle hat and staff,
> And his sandal shoon.
> Queen: Alas, sweet lady, what imports this song?
> Ophelia: Say you? Nay, pray you, mark.
> [sings] He is dead and gone, lady,
> He is dead and gone;
> At his head a grass-green turf,
> At his heels a stone.
> (*Hamlet* IV: 5, 21–32)

Similarly, when Edgar wishes to counterfeit madness in his dealings with King
Lear, he does so by frequently quoting song lines (*King Lear* III: 3, 50 ff.). Feste
does the same in his dialogue with Malvolio in prison (*Twelfth Night* IV: 2, 79 ff.).
This behavior appears to have been a stock device for representing madness on
the Elizabethan stage. If so, it demonstrated a cultural awareness of the likelihood of complications in the complex task of receiving lyric songs empathically.

Shakespeare, then, presents as laudable the ability to match song to mood
(either in a performer or in a person calling for performance), and he expects a
competent audience member to appreciate a song by identifying with the sentiment expressed in its melody and words. This empathic response hinges on
the ease with which an inscribed feeling or situation can be recognized by the
audience and the seeming sincerity of the singer's performance. Conventions of
melody and text are thus in this light important for facilitating audience recognition and empathy but are supplemented by the (feigned) authenticity of the
performer's embodiment of the song's emotions. The tendency to believe that
the song's stated sentiments or viewpoints actually belong to the singer personally, however, is portrayed as naive, something that can lead innocent maidens,
for instance, into falling foolishly in love. Ultimately, the real sentiments of importance in a lyric performance situation belong to the audience who has requested or permitted the performance to occur. And a potential audience who

refuses to engage in such empathy is portrayed as defective in intellect or heart and therefore worthy only of distrust. A further danger of the empathic act lies in the possibility of overidentifying with a song's contents, failing to reestablish a distance between self and inscribed speaker at the end of the performance and eliding the generic axis of interpretation so completely with the personal that the two become confounded. The resulting confusion is to be found in the ravings of the inebriated and the mad, or sometimes in the sham ravings of those wishing to counterfeit a state of impaired judgment.

The oral lyrics of northern Europe, like the popular songs of the modern music industry, show a perennial tendency toward convention, a reliance on the generic axis that both eases and accentuates the performative artistry of the song. In an elite aesthetic framework privileging originality and uniqueness, such a tendency may seem lamentable. Yet it is highly functional in living lyric traditions. As the above examination of Shakespeare's lyric passages demonstrates, conventions can help a performer to connect with the likely emotional state of an audience, drawing on established images not out of a lack of creativity but as an act of performative efficiency and skill. A performer must link a lyric to an audience's likely states of mind in as immediate and powerful a manner as possible, so that the real work of the lyric performance—the creation of an audience's empathy—may occur. In so doing, the performer must walk a fine line between effective familiarity and the recognition of insincerity or triteness. So, too, the audience must be careful both to empathize and to read the performance and its content as fictive. Throughout this complex transaction, performer and audience alike have crucial roles to play.

CHAPTER 6

Attribution and the Imagined Performer

> The poet is snatched from us by death, his body falls into the
> earth, but the movement which he has aroused remains, and
> his poems raise a little, quiet, gentle wave upon the water of
> life which floats far out from the poet's own native place.
>
> Douglas Hyde, *Songs Ascribed to Raftery* ([1901] 1903)

In the modern reception of popular lyric, the singer-songwriter holds the spot-light to such an extent that it is often difficult to imagine it any other way. We may listen to a song at first for its tune or words, but if we become interested in it to any real degree, our attention usually turns to its creator or performer. We seek comprehension of the song in the biography, career, or personal views of a human subjectivity that the song seems to connect us with. As Simon Frith (1998: 171) has shown, performers may use this tendency to their advantage, cre-ating more or less fictive personae that their songs purport to explore. It would be hard to understand the careers and success of twentieth-century singers such as Mick Jagger, Elvis Presley, Dolly Parton, or Madonna—diverse though their musical styles may be—without reference to this interplay between the inter-pretive demands of the audience and the self-styling strategies of the performer, conveyed through that barrage of interviews, public appearances, concert tours, album art, webpages, and the like that constitute "publicity." Sometimes the "star" persona may long outlive the actual performer.

This tendency toward attribution—that is, toward interpreting a lyric by associating it with its creator—may seem quintessentially modern, and not only because it so dominates the contemporary popular music industry. As discussed in chapter 1, a scholarly commitment to the "anonymous" or "collective" creator has often limited the ways in which folklorists have approached lyrics or their performers. As singers became conceptualized as "tradition bearers" rather than "creators," they seemed far distant from the conscious, calculating machinations of a modern singer or publicist. Scholars have tended to portray traditional singers as largely innocent community members, performing for a small circle of family and friends. At the same time, their music-making, through the agency of the collector or scholar, could be recognized as the expression of a national or cultural identity, an example of "authentic" collective *Volkspoesie* after the model of Herder (see Bendix 1997). Such symbolic designations, however, remained part of the apparatus and powers of the scholar, not the performer. The traditional singer, as a member of the "common folk," was usually expected to remain outside of this discussion or its presentation, even when the singer might have considerable knowledge, strong opinions, and an economic stake in the topic, as Roger D. Abrahams (1970) has shown in his thoughtful examination of Almeda Riddle. A singer's aura of authenticity could easily be damaged by a display of cognizance regarding the formal study of folk music.

The poets and musicians discussed in this chapter—though diverse in terms of tradition—share similar situations and careers, ones that hinge on the practice and manipulation of the interpretive potential of attribution. Their activities are known to us today largely because of the attributive lore that surrounded their works in oral tradition and that eventually followed their works into written collections and analysis. This attributive lore appears nominally specific or unique to each singer in particular; in practice, however, the biographical, too, becomes traditional in form and content. The image of the poet-singer tends toward certain characteristics regardless of culture or period, implying norms by which audiences use biographical details to interpret and appreciate the songs they attribute to particular singers.

ATTRIBUTION IN THE CELTIC LYRIC TRADITION

Perhaps no other part of northern Europe shows such a rich devotion to the hermeneutic option of attribution as the Celtic-language regions of Britain and Ireland. Medieval texts from Ireland and Wales frequently include accounts of artful and revered poet-singers who use their poetry to praise, remember, and influence kings and nobles.

Suibhne geilt (Mad Sweeney) furnishes an apt and early example. According to the text *Buile Suibhne* (O'Keefe 1913; Dillon 1948: 94–100), Suibhne, a seventh-century king, was said to have lost his wits as a result of a curse placed on him by Saint Rónán. The saint, provoked by Suibhne's attempted destruction of his psalter and murder of some of his disciples, dooms Suibhne to a period of insanity, during which he can find no comfort in human company, clothes, or housing. During the subsequent Battle of Magh Rath (637), Suibhne is suddenly struck with frenzy and flees from the field, spending the coming years alone in various mountains and glens throughout Ireland. In his wanderings, he becomes birdlike, capable of flight and impressive leaps and sprints, all the while reciting poignant lyrics about his unhappy situation. Typical is the long lyric that begins as follows:

> Anocht is fúar an snechta,
> Fodeachta is búan mo bhochta,
> Nidom neirt isin deabuidh .
> Im geilt romgeoghuin gorta.
>
> Atchid cach nidom chuchtach,
> As lom i snáth mo cheirteach,
> Suibhne mh'ainm o Ros Ercain,
> As misi an gealtán gealtach.
>
> Nidom fois o thig aghaidh,
> Ni thaidlenn mo chois conair,
> Nocha bíu sonna a ccíana,
> Domeccad ialla omhain.

> ————

> Cold is the snow tonight,
> Lasting now is my poverty,
> There is no strength in me for fight,
> Famine has wounded me, madman as I am.
>
> All see that I am not shapely,
> Bare of thread is my tattered garment,
> Suibhne of Ros Earcain is my name,
> The crazy madman am I.

I rest not when night comes,
My foot frequents no trodden way,
I bide not here for long,
The bonds of terror come upon me.
    (O'Keefe 1913, 28–31)

The lyric itself calls forth both sympathy for the beset Suibhne and esteem for his poetic gifts. In both ways, Suibhne as a personality is highlighted in the song as well as in the narratives that accompany it. Suibhne's tale is based on quasi-historical traditions surrounding the Battle of Magh Rath, infused with the motif of the Wild Man of the Woods (O'Keefe 1913: xxxv), and seems to have taken shape sometime during the High Middle Ages. Its element of the feather-sprouting accursed king echoes the experience of Nebuchadnezzar in the Book of Daniel (4:30), who rejoices via lyric himself after his time of curse is over (see Sayers 1992). The poems attributed to Suibhne date from the ninth through twelfth centuries. Poems composed in the persona or manner of Suibhne, of course, need not have been composed by a historical Suibhne at all. Rather, it is the attribution to him alone—the creation of a poem that seems to fit with the persona and biography of this famed poet-king—that gives the Suibhne lyrics their context for interpretation.

Royal poet figures are recurrent in northern Europe; kings such as Richard the Lionhearted and Henry VIII are credited with lyric compositions. Yet in practice, the poet-singer of attributive lore tends more often to be a professional performer. The Welsh Gwion Bach, or Taliesin, provides a valuable example from Wales (Ford 1977: 159–81). In manuscripts dated to the sixteenth century and after but clearly drawing on earlier material, the colorful life and career of Taliesin is detailed. He is said to have lived in the era of King Arthur, as well as the succeeding king Maelgwn of Gwynedd. Accounts depict the young Gwion Bach using guile to gain for himself the benefits of a magic brew that fills him with wisdom and prophecy. After a magical rebirth, he comes to live with the noble Elphin and his wife, who raise him with tenderness and love. Renamed Taliesin, he eventually uses his skills to rescue his adopted father/ noble patron from the taunts and censure of King Maelgwn, showing himself more skilled in poetry than the king's own bards. Taliesin saves his master from imprisonment and poverty while displaying all the while an unmatched skill in poetry. Regarding the relation of this narrative to Taliesin's various poems, Ford writes:

The poems in the tale present a special problem. They were not considered an integral part of the tale, and many manuscripts omit them entirely. Elsewhere, we find the poems, but without the prose or separated from it. Even where the poems are integrated with the text, there is little agreement on their order from one manuscript to the next. (162)

Here, then, we find what appears the same relation between lyric and narrative that we saw in the discussion of Deirdre in chapter 2. The act of attribution situates and explicates the lyrics for their audiences, even if the background account is not present in the performance or the narrative is given without inclusion of the lyrics. And a certain image of Taliesin emerges from both sources: inventive, emotive, and politically canny, the poet uses his intellect as well as his artistic gifts to advance his patron's career, gaining a secure life and career for himself through his lord's success.

As these tales indicate, the trade of the bard enjoyed high esteem in Welsh tradition. The Laws of Hywel Dda, ascribed to the tenth century but first appearing in manuscripts of the twelfth and thirteenth centuries, speak of several classes of poet (Edwards 1996: 4). The *pencerdd* was the highest of these, a professional poet whose superior gifts had been proven in competitions and who now held the right to take pupils. Below him ranked the household bard, or *bardd teulu*, who performed specific poetic duties for the court, such as singing to the troops before battle or entertaining the queen. On a lower level was the *cerddor*, whose duties seem to have included lighter or more satirical entertainment. Edwards also speaks of a subclass of folk poets too lowly to merit attention in the laws or poems of their betters but popular nonetheless with the populace as a whole. Scholars have increasingly explored the interrelations of these different groups and the influences that entered Welsh poetry from high as well as low as a result. At all levels, attribution served as a central and expected means of interpreting poetic works.

The notoriety of the bard continued through the Gogynfeirdd poets of the twelfth and thirteenth centuries and down to the Cywyddwyr of the fourteenth. During this latter period, the poets Dafydd ap Gwilym and Iolo Goch emerged as particularly prominent artists. They serve below as illustrations of the profiles and careers such professionals could experience while making a circuit of aristocratic households, exchanging poetry for hospitality and reward.

Dafydd ap Gwilym was active in the mid-fourteenth century. Born in Cardiganshire of a notable family, he may have enjoyed a partial income from inherited land rents (Thomas 2001: xii). But he was also clearly a wandering poet, performing at the homes of the gentry as well as (apparently) at taverns. His poems include religious lyrics of deep solemnity, as well as wry, predominantly narrative poems regarding lovers' trysts and travails, composed in the Ovidian manner of continental lyric (Bromwich 1986: 2). Many of these focus on his longstanding love of two women, Morfudd, daughter of Madog Lawgam of Merioneth, and Dyddgu, daughter of Ieuan son of Gruffudd of south Cardiganshire (Thomas 2001: xxi). In various poems, Dafydd addresses them directly or relates his adventures in their pursuit despite their husbands' wishes. More serious than many, but particularly beautiful in its lyric imagery, is his poem addressed to the wind:

> Yr wybrwynt helynt hylaw
> Agwrdd drwst a gerdda draw,
> Gŵr eres wyd garw ei sain,
> Drud byd heb droed heb adain.
> Uthr yw mor aruthr y'th roed,
> O bantri wybr heb untroed,
> A buaned y rhedy
> Yr awron dros y fron fry.
> Nid rhaid march buan danad,
> Neu bont ar aber, na bad.
> Ni boddy, neu'th rybuddiwyd,
> Nid ai ynglŷn diongl wyd.
> Nythod ddwyn, cyd nithud ddail,
> Ni'th dditia neb, ni'th etail
> Na llu rhugl, na llaw rhaglaw,
> Na llafn glas na llif na glaw.
> Ni'th ddeil swyddog na theulu
> I'th ddydd, nithydd blaenwydd blu.
> Ni'th lladd mab mam, gam gymwyll,
> Ni'th lysg tân, ni'th lesga twyll.
> Ni'th wŷl drem, noethwal dramawr,
> Neu'th glyw mil, nyth y glaw mawr;
> Noter wybr natur ebrwydd,
> Neitiwr gwiw dros nawtir gŵydd.

Rad Duw wyd ar hyd daear,
Rhuad blin doriad blaen dâr.
Sych natur, creadur craff,
Seirniawg wybr, siwrnai gobraff.
Saethydd ar froydd eiry fry
Seithug eisingrug songry.
Dywed ym, diwyd emyn,
Dy hynt, di ogleddwynt glyn.
Drycin yn ymefin môr,
Drythyllfab ar draethellfor.
Huawdl awdr, hudol ydwyd,
Hëwr, dyludwr dail wyd.
Hyrddiwr, breiniol chwarddwr bryn,
Hwylbrenwyllt heli bronwyn.

Hydoedd y byd a hedy,
Hin y fron, bydd heno fry,
Och ŵr, a dos Uwch Aeron
Yn glaer deg, yn eglur dôn.
Nac aro di, nac eiriach,
Nac ofna er Bwa Bach
Cyhuddgwyn wenwyn weini;
Caeth yw'r wlad a'i maeth i mi.
Gwae fi pan roddais i serch
Gobrudd ar Forfodd, f'eurferch;
Rhiain a'm gwnaeth yn gaethwlad,
Rhed fry rhod a thŷ ei thad.

Cur y ddôr, pâr egori
Cyn y dydd i'm cennad i.
A chais ffordd ati, o chaid,
A chŵyn lais fy uchenaid.
Deuy o'r sygnau diwael,
Dywed hyn i'm diwyd hael:
Er hyd yn y byd y bwyf,
Corodyn cywir ydwyf.

Ys gwae fy wyneb hebddi,
Os gwir nad anghywir hi.
Dos fry, ti a wely wen,
Dos at feinwen felenllwyd,
Debre'n iach, da wybren wyd.

————————

Sky wind of impetuous course
Who travels yonder with your mighty shout,
You are a strange being, with a blustering shout,
Most reckless in the world, without foot or wing.
It is strange how marvelously you were sent
Lacking a foot, from out the store-house of the sky,
And how swiftly it is you run
This moment now across the slope above.
No need for a swift horse under you,
Nor bridge nor boat at river-mouth,
You will not drown: you have been indeed forewarned,
You have no corners, you will not get entangled.
Though you might winnow leaves, seizing the nests,
None will indict you, neither swift troop
Nor hand of magistrate will hold you back,
No blue blade nor flood nor rain,
Neither officer nor retinue can hold you
In your life-time, scatterer of the
tree-tops' feathers;
No mother's son can strike you [it would be] wrong [even] to mention it,
No fire burns you, nor treachery restrains you.
No eye can see you with your great barren wall,
[but] a thousand hear you, nest of the great rain,
swift-natured annotator of the clouds,
fair leaper across nine fallow lands.

You are God's blessing over all the earth,
With harsh roar shattering the tops of oaks:
Your nature dry, tenacious creature,

Trampler of clouds, a mighty journey,
Shooter upon the snow-fields up above
Of futile noisy piles of chaff.
Tell me, [my] devoted jewel,
Your journey North Wind of the valley?
[When] bad weather agitates the sea
you are a reveler upon the shore.
Eloquent author, you are an enchanter,
You are a sower, a pursuer of leaves,
A privileged jester on the hill—you are a hurler
Of wild masts on the white-breasted sea.

You fly the full length of the world,
The hill's limit: be above tonight,
Ah, man, and go to Uwch Aeron,
[be] gentle and kind, with voice easily heard.
Do not stop, do no hold back
Nor fear, in spite of the Bwa Bach
—that whining accuser, serving jealousy—
that land which nourished her is closed to me.
Woe is me that I placed serious love
On Morfudd, on my golden girl—
A maiden who has made me exiled from the land—
Run upwards [now] towards her father's house.

Beat on the door, make it be opened
Before day [comes], to my messenger
And find a way to her, if it may be had,
And, with complaining, voice my sighs.
You come from the unchanging planets:
Say this to my faithful generous [girl]:
However long I may be in the world,
I shall remain her faithful follower.
Without her all my looks are sorrowful—
If it be true she is not faithless to me.
Go up, and you will see the fair girl:
Go down, you darling of the sky,

Go to the pale, fair, slender maid
And come back safely: you are the sky's treasure.
(Bromwich 1982: 104–6)

The poem's images of the wind are timeless and complete in themselves and would seemingly not announce any one composer over another. Yet the poem's references to Morfudd and to Bwa Bach ("Little crook-back," apparently a derogatory nickname for Morfudd's cuckolded husband; Thomas 2001: 228) inform the knowing audience that the speaker is Dafydd ap Gwilym. The poem's enduring images are thus glossed by the persona of a composer-speaker, whose career of womanizing and poetry was well known to his contemporaries and their descendants. Attribution helps to clarify details of the poem, presenting the poet as the key to its existence and meaning. The poem can be experienced and enjoyed without knowledge of who Dafydd or Morfudd was, but crucially, it was the expectation of both performer and audience that their identities would be known and their subjectivities glimpsed through the images of the lyric itself.

Of course, we cannot be certain that the poem above was composed by Dafydd ap Gwilym; it survives today because of its inclusion in manuscripts preserved over the centuries. Other poems, similarly, are preserved alongside it, many of these attributed to the same poet. In his authoritative edition of Dafydd ap Gwilym's works, Thomas Parry (1952) accepted as "authentic" some 150 surviving poems while rejecting as "apocryphal" some 177 (Fulton 1996: xiv). His judgments were based on language, style, and content and have been much debated by scholars since. Nonetheless, it is clear that for generations of Welsh audiences from the fourteenth century onward, the attribution of works to Dafydd ap Gwilym was a meaningful and effective means of identifying and evaluating poems.

Although scholars debate the details of poems actually composed by Dafydd ap Gwilym, they readily assent to the fact that what little we know about the poet comes from his poems themselves. Indeed, in these the poet-speaker Dafydd seems intent on cultivating and maintaining a variable and complex persona. He sometimes rises to heights of seriousness and religious fervor. But equally likely are his playful and self-deprecatory tales of comeuppances, intrigues, squabbles, and foibles. An ode to Jesus (Thomas 2001: 1–2) is offset by a denial of having ever been schooled as a monk (74–76) and a scathing rejection of a friar's call to chastity (270–71). In a poem of singular inventiveness, he debates his failings with his shadow (276–77), and in another poem long rejected as apocryphal, he similarly addresses his penis (317–18). As a wandering poet, it was important to

Dafydd ap Gwilym that his reputation precede him, so that audiences would be more likely to afford him attention and payment. And thus, he appears to have indulged expressly in the kinds of self-depiction and self-promotion that made subsequent attribution by his audiences both natural and effective.

Iolo Goch survives in fewer poems but more biographical detail than his illustrious counterpart. Also born in the first half of the fourteenth century, his career overlapped with Dafydd's, for whom he wrote a poignant elegy.

Marwnad Dafydd ap Gwilym

"Hudol doe fu hoedl Dafydd,
Howy o ddyn pe hwy fai'i ddydd,
Diungor awdl, da angerdd,
Ap Gwilym Gam, gwlm y gerdd.
Lluniodd wawd wrth y llinyn,
Llyna arfer dda ar ddyn.
Mau ddarpar, mi a ddirpwr
Marwnad o gariad y gŵr.
Gem oedd y sirroedd a'u swch,
A thegan gwlad a'i thegwch,
Mold y digrifwch a'i modd,
Ymwared im am wiwrodd,
Hebog merched Deheubarth,
Heb hwn, od gwn, aed yn garth.
Cywydd pob cethlydd coethlawn,
Canys aeth, cwynofus iawn."

"Tydi gi, taw di gywydd!
Nid da'r byd, nid hir y bydd.
Tra fu Ddafydd, gelfydd gân,
Ydd oeddudd barchus ddiddan;
Ach ni bydd oherwydd hyn
Gwedy ef gwiw dy ofyn.
Bwrier a wëer o wawd
A'i deuflaen ar y daflawd.
Ethyw pensel yr ieithoedd,
Eithr pe byw athro pawb oedd.

Uthr fy nghwyn o frwyn fraw,
Athroddysg oedd uthr ynddaw,
A thaeliwr serch i ferch fu
A thelyn llys a'i theulu,
A thrysorer clêr a'u clod
A thryfer brwydr a thrafod
A thruan heb athrywyn,
A thraha fu difa'r dyn,
A thrawst beirdd, athrist y byd,
A thrachefn ni thrachyfyd;
Athro grym glewlym gloywlef
A thëyrn oedd, aeth i'r nef."

————————

[The Verse:]
"Dafydd's life was enchanted yesterday,
a fine man had his day been longer,
many-stranded ode, good artistry,
son of Gwilym Gam, knot of song.
He fashioned praise straight along the line,
There a good custom for a man.
My provision, I will make
An elegy of love for the man.
He was the jewel of the shires and their tip
And the toy of the country and its beauty,
The mould of entertainment and its manner.
My salvation for a fine gift,
The hawk of the girls of Deheubarth,
Without him, indeed, let it turn to rubbish.
The *cywydd* of every refined singer
Is grieving deeply because he has gone."

[The Poet:]
"You dog, shut up, you *cywydd!*
The world is not good, it will not last long.

Whilst Dafydd was alive, skilful song,
You were respectable and merry;
And because of this it will not be
Fitting to request you after him.
Let whatever praise is woven
And its two ends be thrown into the loft.
The penoncel of language has gone,
If only he were alive he would be everyone's teacher.
Immense is my complaint because of grievous shock,
Learning was immense in him,
And he was tailor of love to a girl
And the harp of a court and its retinue
And treasurer of minstrels and their praise
And trident of battle and conflict,
And pitiful without mitigation
And presumption was the destruction of the man,
And the beam of poets, most sorrowful is the world,
And he will not rise up again,
A strong, bold, sharp, clear-voiced teacher
And lord was he, he went to heaven."
   (Johnston 1993: 88–91)

In an inventive and beautiful lyric dialogue, Iolo Goch here depicts an argument between a poet-speaker (presumably himself) and the verse form that Dafydd ap Gwilym had done so much to develop (the *cywydd*). The verse declares that it will memorialize Dafydd: "My provision, I will make / an elegy of love for the man." This represents exactly the function and effect of bardic poetry during the era: it kept alive the memory of poets or subjects while these figures in turn helped gloss the verse itself. Yet the grieving speaker retorts that verse cannot simply create itself; it needs great geniuses like Dafydd, and once these have gone, the form cannot hope to enjoy the same success: "The world is not good, it will not last long." The speaker points to a crucial interreliance of poet and poem, a relation that assuredly provided an economic foundation for the poet but also ensured the survival of the poetry and its tradition from one generation to the next. Attribution was part of a framework of evaluation and interpretation that helped to maintain the tradition through the course of centuries.

The corpus of poems attributed to Iolo Goch includes serious praises and elegies for figures like the sons of Tudur Fychan and Owain Glyndŵr, political figures whose names and actions help to date the poems and the poet. At other points, his repertoire turns more humorous, as he chides his beard for scaring away a young love (Johnston 1993: 102–5), or satirical, as he berates one Madog ap Hywel for a lack of hospitality:

Costiaf i Fadog, castyn untroediog,
Costog cynghafog, hufen amcaff,
Cystuddfab Hywel, costiai ei ochel,
Costrel aelisel nid ail Asaff,
Custos gwartheg cadw, cawstyau achadw,
Cwd rhwd brwd bradw, breudwrch rhybraff,
Cildwrnel gwanleddf, celwrn bramsachleddf,
Cail mail mileinddeddf, neud cynneddf caff,
Cwlm ysgwthr, twnffed, calon Mahumed,
Caled er byrred, ni ŵyr barraff,
Calgrwn bacwn bocs cyfled fflaced fflocs,
Cawldrwm hocs llawn crocs, crocer wrth raff,
Colwydd bugail Pedr, colerau wystn gledr,
Celwydd fedr, cwffl lledr, llwdn mewn ysgraff,
Cymwrn burm ysgai, cymaint â dimai
I gan y bawai ni graffai'r graff.

———————

I will provide for Madog, one-legged scoundrel,
Grasping cur, grabbing cream,
Hywel's troublesome son, he had to be avoided,
Low-browed flagon, no second Asaph,
Keeper of store cattle guarding cheeseries,
Fetid tattered bag of rust, feeble overweight mole,
Flacid tub, bucket whining like a sack of farts,
Churlish sheep trough, it's a grasping nature,
Carved knot, funnel, Mahomet's heart,
Hard despite his shortness, he doesn't know what a paragraph is,

Blunt-pricked boxwood bacon as wide as a pack of wool,
Cauldron of mallows full of deceit, may he be hanged by a rope,
Neck of Peter's shepherd, collars like a wizened trellice,
Skill in lying, leather cowl, young animal in a boat,
Pile of scummy yeast, pincers could not seize
So much as a halfpenny from the filthy wretch.
   (Johnston 1993: 154–55)

The poem's stinging metaphors are shaped both by the ideas of honor of Iolo Goch's day and by the verbal requirements of the poetic form. Through his memorable string of barbed characterizations, the poet ensures that the name of Madog ap Hywel will be remembered ever after not for any meritorious deeds but rather for his failings. The bard satirizes the stingy for more than merely personal reasons, however. His entire profession, the tradition of poetic composition and performance that he embodied, relied integrally on respect for and patronage of the poet. Thus, this satire against Madog ap Hywel becomes a punishment of miserliness, an underscoring of the dangers of offending a poet, and finally, an advertisement of the poetic prowess of its creator, Iolo Goch. He seeks to remind his audience of this considerable heritage of his trade and to exercise his prerogative to censure those who fail to evince proper respect and support for his office. Yet, in the long run, his poem is remembered as much through its attribution to him as through its vituperative tone and content: the poet becomes one with his works and serves ultimately as a prime source of meaning for his texts. We come to see Iolo Goch—like many of the poet-singers discussed below—as an artist with a temper.

The bardic system of Wales had its counterpart in Ireland. An eighteenth-century Irish account of a bardic school describes a winter course of studies for poets-in-training, in which young men were taught to compose poems in the elaborate meters and diction of the classic tradition (Bergin 1970: 5 ff.). Although the composition occurred orally (while sequestered in a dark room), the poems were thereafter committed to writing and, indeed, were taught to a second performer—a *reacaire,* or reciter—who would perform them to the accompaniment of the harp at aristocratic banquets or festivals. As in Wales, attributive copies of various poems by these poets survive in Irish manuscripts, drawing on a centuries-old stock of poetic forms, vocabulary, and imagery while addressing topics or recipients in the poet's own day. And as in the case of Iolo Goch, above,

Irish poets struggled to maintain the respect and prestige of their demanding art, despite eventually declining economic support and ebbing popular interest. As it is put in a poem attributed to a disgruntled poet Mathghamhain Ó Hifearnáin of the early seventeenth century:

Ceist! Cia do cheinneóchadh dán?
A chiall is ceirteólas suadh:
An ngéabhadh, nó an áil le haon,
Dán saor do-bhéaradh go buan?

———————

Question! Who will buy a poem?
Its meaning is genuine learning of scholars.
Will any take, or does any lack,
A noble poem that shall make him immortal?
   (Bergin 1970: 145, 279)

The speaker reminds his audience that poetry can bring them immortal fame, just as it can bring infamy to the victims of its satires. Yet, in the long run, it was the poet who most benefited from this immortality, for it was by his name and career that the poem would most likely be interpreted in coming generations.

It is important to note for the sake of the discussion of Carolan below that these poets were usually distinguished from harper-reciters (Walker 1786: 59; Connellan 1860). John Derrick depicts both a harper playing and a poet reciting at an aristocratic feast in his 1581 work, *The Image of Irelande* (Buckley 1999). In his *View of the State of Ireland*, Spenser writes, "Their verses are taken up with a general applause and usually sung at all feasts and meetings by certain other persons, whose proper function that is" (quoted in Walker 1786: 134). A now-anonymous bardic poem from the sixteenth century begins:

Triall, a reacaire, reac m'fhuighle,
Imthigh go grod, ná gabh sgís
Gan dol d'fhéaghain chin ar ccoimhghe:
Fill ré sgéulaibh oirne arís.

———————

Go, my reciter, recite my words;
Depart speedily, let no weariness
Keep thee from going to see the head of our protection,
Turn again to me with tidings.
    (Bergin 1970: 200, 306)

Several extant bardic poems are addressed to harpers; both the sixteenth-century Fear Flatha Ó Gnimh and an unknown contemporary composed poems addressing the same, apparently famous harper Nioclás Dall (i.e., Nicholas the Blind) (Bergin 1970: 112–14, 197–99), praising his skill in performance while demonstrating their own skills at making literary and mythological allusions to great musicians of the past.

Although the evidence above suggests a clear and highly formalized division between poet and harper-reciter, the latter appears to have also enjoyed some performative autonomy. Spenser notes, "Under the present reign we find Bards of an inferior rank, or rather, Minstrels, strolling in large companies amongst the Nobility and Gentry" (Walker 1786: 142). In his *De rebus in Hibernia gestis* (1584), Stanihurst writes, "A harper attends at the feasts; he is often blind, and by no means skilled in music" (Connellan 1860: 161). He goes so far as to mention a particular harper, Crucius, who is exceptionally skilled in the instrument and justly famed for his playing (Walker 1786: 145). The seventeenth-century Irish historian Keating recounts the harper Craftiny's wooing of a woman in Gaul (Connellan 1860: 162). He selects and performs an ode to win her heart. Like Nioclás Dall above, however, Craftiny's art appears to be in his playing, not in his verse-craft. That attribution could and did also occur within this seemingly humbler branch of Irish performance is a finding I explore in more detail below.

CAROLAN

Toirdhealbhach Ó Cearbhalláin (anglicized Turlough Carolan) illustrates in many ways the typical life and fortunes of an Irish itinerant musician-poet, as both a continuation of past roles for harpers and an assumption of the more prestigious role of poet vacated by the decline of the bardic tradition. Carolan was born in 1670 in County Meath, the son of a craftsman or farmer named

John Carolan. At around the age of fourteen, he moved with his family to the area of Roscommon and Leitrim, where his father seems to have received employment at one of the manor houses. The aristocratic Mrs. MacDermott Rae of the Ballyfarnon estate took an interest in the young Carolan and provided him with an education. Carolan also became acquainted with the O'Conor family of Belanagare and other local notables who became his primary patrons later in life. Sometime in his after teenage years, Carolan contracted smallpox and was left blind as a result. Mrs. MacDermott Rae arranged for him to learn the harp from a local harper and subsequently provided him with a horse, a guide, and money to begin his career as an itinerant musician.

Despite personal tragedies, Carolan was able to achieve a good degree of social and economic solidity. He married a woman named Mary Maguire and settled with her in a small home in Mohill, Country Leitrim. Together, they raised seven children. Carolan traveled broadly in his career, visiting various estates in the districts of Connacht, Leinster, Ulster, and Munster. He also visited Dublin on a number of occasions. His pattern of visiting was nearly always the same: he accepted the invitation of an aristocrat, journeyed to his home by horse, with the help of a guide, and stayed for a period of days or weeks. He entertained for the household, composed songs for family members, and occasionally taught tunes to young gentlemen or ladies. On occasion— either at a manor (a "big house") or on the road between stops—he met with other harpers, with whom he shared drinks and vied for status as the region's finest player. He was not known as a particularly good musician, having taken up the harp only as a young adult, but excelled far beyond his contemporaries in his musical and poetic compositions, many of which became common parts of other harpers' repertoires. Combining an expert command of Irish music with the influences of Italian masters (including Vivaldi, Corelli, and Geminiani, the latter of whom he met personally at the estate of one of his patrons; O'Sullivan 1958: vol. 1, 144), Carolan's music helped to reshape the tradition even while his poetry preserved the image of an ancient bardic profession.

The stories surrounding Carolan and his songs became a widespread and cohesive body of local tradition, one that Carolan himself appears to have carefully monitored and maintained. The lyric *Carolan's Receipt*, for instance (also known as *Dr. John Stafford*, or *Stafford's Receipt*; O'Sullivan 1958, vol. 2: 102–3, 249), praises drink and a Dr. Stafford who was generous in giving it. Its melody is reproduced below as transcribed by Donal O'Sullivan (1958: vol. 2, 248).

EXAMPLE 6.1

The song's first half is reproduced below as rendered and translated in James Hardiman's *Irish Minstrelsy; or, the Bardic Remains of Ireland* (1831: 22–25).

Má's tinn nó slán do thárlaidheas féin,
Ghluaiseas tráth 's dob fhearrde mé
Ar cuairt chum Seóin chum sócamhail d'fhagháil,
An Stafardach breágh sásta, nach gnáth gan chéill.
Is i dtaca an mheódhain oidhche do bhíodh sinn ag ól,
Agus ar maidin arís cordial:
'Sé mheas sé ó mhéinn mhaith gurb é súd an gléas
Le Cearbhalláin caoch do bheódhughadh!

Seal ar misge, seal ar buile,
Réabadh téad 's ag dul ar mire,
An faisiun sin do chleachtamar ní sgarfam leis go deó!
Deirim arís é
Is innsim don dtír é,
Má's maith libh do bheith saoighlach bídhidh choidhche ag ól!

When in sickness or in sorrow I have chanc'd to be,
My hopes my dear Stafford were plac'd in thee,
For thy friendly care and skill,
And thy drink more cheering still,
Left the jolly-hearted bard from each evil free:
At midnight all merrily our cups went round;
Our joys in the morning the gay cordial crown'd;
For the past had plainly shown,
That in this, and this alone,
Old Turlough unfailingly true comfort found:
Drinking, drinking,
Never thinking,
Roaring, raking,
Harpstrings breaking,—
Oh! This is my delight—'tis the life for me;
Then let glasses overflowing,
Still o'er the board keep going,
Bright gleams of bliss bestowing,
On the sons of glee.

Although the song has evident narrative contents and mentions both John Stafford and Carolan by name, the prose narrative behind it gives further details. As first recounted in print by Walker (1786: 83–84), Carolan composed the song after resuming his habit of heavy drinking following an arduous six weeks of doctor-imposed abstinence. Having lost all sense of creativity during this period of sobriety, Carolan finally chose the invigoration of drink and fancy over the sureties of health. While the song depicts Dr. Stafford as a willing accomplice in Carolan's drinking, the narrative signals the irony of the poem, as Stafford had endeavored to break the harper of his habit. By the eighteenth century, the work was often known by its tune alone, and in many versions Stafford is described as the pharmacist or shopkeeper who gave Carolan the drink that knocked him off the wagon. In any case, the narrative functions not simply to explain the song's contents but also to connect it specifically with the famed and imperfect Carolan. Once the linkage to Carolan has been made, the song can be seen within a broader array of Carolan's poems, a number of which specifically praise strong drink. Carolan's foibles became as much a source of notoriety as his virtues, helping to sketch the image of a fully fledged individual in the minds of audience members. They were foibles, however, that were more or less predictable in attributive lore about poet-singers: creative and temperamental, they are frequently given to strong appetites in the area of women and drink.

The attributive focus on the poet or musician easily led to competition between rival stars. The notoriety of being a great performer could not be shared with many before any one artist was pushed into obscurity. And so we often find performers engaging in overt contests of skill and fame with their contemporaries. Dafydd ap Gwilym measured wit with Gruffudd Gryg (see Thomas 2001: 288–306); Carolan found his challenger in Cathaoir Mac Cába (Charles MacCabe) (O'Sullivan 1958: vol. 1, 67 ff.). Narratives recount that MacCabe and Carolan engaged in a drinking bout, with the stipulation that the one inebriated first would have to pay for the night's drinks. When MacCabe at length fell into a drunken stupor, Carolan tied a bag over his head and had a derisive sign written on it. He also composed a lampoon about his friend, which was remembered thereafter. MacCabe also played his share of tricks on Carolan. Once, when meeting his friend en route from one manor to another, MacCabe (who was sighted) convinced Carolan that the nearby graveyard held the newly dug grave of Charles MacCabe. A distraught Carolan asked to be led to the grave, where he composed a moving elegy to his friend, only to be thanked in person for it by the laughing MacCabe (O'Sullivan 1958: vol. 1, 70–71). The melody of Carolan's lament survived as a popular tune in Ireland, and is reproduced below.

EXAMPLE 6.2

Its words and translation, as presented by Hardiman, are as follows:

Nach í so an chuairt easbadhach, do lagaidh mé th'réis mo shiúbhail!
Air uaigh mo charaid, 's me falcadh na n-déar go h-úr;
Ní bh-fuair mé agam mo thaithneamh, a's radhare mo shúl;
Acht cruaidh-leac dhaingean, a's leabadh de'n g-cré bhídh cúmhang.

Ní tréan me a' labhairt, 's ní mheasaim gur cuis náire,
Is caídhean bhocht seoithte me, ó chailleas mo chúl báire,
Ní'l pém ní'l reanaid, ní'l galair chomh cruadh craidhte,
Le h-eag na g-carad, nó searadh, na g-companach.

───────

Oh! What a baffled visit mine hath been,
How long my journey, and how dark my lot;
And have I toil'd thro' each fatiguing scene,
To meet my friend—and yet to find him not?

Sight of my eyes!—lost solace of my mind!
To see—to hear thee—eagerly I sped;
In vain I came—no trace of thee I find—
Save the cold flag that shades thy narrow bed.

My voice is low—my mood of mirth is o'er,
I droop in sadness like the widowed dove;
Talk, talk of tortures! Talk of pain no more,
Nought strikes us like the death of those we love.
    (Hardiman [1831] 1971: 95–96, 94–95)

A number of Carolan's surviving airs and poems are dedicated to Bridget Cruise. Expectedly, prose narratives connected with these works designate Bridget as Carolan's first love, who he was unable to win despite his poetic and musical gifts. A particular narrative recounts how an older Carolan—by now blind and married and in the midst of a pilgrimage—recognized Bridget again by the mere touch of her hand (O'Sullivan 1958: vol. 1, 64 ff.). It is noteworthy that Carolan seems to have been expert at spreading such stories himself: many of the tales, if true at all, could not have survived without Carolan's own telling. And at least one of his poems is an unabashed encomium in praise of himself (O'Sullivan 1958: vol. 1, 160). Clearly, self-representation and self-promotion were part of the harper's career apparatus, as they are for an ambitious modern singer-songwriter today.

Such attributive lore can be recognized as a continuation of earlier traditions of attribution within Irish lyric. At the same time, discourse concerning Carolan helped to establish this notion of the colorful bard among the intellectual elite of Britain and Ireland, who had been prepared for such an appraisal through the figure of the blind Ossian in James Macpherson's *Fragments of Ancient Poetry* (1760; Gaskill 1996) and its enthusiastic promotion by Hugh Blair in his "Critical Dissertation on the Poems of Ossian" (1765; Gaskill 1996). Although Charles O'Conor of Belanagare (1766)—who as a young man learned harp tunes from Carolan, and for whom Carolan composed at least one panegyric—did not regard the harper as anything like the bards of antiquity, many writers soon did. The persona of the native bard—learned in the traditions of the ancient past, humbled by the limitations of blindness, and skilled in the performance of lyric song—gained its quintessential literary expression in Scott's "Lay of the Last Minstrel" (1805) and helped to constitute what Maureen McLane (2001, 2002) has described as the "romance of orality" in eighteenth- and nineteenth-century literature. It was an image that became linked to Carolan in particular through the writings of Oliver Goldsmith (1760; Ó Máille 1916: 39–40), followed thereafter by works such as Joseph Cooper Walker's *Historical Memoirs of the Irish Bards* (1786), Edward O'Reilly's *Irish Writers* ([1820] 1970), James Hardiman's *Irish Minstrelsy* ([1831] 1971), and Edward Bunting's *Ancient Music of Ireland* ([1840] 1969).

The Carolan who emerges from the mass of tales told about his life and music is a figure of esteem as well as pity. Blind, dependent on patrons, and given to faults like heavy drinking, he can seem lowly and pathetic. At the same time, his talent, temper, and artistic success bespeak a man with ample cause for pride. It is in the juxtaposition of these opposing perspectives that the songs attributed to Carolan gain their particular interpretive interest.

CARL MICHAEL BELLMAN AND THE MINSTRELSY OF THE NORTH

Whereas Irish tradition made a distinction between the poet and the musician who performed the poems, the image of the poet-musician enjoyed preeminence in other parts of northern Europe, including Scandinavia. In Sweden during the eighteenth century, Carl Michael Bellman drew on the image of the continental minstrel, as well as the Scandinavian skald, to create a profile for himself in the court of King Gustav III. His career, like that of Dafydd ap Gwilyn, Iolo Goch, or Carolan, depended integrally on a system of attribution, maintained and manipulated by Bellman himself in the songs he wrote and performed. Bellman's songs and reputation live on in Scandinavian oral tradition as favorite items of entertainment today.

As noted in chapter 2, the Icelandic sagas preserve narratives of great skalds of the past. Court poets there developed elaborate poetic meters, complex embedded metaphors, and royal or aristocratic themes aimed at currying the praise of powerful leaders. Skalds became attached to particular courts, where they mostly composed praise poetry for their patrons or poetic records of battle victories or defeats. As the sagas make use of the praise poems or elegies of skalds of the past, they also often include the skalds as characters in their works, sometimes making them the outright heroes of their narratives.

During the centuries that followed the Viking age, however, Scandinavian court entertainment shifted markedly toward the instrumental performances of chamber ensembles and the performance of courtly lyric, artistic genres that spread north from the refined and prestigious courts of central and southern Europe. Bellman made a living for himself in this context, combining contemporary interests in continental music and burlesques with a prodigious command of his native Swedish language. While sometimes writing works of praise for his king, or creating solemn songs of religious fervor, his most famous and beloved creations depict the Bacchanalian excesses of a group of fictionalized cavorters in the taverns of the Swedish capital. These songs became identified ever after as "Bellman songs," and still rely today on association with their creator for much of their interpretation and esteem in modern Scandinavia.

Carl Michael Bellman was born in 1740, the eldest son of a court official of German-Swedish background (Huldén 1994). He received an excellent education and eventually found favor in the court of Gustav III, where his patriotic songs secured royal favor and patronage in the 1770s. His serious songs curried favor among those of great dignity and weight, but Bellman also showed a playful side in his musical retellings of biblical narratives, rendered farcical and ironic (Huldén 1994: 47–54). Many of his most playful and even bawdy ditties were composed in the 1760s, on the basis of his observations and experiences of the drinking life of Stockholm. In 1790 he published a collection of these songs, *Fredmans Epistlar* (The Epistles of Fredman), and a second collection, *Fredmans Sånger* (The Songs of Fredman), appeared in 1791.

Where earlier court poets unambiguously attributed their works to themselves, Bellman erected a two-layered attribution. On the surface, the songs contained in his books were supposed to represent the views and words of a watchmaker named Fredman, or one of his circle of similarly wastrel friends. The song texts explicitly mention characters in this fictive cadre and the lyrics' speakers are typically identified as one or another of the friends. On a deeper level, Bellman clearly intended that he would be known as his works' composer and first performer, as he made plain in the preface to his first book: "The following collection of Fredman's 82 epistles are edited, preserved, and made known by me, both in terms of poems and melodies" (Bellman 1790: n.p.). Bellman took pleasure in creating an imaginary world of drinking buddies in his songs, but he also relied on his audiences' knowing attribution of the songs to him personally.

The Fredman of Bellman's confection was based lightly on a historical personage. Jean Fredman was born around 1712 and died in 1767. His career included great successes, such as the repair of the main clock in the tower of Storkyrkan in the center of Stockholm, and he was named court watchmaker in 1745. But an unfortunate marriage and eventual alcoholism stripped him of all dignities, and he died in wretched poverty at the age of fifty-five (Hulden 1994: 120–21). In Bellman's songs, Fredman is a hopeless boozer whose daily revels in the service of the Temple of Bacchus are matched only by those of his similarly impaired companions. Typical of Bellman's wit is his Epistle 27, a portrayal of Fredman's last thoughts.

EXAMPLE 6.3

No: 27.
Fredmans Epistel,
Som är deß sista tankar.

Gubben är gammal, urverket dras,
Visaren visar, timmar ilar.
Döden sitt timglas har stält vid mit glas,
Kring buteljen strött sina pilar.
Törstig ja skådar min Stjerna och Sol.
Vandringsman hör nu min Basfiol
V:cello - - - Movitz, din tjenare hvilar.

Klaraste sköte, ljustiga barm!
Sorgligt de blommors lif föröddes,
Som gaf min far, til min sveda och harm,
Vällust i den sang där jag föddes.
Men båda sofva. Gutår i förtret!
Sjung Movitz, sjung om hur ögat gret
V:cello - - - Vid de Cypresser som ströddes.

Raglande skugga, brusiger min,
Skapad at Bacchus gå til handa;
Bläddriger tunga af bränvin och vin,
Känn der far min, känn där hans anda.
Fröja och Bacchus gaf kring den et sken,
Movitz lät bland mina faders ben
V:cello - - - Detta mit stoft få sig blanda.
   (Bellman 1790: 77)

———

Fredman's Epistle no. 27
Which are his last thoughts.

Aged am I, my watch is wound up
Hurrying hands its hours are skewing,
Death has an hourglass placed by my cup,

My bottle with his arrows bestrewing.
Thirsty I gaze on my sun and my star.
Wanderer, hear my lament from afar.
'cello - - - Movitz, to rest I am going.

Clearest of wombs, delightful embrace,
Flower whose being in sorrow was wasted,
Which in a birth-bed the cause of my days
My father voluptuous tasted.
Both are now sleeping! To bed they have crept.
Sing Movitz, sing how the eye it wept
'cello - - - Where, 'neath a cypress they rested.

Staggering shade, red-visag'd and drear,
Bacchus alone did thee inherit;
Slobbering accents of brandy and beer—
Know then of thy father, see there his spirit!
Fröja and Bacchus once lent thee a glow.
Movitz, with forefathers' bones below
'cello - - - Let now my ashes be buried.
        (Britten Austin 1990: 42–43)

The song's images play on the character and experiences of the fictionalized Fredman: he uses timekeeping metaphors to describe the approach of death, while he
holds on to his devotion to both the classical god Bacchus and the Scandinavian
goddess of love, Fröja (Freyja). In the text, space is given also to an instrumental
interlude on the violincello, and the speaker calls to his friend Movitz. Crucially,
the real interpretive foundation of the song lies in its attribution to Bellman himself, the creator-performer only slightly out of the spotlight in the text.

    Bellman became immensely popular after the publication of his songs and
has remained a favorite of Swedes ever since. In his day, he became the subject of
numerous paintings and written characterizations, even as his financial situation
deteriorated later in life (Kretz, Nilsson, and Stålmarck 1994; Nyström 1994). As
in the case of Robert Burns of Scotland, clubs developed to sing and celebrate his
persona. Bellman songs are regularly performed in Scandinavia today as humorous verses, drinking songs, and means of building comaraderie among strang-
ers and friends. They demonstrate both the importance of attribution as an

interpretive device in Scandinavian lyric and the popularity of certain varieties
of lyric across class and national lines.

RAFTERY

Antoine Ó Reachtabhraigh (1779–1835, anglicized as Anthony Raftery) lived almost exactly a century after Turlough Carolan, in an Ireland in which the harp
had virtually ceased to exist as an itinerant musician's instrument and in which
the crushing stasis of British rule faced serious and concerted challenges from
high and low alike. Blinded, like his predecessor, by childhood smallpox, Raftery,
too, became a wandering musician, playing the fiddle for a living and composing
long and celebrated poems in his native Irish. The attributive lore surrounding
Raftery—known in oral tradition as Reachtuire, Reachturigh, Reachturaigh,
Raifteri (Hyde 1903: 29–31)—offers another valuable illustration of the role of
attribution in lyric interpretation.

Like Carolan before him, Raftery was known as lacking in musical skill, a
fault offset by his masterful poetry (Hyde [1903] 1973: 13). Also like his predecessor, he used his poems to curry favor: one of his most famous lyrics, *Contae
Mhuigh Eo* (County Mayo) was said to have been composed in part to win back
the affections of his estranged former patron, Frank Taafe. The song's melody
was transcribed by Eibhlín Bean Uí Choisdealbha and is presented below as in
Máire Nic Domhnaill Gairbhí (2000: 33).

EXAMPLE 6.4

Frank Taafe is mentioned by name in the song's final stanza, which Hyde recorded as follows:

Fághann d'íleachta 's baintreabhach cabhair a's réidhteach
Slighe bró a's éadaigh, a's talamh gan cíos,
Sgoláiridhe bochta sgríobh, sgoil, agus léigheann ann,
Lucht iarrata na déirce ann, ag tarraing 's ag triall.
Sháruigh sé an domhan in a h-uile dheagh-thréithribh
Thug Raifteri an chraebh dó ar a bhfacaidh sé riamh,
Sé deireadh na cainte: saoghal fad ag Franc Taafe ann
Sliocht Loinnsigh na féile nár choigil an fiadhach.

———————

The orphan and the widow get assistance and redemption,
A way to get food and clothes, and land without rent;
Poor scholars get writing and schooling and learning there,
And the people who ask alms are drawing and journeying there.
It overcame the world for all its good qualities,
And Raftery has awarded it the branch, over all that he ever saw;
The end of the talk is this: Long life to Frank Taafe in it,
The descendent of the Lynch of hospitality, who never spared the hunt.
    (Hyde [1903] 1973: 104–5)

For the bulk of the poem, Raftery presents himself as an authority on his native county's many blessings; he notes its benevolence to the poor and the needy and compliments Taafe in particular for his generosity (Hyde [1903] 1973: 93–97; O'Flynn 1998: 76–77). The story associated with the song claims that Raftery composed it as part of a wager with a Galway singer regarding who could praise his home county best. Raftery's song so overwhelmed his competitor that the latter could think of nothing to say of Galway. The narrative also seeks to explain why the Mayo fiddler spent the bulk of his adult life performing not in his native county but in the remoter Galway: purportedly he was exiled from his home district by Taafe after he accidentally drowned one of Taafe's favorite horses. Taafe is said to have begrudged the generous gesture embodied in the song's final lines because his name came only at the end and without any honorific title.

Often attributive lore connected with Raftery, like that of his predecessors, locates the meanings of songs in the singer's web of personal relations. Where Dafydd ap Gwilym composed lyrics in honor of Morfudd and Dyddgu and

Carolan for his first love, Bridget Cruise, Raftery was said to have carried a torch for Mary Hynes, a woman who had died a century before his time (Nic Domhnaill Gairbhí 2000: 39–40). Nic Domhnaill Gairbhí's transcription of the song is presented below.

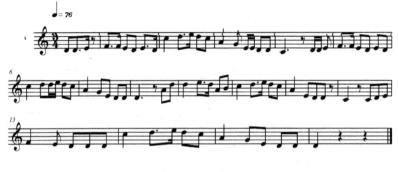

EXAMPLE 6.5

Raftery's lyric in Mary's honor became one of the best known of his repertoire. In it, he mingles narrative details with loving description of Mary's generosity and pleasant nature.

> Dul chuig an Aifrionn dam le toil na nGrásta,
> Do bhí an lá báisteach, agus d'árduigh gaoth,
> Casadh an ainnir liom le taoibh Chilltartain
> Agus thuit mé láithreach in ngrádh le mnaoi.
> Labhair mé léi, go múinte mánla
> 'S do réir a cáilleacht 's eadh d'fhreagair sí,
> 'Sé dubhairt sí, "Raifteri tá m'inntinn sásta
> agus gluais go lá liom go Bail'-ui-liagh.
>
> Nuair fuair mé an tairisgint níor leig mé ar cáirde é,
> Rinne mé gáire agus gheit mo chroidhe,
> Ní raibh le dul againn acht trasna páirce
> 'S ní thug muid an lá linn acht go tóin an tighe.
> Leagadh chugainn bord a raibh gloine a's cárta air,
> agus cúilfhionn fáinneach le m'ais 'na suidhe,
> 'Sé dubhairt sí "Raifteri, bi'g ól 's céad fáilte,
> Tá 'n soiléar láidir i mBail'-ui-laigh."

Is aoibhinn aéreach ar thaoibh an ti léibhe
Ag breathnughadh síos ar Bhail'-ui-liagh,
Ag siúbhal sna gleanntaibh 'baint cnó agus sméara,
'S geall ceileabhar éan ann le ceóltaibh sidhe.
Cia'n bhrigh san méad sin go bhfáightheá léargus,
Ar bhláth na gcraébh atá le n-a thaoibh,
Ní'l maith d'á seunadh a's ná ceil ar aenne,
'Sí spéir na gréine agus grádh mo chroidhe.

————————

Going to Mass of me, God was gracious,
The day came rainy and the wind did blow,
And near Kiltartan I met a maiden
Whose love enslaved me and left me low.
I spoke to her gently, the courteous maiden,
And gently and gaily she answered so:
"Come, Raftery, with me, and let me take you
to Ballylee, where I have to go."

When I got the offer, I did not put off,
I laughed, and my heart bounded;
We had only to go across the field,
And we only brought the day to the back of the house.
There was laid for us a table on which was a glass and quart,
And the ringletted coolun beside me sitting,
'Twas what she said, "Raftery, be drinking, and a hundred welcomes,
The cellar is strong in Ballylee."

It is lovely and airy on the side of the mountain,
Looking down upon Ballylee,
Walking in the grass, picking nuts and blackberries,
The warbling of birds there is all as one as fairy music.
What is the good of all that, till you get a sight
Of the blossom of the branches who is by its side;
There is no use in denying it, and conceal it from no one,
She is the sky of the sun and the love of my heart.

(Hyde [1903] 1973: 330–31)

Raftery also composed lyrics for women he had met and loved, including Nancy Branach (Walsh), Bríghdín Bheusaigh (Brigit Vesey), and Mary Staunton. And although Mary Hynes had died long before Raftery's time, later audiences assumed the two were personally acquainted. Under the tutelage of Lady Gregory, William Butler Yeats composed a poem that reflects this assumption (*The Tower*; quoted in Daly 1973: xi). And one of Hyde's informants attributed Mary's tragically short life to the fact that Raftery had composed a song about her:

> I often heard talk of people who would give him a lift on their car, and when he would ask what their name was they would not tell him, for fear he'd put it in a song. . . . He praised Mary Hynes and Breedyeen Vasey, and both of them had a troubled life. Mary Hynes died miserable in the middle of a bog, and a neighbor of hers said "The sorra long alive a person will be who has a song composed for them." (Hyde [1903] 1973, 17)

With the skills of praise came the power of lampoon. Raftery, like poets before him, was credited with the ability to intimidate others by the very threat of a critical verse. Hardiman collected an anecdote about Carolan in which the blind harper stopped for the night outside the house of the prosperous farmer Laughlin Monaghan. Knocking on the door of the house late at night, he was initially turned away by a disgruntled Mrs. Monaghan, until the panicked farmer, fearing a scandalous lampoon, rushed after him and convinced him to spend the night (O'Sullivan 1958: vol. 1, 42). Douglas Hyde records a similar story of Raftery, in which a local farmer passed by the fiddler without offering him a ride, pretending not to see him. The affronted Raftery retorted in verse so that the panicked farmer immediately responded, "O, Mr. Raftery, I didn't know it was you was in it. Won't you get up and sit on the car?" (17). More vindictive than his predecessor, Raftery was said to have cursed or lampooned people who angered him even after their deaths, and his friend Calaman depicts him as a sharp-tongued bully:

> Ag searsál na tíre, agus ag sgóladh na ndaoine,
> Agus ag tógbháil na cíosa in sna bailteachaibh,
> Agus mar bhfágh' raisean dídion agus a bholg do líonadh,
> Béidh a dheimheas i bhfaobhar a' brerradh aige!

———

Charging the country and scolding the people,
And raising the rent in the villages,
And unless he gets shelter and his belly to be filled,
He will have his scissors with sharp edge a-cutting.
     (Hyde [1903] 1973: 38–39)

Raftery's self-portrayal, however, seems to indulge in the plaintive as well, as he describes himself in terms far humbler than those Carolan used in his portrait of himself.

Mise Raifteiri an file,
Lán dóchais agus grádh,
Le súilibh gan solus
Le ciúnas gan crádh.

Dul siar ar m'aistear
Le solus mo chroidhe,
Fann agus tuirseach
Go deaireadh no shlighe.

Féach anois mé
Agus m'aghaidh ar bhalla
Ag seinm ceóil
Do phócaibh falamh.

———

I am Raftery the poet,
Full of hope and love,
With eyes that have no light,
With gentleness that has no misery.

Going west upon my pilgrimage,
By the light of my heart,

Feeble and tired,
To the end of my road.

Behold me now,
And my face to a wall,
a-playing music
unto empty pockets.
  (Hyde [1903] 1973: 40–41)

Despite the poignancy of this song, Raftery was able to make a living from his art; he married and raised a family. Anecdotes about him focus on his love of liquor and women (Hyde [1903] 1973: 37–39), and his oeuvre contains songs in praise of whiskey and a humorous argument between a drinker and his drink (184–91). Yet, in contrast to Carolan, he also spoke out on political matters, composing songs, for instance, to incite his fellow Irishmen to support the Catholic Association (112–23), to elect Daniel O'Connell of Clare to Parliament (258–71), and to decry the execution of captured Whiteboy Anthony O'Daly (122–33). These songs seem to have derived at least some of their power through association with the singer himself, so that at the end of one of his powerful invectives, Raftery boldly declares:

'Sé Raifteri do mhínigh 's do chuir síos a aithris seo
Adeir go mbéidh Gallaibh le fánaidh.

———————

It is Raferty who has explained and put down this recitation,
Who says the foreigners shall be scattered.
  (122–23)

His name itself bolstered the credibility of his prophecy.

Another source of similarity between the attributive anecdotes told of Carolan and of Raftery is the degree to which each is credited with supernatural abilities. Walker recounts an apparently well-known tale of Carolan's prediction of the early death of a certain girl (O'Sullivan 1958: vol. 1, 42). When asked to compose a song about her, the harper could not, attributing his lack of inspiration to melancholy about the girl's likely death. She was said to have died the next year. Raftery, too, was said to have predicted the time, place, and manner of his own death (Hyde [1903] 1973: 7, 47) after seeing a vision during his sleep. His dialogue with Death at the time was the subject of one of his lyrics (371) and became common knowledge among his contemporaries (49). It is not surprising in this connection to note that Carolan's skull was used by peasants as a cure for epilepsy. Whereas elite admirers such as Charles O'Conor came to regard Carolan's skull in the recess of the church wall at Kilronan as a melancholic memento mori, local peasants were known to boil milk in it or grind up pieces to add to water in their quest to access its supernatural powers (O'Sullivan 1958: vol. 1, 117–18).

KREETA HAAPASALO

In nineteenth-century Finland, a female performer became an iconic image of Finnish folk culture for her century and thereafter. This woman was Kreeta (Greta) Jakob's Daughter (1813–93). As Kreeta Haapasalo—named for one of the crofter farms she lived on in Kokkola parish, Ostrobothnia—she became legendary. She played the kantele and sang in the drawing rooms of Finnish gentry in Finland and abroad. She provided the intelligentsia of her day, as well as Finns in general in later generations, with a powerful symbol of Finnish folk music, the Finnish peasant, and Finnish identity. It is difficult today to study the kantele or Finnish folk song without coming upon her name.

Kreeta Haapasalo was born in 1813 in the village of Järvelä, in the vicinity of Kaustinen. At the age of six, she began to learn the kantele from a neighboring farmer who played regularly in his home. As a teenager, she entered service, cleaning and sewing from door to door, and received the advice of an itinerant tailor that she should play and sing for a living. Although she did not act on the advice immediately, she nonetheless thought about it during the following years. She worked for a time at the farm of her elder sister and brother-in-law before eventually marrying and starting a family of her own. Kreeta and her husband had eleven children, two of whom died in infancy. As an adult, her fortunes varied, apparently because of her husband's drinking, and the family was obliged to move numerous times, renting or buying land as their finances permitted. By the late 1840s, famine and desperation led her to take seriously the advice she had received earlier, and she undertook her first musical pere-grinations, singing door to door in her own locale. Soon, she was headed to local cities as well. With a couple of children in tow and her mother at home to look after the rest, Kreeta began to travel to larger cities and arrived in Hel-sinki in January 1853. Her success there, and in other cities, grew largely out of favorable publicity: she was discovered and celebrated as an embodiment of the true Finnish folk singer by the famed writer and nationalist Zachris Tope-lius. During the 1850s and 1860s, she was able to tour St. Petersburg and Stock-holm as well. Dressed always in simple peasant attire, she became a favored subject for nationalist painters and through them, was transformed into the very image of the Finnish peasant woman. In 1887 she was honored as a special guest at the Jyväskylä Song Festival, an event that capped her career. She died in 1893.

In her career as a performer, Haapasalo was not able to follow well-estab-lished models, as were Carolan and Raftery. Irish society regarded itinerant musicians with tolerance and even favor, especially if they were blind and pre-sumably unable to support themselves otherwise. Women also participated in such itineracy; the diaries of Charles O'Conor indicate that he learned harp tunes from the blind harper Mary Connellan as well as from Carolan (O'Sullivan 1958: 63). In some respects, he seems to have appreciated Connellan's playing more than Carolan's. In Finland, the situation was different. Itinerant trades-people abounded, and women and men regularly traveled from estate to estate or farm to farm offering skills in washing, mending, sewing, tool repair, and the like. In general, however, itinerants walked an uneasy line between being recog-nized as valuable contributors to society and being castigated as mere beggars or vagrants (Laitinen 1990: 9–10). Music-making was not one of the standard offer-ings of such craftsmen, and Haapasalo opened herself to charges of laziness and vice in offering it door to door.

Part of the persona that Topelius helped to convey of Haapasalo in his cru-cial newspaper report of 1853 was her dual readiness to perform and her protests that she was compelled to do so by financial hardship. In her autobiography of 1887, she mentions telling a local woman who questioned her about her playing that she was happy that she did more than just live at a farm thinking of noth-ing all day (Kolehmainen and Valo 1990: 78). On the other hand, when a local minister suggested that she might be displaying pride about her career, she pro-tested that a person obliged to travel about in search of a living could scarcely

feel proud (79). In Helsinki and elsewhere after 1853, she began her performances
with a song that declares forcefully (but somewhat cryptically) her own views
of her itineracy. The song is presented as transcribed by Ilmari Krohn and colleagues (1933: no. 1703).

EXAMPLE 6.6

Lapseni minun kotia huonolle hoidolle jäi.
Minun täytyy kulkia ympäri maata näin.

Elatusta hakien, kuin lintu pojilleen
Siksi että he joutuvat siivilleen.

Eipä tämä raskahaksi käsilleni käy,
Mutta sydämelleni, joka ei ulos näy.

Minä mielelläni ne päivät kulkisin vaikka vuorten rotkoissa,
Ennenkun minä näin kävisin näissä herrain hoveissa.

Mutta minun puutokseni ei siitä vähenisi, eikä leipäni enänis.
Sentähden tyytyväisyydellä käyn ovista oville.

Minä luulen, että olis paljon keviämpi vetää kiviä kelkassa,
Kun se että käydä katuja kantele käsissä.

Itku se oli minulla aina vuorovärssynä
Kun minä tämän ylösajattelin tiellä käydessäin.

Kun minun leipäni on pantu niin pieneks ja hajotettu niin leviälle,
Jota minun pitää koota murheella ja pelvolla.

Mutta minä luotan Luojani päälle, joka voi minua lohduttaa
Ja ilman mitään vaarata minua kotia johdattaa.
   (Kolehmainen and Valo 1990: 73–74)

———————

My children I left behind me to uncertain care.
It is my lot to walk this way, about this land to fare.

Searching for some sustenance, as a bird for its young ones might,
This is the reason why they take to their flight.

This labor is not difficult, callousing my hands,
But upon my heart it weighs, so that no one understands.

Rather would I spend my days trudging a craggy mountainside
Than that I should visit thus, in a lofty manor bide.

But my lack would not thus lessen, nor my bread extend.
Thus with resignation, I go door to door this way.

I think it would be lighter far, to pull rocks in a sleigh,
Than to frequent the streets, with kantele in hand.

A cry was ever in my heart, I trod on weary feet,
When I composed this song you hear, walking on the street.

My scraps of bread are slivered so and strewn both far and near,
So I must go and gather them, in sorrow and in fear.

But I trust ever in my Lord, who gives me comfort so
And leads me in the safest way back to the home I know.

The song became a kind of trademark for Haapasalo, one that emphasized her
motherly emotions while also demonstrating her artistry. As Heikki Laitinen
(1990) notes in his perceptive overview of Haapasalo's career, it was important
for her to establish herself not as a beggar but as someone who offered a valuable

skill. While beggars had grown in such numbers as to be perceived as a major problem in the famine-prone Grand Duchy of the mid-nineteenth century, the latter could offer the gentry something they craved: a taste of the authentic folk music of the Finnish nation, so powerfully symbolized already by Lönnrot's *Kalevala* (1835) and *Kanteletar* (1840) and by two collections of folk songs arranged for piano: H. A. Reinholm's *Suomen Kansan Laulantoja* (1834–76) and Karl Collan and colleagues' *Valituita Suomalaisia Kansan-Lauluja Pianon mukasoinnolle sovitettuja* ([1857–71] 1988). By interpreting Haapasalo's song as a personal explanation of her plight and need to provide for her starving family, her audiences were able not only to appreciate the poignancy of her lyric but also to justify their support of her unconventional career.

Although the notion of Haapasalo composing her own songs appealed to her elite audiences—who interpreted them unquestioningly as expressions of personal experience—they also wanted to hear from her what they had come to regard as the gems of Finnish folk music. As few collections of folk songs existed at this time, these gems were drawn from a very small pool of published sources. These comprised most notably the introduction to Lönnrot's *Kanteletar,* which includes some musical notations as well as a selection of "newer" (i.e., rhymed) folk songs of the type common in western and southern Finland, Reinholm's songbook and Collan's collection. Both the *Kanteletar* and Reinholm's work contained the lyric *Minun kultani kaukana kukkuu,* which soon emerged as one of the most requested songs in Haapasalo's repertoire (Laitinen 1990: 18). It is presented below, as transcribed by Krohn and colleagues (1933: no. 1560).

EXAMPLE 6.7

Kultani kukkuu, kaukana kukkuu,
Saimaan rannalla ruikuttaa;

Ei ole ruuhta rannalla,
Joka minun kultani kannattaa.

Ikävä on aikani, päivät on pitkät,
Surutont' en hetkeä muistakaan;
Voi, mikä lienee tullutkaan,
Kun jo ei kultani kuulukan!

Toivon riemu ja autuuen aika
Suruani harvoin lievittää;
Rintani on kuin järven jää—
Kukapa sen viimeinki lämmittää?

Kotka se lenteli taivahan alla,
Sorsa se souteli aalloilla;
Kulta on Saimaan rannalla,
Lähteä ei tohi tuulelta.

Tuuli on tuima ja ankarat aallot,
Ruuhet on rannalla pienoiset;
Ruuhet on rannalla pienoiset,
Kultani sormet on hienoiset.

Elä lähe, kultani, aaltojen valtaan!—
Aallot ne pian sinun pettäisi.
Sitte ei suru mua heittäisi,
Ennen kuin multaki peittäisi.
    (Lönnrot [1840–41] 1982: xiii–xiv)

———————

My love calls, from afar calls,
Splashes from Saima's shores;
No boat sits upon the shore,
To carry my love to me.

Tedious my hours, long are my days,
Not a moment I spend without sorrow;

Oh, what could have happened thus
That of my love I nothing hear.

I hope for joy and a time of blessing
My sorrow seldom lightens;
My breast is like ice on a lake—
Who at last can warm it?

The eagle it flies beneath the heavens,
The duck it paddles upon the waves,
My love is on the shore of the Saima,
But no wind to blow toward home.

The wind is hard and heavy the waves,
The boats on the shore are but small;
The boats on the shore are but small,
My love's fingers are fine.

Go not, beloved, into the waves' grip—
The waves will soon engulf you.
Then would sorrow never leave my side,
Until the ground engulfs me.

Performing a published song did not mark Haapasalo as inauthentic: on the contrary, as Laitinen (1990) shows. By doing so, she demonstrated her unity with the canon of Finnish folk songs as then known and also met the aesthetic tastes and expectations of her paying audience. Quintessentially, this taste tended toward the melancholic: as Haapasalo herself noted in appraising her success, it was the sorrow of her voice they enjoyed (Laitinen 1990: 20). In folk dress, with small children by her side, Haapasalo easily personified the mournful speakers of such lyrics, especially in the eyes of the urban bourgeoisie and gentry.

Haapasalo developed her repertoire to meet her audience's tastes, sometimes combining songs and melodies in new ways or altering the lines of songs to better fit her audience's expectations. Sometimes, however, she seems to have resisted a complete equation with her songs' contents. Early on in her career, she performed the lyric *Turvaton* (Without Shelter) from the *Kanteletar* in a manner that would present her, predictably, as the powerless speaker her audiences had come to expect. The song's opening lines typify its tone.

Onneton olin minä olessani,
Onneton tähän kylään tullessani;

Onnettomaksi olen minä luotu,
Ei ole minulle ilopäivää suotu.

————————

Hapless was I living,
Hapless when I came to this village.

Hapless have I been created,
No day of joy granted me.
   (Lönnrot [1840–41] 1982: xvi)

In a version of the song collected later in her career, Haapasalo altered, perhaps even parodied, the song's lines, representing herself not as a powerless victim but as the fortunate recipient of many good turns of events:

Onni on ollut mulla ollessani,
Onni on ollut joka kylään tullessani.

Onnettomaks ei ole minuakaan luotu
Oli tämä kantele toki mulle suotu.
   (Laitinen 1990: 19)

————————

Lucky have I been,
Lucky when I came to this village.

Hapless have I not been created,
This kantele was granted to me.

In this way, Haapasalo's repertoire did indeed come to reflect directly her life experiences and perceptions. But it also remained, as Frith puts it, a stylized self-representation, one consciously deployed to meet audience interests and secure the success and income of the performer: "No pains sir; I take pleasure in singing, sir" (*Twelfth Night* II: 4, 70).

While certain aspects of Haapasalo's career distinguish her from her male counterparts, most of her experiences mirror those of the other itinerant performers. In every case, we see artists who made careful and conscious choices to present themselves in a favorable light, crafting personae for themselves in their works they chose to perform, the topics they broached, or the lines they chose to include. Often, the performers sought a mixed response: a combination of pity and awe that would touch different audience members in different ways. And by and large, audiences responded; they viewed the poems or songs as reflections of the performers' lives and found meaning in their details through reference to a stylized, often thoroughly predictable biography. In so doing, I argue, audiences carried on a tried-and-true option of lyric interpretation, one that proved profitable to audience and performer alike in the centuries from the mournful mad Suibhne to the melancholic Kreeta Haapasalo. Attribution represented a valuable and distinctive way to find meaning in lyric songs.

CHAPTER 7

Personal Meanings in the Performance
of One Man's Repertoire

When there're brighter days in Ireland,
I'll come back and marry thee
> Michael Lyne, *Three-Leafed Shamrock I Adore Thee* (1998)

Of all the interpretive options explored in these pages, personalization is perhaps the most secondary and yet the most inevitable. "Secondary" in the sense that—unless one has composed the song oneself in response to events or experiences in one's own life—the song arrives with a form and content already intact: a set of nascent meanings that, as this study has outlined, a competent audience is challenged to decode and only then, if warranted, relate to personal experiences.

Personalization is inevitable, of course, because the experience of art is always personal, subjective. And this tendency is even more pronounced when the work of art—as in the case of the lyric—foregrounds subjectivity itself, compelling the audience to contemplate the feelings and perceptions of an absent, inscribed speaker. Because of this basic subjectivity of the aesthetic experience, a lyric song that passes into one's passive or active repertoire acquires in the process a set of meanings that are specific to the persona, time, and circumstances of the listener, meanings that may become evident when the listener in turn chooses to reperform the song for another audience. In this act, the personal becomes potentially public, and we have moved toward that end of the interpretive axis discussed in the previous chapter: attribution. Performing a song invites an audience to consider the possibilities of personal meanings, to intertwine the supposed emotions of the performer, composer, and lyric speaker into some organic whole. Certainly, learning and maintaining a song in one's active repertoire takes a strong commitment, and thus, it should come as no

212

FIGURE 7.1

Michael and Lizzy Lyne
outside their home,
Longwood, County
Meath, Ireland, 1998.

surprise that singers may identify with their songs in strong and shaping ways
and that audiences in turn may expect them to do so.

In this chapter I highlight some of the personalizing tendencies that can
come into play in lyric songs through an analysis of the repertoire and discourse
of one traditional singer, Michael Lyne of Longwood, County Meath, Ireland.
Michael ("Mick"), my granduncle, performed his songs for me in 1998, when
I visited him and his wife, Lizzy, on their farm. The viewpoints that emerged
in our discussions, and which I report here, were certainly shaped in some ways
by my relationship with Mick and Lizzy. At the same time, however, Mick's
repertoire—and the personal meanings he attached to his various songs—did
not vary a great deal from performance to performance: they were part of a
stable relation that Mick had formed with songs that he felt summed up his
own life and the historical and political events that shaped it. The "personal"

that I detail below in the discussion of Mick's repertoire is actually quite public, a set of meanings negotiated between Mick and his audiences over the course of many years. Yet at the same time, this public personal held deep meaning for Mick, and he assented to it readily through his singing and words. As I want to demonstrate, traditional lyric hermeneutics includes normative means by which audience members (and performers) are expected or are able to personalize their experiences of lyric songs.

MICK AND LIZZY LYNE

Mick Lyne's voice rises in a thin quaver, embellished by the nearly endless grace notes typical of Kerry Gaeltacht *sean-nós* singing. At high points in his rendition, his voice mingles with the earthier, robust tones of Lizzy, Mick's West Meath bride of twenty-seven years. It is the second marriage for both: their courtship began in pubs after the deaths of their first spouses and when Mick's six children and Lizzy's two sons were raised and moved away. I sit by, tape recorder in hand, the grandson of Mick's eldest sister, Nora ("Noney"), who emigrated to America when Mick was only a child. Mick, Noney's youngest brother, is singing me his repertoire. The date is July 17, 1998.

Few performative genres delineate the passage from normal discourse into performance as clearly and cogently as Irish lyric singing. The performer closes his eyes or stares off toward some otherworldly spot, his voice, mannerisms, and tone transformed. He maintains this performative frame until the final syllables of his song, when he slips, tired but seemingly fulfilled, back into the conversational tone of his world. Yet elements trail Mick from this world to the next, and he would be a poor performer in Irish eyes if they did not. Mick takes stock of his audience, of the issues of the day, and, most crucially, of himself, creating a performance that uses a stable repertoire to situate and present a personal identity. This moment involved me as Mick and Lizzy's guest in the political events then occurring in Northern Ireland and in the wider context of a changing Ireland. Mick's performance finds some of its meaning in each of these contexts but only with the cooperation and collaboration of audience members. To a greater extent, Mick's songs find their meaning in a set of attitudes that Mick and his audience share regarding lyric songs, their purpose, and their relation to their singers. This shared understanding informs and shapes what can be called the "personal" meanings of Mick's repertoire.

In chapters 1 and 2, we saw that a narrativized hermeneutics—the inter-pretation of a lyric through reference to an evident or submerged narrative—is normative in Ireland. Evidence of this norm can be found in medieval texts as well as in nineteenth-century folk song collections and remains strongly opera-tive in the Irish lyric tradition of today. In chapters 3 and 4, on the other hand, we saw that lyrics also invite a personal interpretation, one that proves especially functional in invocational and religious lyrics, in which the singer or listener is expected to identify with the song's inscribed speaker and situation. This strategy became particularly important to the lyric during the High Middle Ages, when religious lyrics led the faithful to explore and identify with the feelings of Christ and his mother. In chapter 5, we saw that such personalizing could become a normative expectation in the secular tradition as well, so that a person who re-fused to take a song to heart—to empathize, identify with its emotions, how-ever stereotyped in expression or nature—could be said to "fail" as an audience member. And in the previous chapter, we saw that attributive traditions, in which a song takes on meaning through association with its creator or performer, also can occur, especially in areas where lyric singing has become professionalized to some degree. By identifying a song with its performer, an audience makes sense of it as a product of that individual's life experiences, while the canny per-former, aware of this interpretive potential, may shape his repertoire and self-presentation so as to accentuate and facilitate the attribution.

Here I integrate these findings through a focus on the repertoire and un-derstandings of one singer. By examining the songs Mick sings, along with the understandings he and his audience explicitly mention when discussing them, we can sense the shaping and pervasive significance of personalization in lyric hermeneutics, even in a highly narrativized tradition. We can also observe the shaping role of the audience in negotiating the meaning—even the personal meaning—of a given lyric at a given time.

MICK LYNE, A HISTORICAL SKETCH

A man's life is difficult to summarize in any truly accurate or satisfactory man-ner. Yet Mick finds that his repertoire reflects his life, and his audience in Meath accepts this premise as part of their experience of his songs. Thus, it helps to pro-vide a few details about Mick's life, especially those he highlights in his songs. Certainly other joys, sorrows, and concerns exist in Mick's life besides those

mentioned below, but I focus here on the ones that emerge in the interpretation of his lyrics. These are the topics that Mick associates with his repertoire
and that, he believes, his repertoire illuminates.

Mick Lyne was born in 1912 in the tiny village of Baile an Sceilg (Ballinskelligs), a small cluster of farmsteads and fishing cottages on the shores of the Atlantic Ocean in the far west of mountainous County Kerry. The village is noted
for its rugged scenery and maintenance of tradition, and folklorists (e.g., Delargy
1945) have documented its performers and repertoires in detail. Mick grew up
in an Irish-speaking household of seven children, five girls and two boys. His
father provided for the family through a combination of farming and fishing,
and Mick grew up to be both a champion rower and a hardworking farmer.
Mick's brother died in young adulthood during late fighting in the War of Independence (1919–21) prior to the establishment of the Irish Republic.

Migration plays an important role in the social history of Ireland as a whole,
and Mick and his family are no exception in this regard. Especially in the once-
impoverished coastal villages of County Kerry, emigration was constant, and
it has been said that, at least for much of the nineteenth and twentieth centuries, Irishmen themselves constituted the nation's greatest export item. Few
Kerry families, it seems, have no relatives outside the country, be it in the United
States, Canada, England, South Africa, or Australia, and during the second half of
the twentieth century, back-and-forth visiting between migrants (or their descendants) and their relatives in Ireland became more frequent and affordable.
Today, the act of emigration—once marked by tearful partings and a mock wake
and funeral—often has been replaced with temporary foreign sojourns, aimed
at earning cash outside the country and acquiring experience in the outside
world. Mick's repertoire, however, is shaped by the earlier, more poignant understanding of emigration and is powerfully melancholic and cathartic. Without
that understanding of emigration—symbolized in the lyrics by the image of
"Amerikay"—many of Mick's songs would make little sense, to him or to his
audience.

Three of Mick's oldest sisters, including my grandmother, emigrated to
America as teenagers and worked as domestic servants in wealthy households
in the East. One sister soon tired of the adventure and returned to Ireland; the
other two remained in the United States, eventually married, and raised families of their own. My mother, Mary O'Conor, the daughter of Noney and Denis
O'Conor, was born into one of those families. Denis was an emigrant from the

town of Caherciveen, not far from Ballinskelligs. Mick knew Denis somewhat before his emigration, but he and Noney met in the United States.

In 1960 Mick and his five daughters and son were resettled in County Meath under an Irish government program intended to lessen the overcrowding of the western districts. Large Midlands estates, blessed with fertile soil and gentle terrain, were parceled out to western farmers, an arrangement that provoked no small degree of resentment among longtime residents of the county. Mick and his daughters recall clearly the ridicule and distrust that they sometimes experienced as newcomers to the region, and nearly forty years after his resettlement, Mick still considers himself a Kerryman. His songs are a reflection and a device of that identity.

Of Mick's daughters, one, Kathleen, emigrated to the United States, where she stayed in close contact with the families of her immigrant aunts and with her family in Ireland as well. Another daughter, Noreen, emigrated to England for a time and eventually returned to Meath with her husband, Peter, an Irishman born in Liverpool. Of Mick's grandchildren, several were presently living abroad, in England and in Japan. In Ireland's now-thriving economy, however, several other grandchildren remained in close proximity, holding non-agricultural jobs. Mick had just retired from farming himself, leasing his lands to a neighboring farmer, since none of his daughters or their husbands wished to carry on the livelihood. Mick had made a good living as a beef farmer, as hoof and mouth and mad cow disease had not yet devastated the farming economy.

Mick visited America twice during my childhood and always made a point of singing his songs for the assembled families of his sister's children. I recall that he wanted to be tape-recorded when he sang and that he viewed his songs as holding great historical and familial significance. When as a college student I visited Mick in the early 1980s, I was able to see him perform his songs in their prime context, the various pubs and homes of the area surrounding the village of Tandragee, not far from Longwood. I remember during those visits that Mick's repertoire was well known to his friends and that they called for certain songs of his by name, rewarding performances (as was customary) with pints of porter. A few years later, as a graduate student, I visited Mick again and witnessed the same evening entertainment and enjoyed anew Mick's singing, humor, and generous nature. In 1998 I visited with the intent of recording Mick's repertoire; those recordings form the basis of this chapter.[1]

LYRICS AS EMBLEMS OF BELONGING

The focus of personal meaning in Mick's repertoire lies in its connection with County Kerry. As Mick remarked of his songs during our evening of recording, "I picked them all up in Kerry. There's great singers down there." Mick's style of singing and language announce this origin emphatically: Mick sings with a pronounced Kerry accent, more noticeable than that which he shows in ordinary speech. In singing, Mick's [w] sound often becomes an [f] (a feature typical of speakers of Irish Gaelic) and the back vowel [a] often fronts to an [ei]. These features occasionally occur in Mick's prose English as well, but they are especially prominent when he sings. So, too, Mick's renditions evince the grace note ornamentation characteristic of *sean-nós* singing: single grace notes, inserted "cuts" (Irish *casadh),* series of multiple sixteenth notes ("rolls") and a sliding into key (usually mournful) notes from above or below. All embellish his performances, both in Irish and in English. Neither this dialect shift nor the grace note embellishment that Mick employs is typical of other singers I heard in Mick's Meath locale, making them an emphatic reminder that the singer is a westerner. In the transcriptions provided here, I have marked Mick's grace notes so as to emphasize their importance in his performances. I have, however, used regularized spelling of his texts throughout.

Of the twelve songs that Mick performed, two were in Munster Irish, a language outside the expertise of nearly all Mick's Meath friends and acquaintances. Despite their incomprehensibility, however, I remember these songs as being among the audience's favorites during evening pub singing. Friends would ask Mick to sing "something in Irish" and sit back to enjoy, rather reverently, even when the song's content remained a mystery to them. One of these, *Bean Dubh an Ghleanna,* is reproduced below as Mick sang it.

Tá bó 'gam ar a' sliabh, agus tá mé seal 'na diaidh,
Ó chailleas-sa mo chiall le nuachar,
A's á seóladh soir a's siar ins áit a ngabhann an ghrian,
Ó mhaidin's go dtí sí féin tráthnóna.
Nuair a fhéachaim féin anonn ins an áit go mbíonn mo rún
Ritheann óm' shúil sruth deora,
'S a Rí ghil na gcumhacht go bhfóirir ar mo chúis
Gurb í Bean dubh ón nGleann do bhreoigh mé.

EXAMPLE 7.1

Bean dubh a' Ghleanna, bean dubh a b'fhearr liom
Bean dubh ba dheise gáire.

A grua mar an eala, 's a píob mar a' sneachta,
'S a com seang singil álainn.
Níl ógánach cailce ó Bh'le Áth Cliath go Gaillimh,
Ná as siúd go Tuaim Uí Mheára,
Ná go bhfuil ag triall 's ag tarraingt ar eachaibh donna deasa
Ag tnúth leis an bhean dubh álainn.

Do gheobhainnse bean sa Mhumhain, triúr ban i Lúighean,
Bean ó rí geal Seoirse,
Bean na lúba buí, do ghráfadh mé ó chrói,
Bean 'gus dhá mhíle bó léi;

Iníon óg an Iarla, atá go tinn dubhach diacrach
A d'iarraidh mé fháil le pósadh,
'S dá bhfaighinnse féin mo rogha de mhnáibh deasa n' domhain,
'Sí bean dubh ón Ghleann b'fhearr liom.

An té chifeadh mo theacht, 's gan de dhíon air ach seasc
'Na shuí 'muigh ó thaobh an bhóthair,
Nuair aosaíonn suas an tslat ní fhanann uirthi aon mheas,
Ach ag tnúth leis an bhrainse is óige,
'S mo chailín plúrach deas, d'éalaigh uaim le spreas,
Sé mo chúig céad slán go deo léi!

———————

I have a cow on the mountain, and I spend time looking after it,
Since my sense was lost to a spouse.
Moving from East to West in the place where the sun goes
From morning until evening itself.
When I look in the place where my love used to be,
I cry a stream of tears.
And may God almighty help me.
'Twas the dark woman of the glen I pine for.
Dark woman of the glen,
I pine for the dark woman,
Dark woman of the lovely smile.

Her skin is like a swan and her neck is white as snow,
And she is so slender and fair.
There's no youth from Dublin to Galway
Or from Toomevara
Driving fine brown horses
Who yearns not for the beautiful dark woman.

I could get a wife from Munster, or three from Laighean,
A woman from King George
A woman of golden curls, to whom I'd give my heart
Or a woman with two thousand cows,

Or an earl's melancholy young daughter,
Endeavoring to make me marry her.
But if I had my choice of all the fine women of the world
It's the dark woman of the glen I would take.

If you were to see my house with no roof or other fixings
Sitting beside the road
When the rod ages it has no respect;
One longs for the youngest branch,
And so my pretty young girl has eluded me.
My five hundred farewells to her forever.

In his extensive *Irish Traditional Music Tune Index* (2005), Alan Ng identifies two melodies by the title *Bean Dubh an Ghleanna*.[2] The first of these (no. 469) first appears by that name in Francis O. O'Neill's *Music of Ireland* (1903; no. 6). Andrew Kuntz (1996–2005), in his index *The Fiddler's Companion*, regards O'Neill's *The Maiden* (1903: 31, no. 174) as a variation of this same tune. Kuntz sees both melodies as Connemara adaptations of Carolan's *James Plunkett* (O'Sullivan 1958: no. 151), first collected from the harper Charles Byrne and published by Bunting (1840: 26), then reprinted in O'Neill (1903: no. 650). Ng's second melody (Ng 2005: no. 4079) for the song is illustrated by the Cork ensemble Nomos on their album *Set You Free* (1996, track 9). The album notes by Niall Vallely identify the song as common throughout Ireland but state that the present tune is typical of Munster, the district from which Mick comes. Indeed, Mick's version above seems to be a variation of this latter melody.

Chris Cranford (2003), on a website devoted to slow air texts, describes *Bean Dubh an Ghleanna* as "a classic love song in the Irish tradition." And, indeed, its protests of love for the dark woman and the intimation in the final stanza that the speaker's hopes have been dashed are reminiscent of the narrative *míniú* associated with *Casadh an tSúgáin,* discussed in chapter 1. Mick takes the ailment described in the first stanza ("Since my sense was lost to a spouse") as something other than love sickness, however, as I discuss below. In any case, Mick's audience does not seem to have taken much interest in the content or meaning of the song itself, other than the fact that it is in Irish. When I asked about its details, Lizzy, who is always at Mick's side during singing sessions, seemed unfamiliar with its story. Our conversation proceeded as follows:

L: Michael. Explain what the song's about. This fella—
M: He was herding; and he was herding cows and,
      The black woman flew at him.
           And she was going to take his life.
    And he composed that song for her—
        Amid the cows and the stones.
    And he was herding the cows,
          And he said that he was a poor man and all that kind of thing,
             And it all came into the song.
    And he escaped from her and they didn't kiss.
    She was a *witch*—
        There were witches at that time.
          Down in Kerry.
      They'd take you at night and they'd—
T: Oh, I see, and what period would that be?
M: Pardon?
T: When would that be?
L: When would that be?
T: Yeah, what year or what century?
M: Oh, that was—
L: 18—
M: That was 1902.
T: Ah-ha!
M: Yeah, going back to that year. Yes.

In Mick's telling, the dark woman forces the poet to compose the present song in her praise. She nearly succeeds in getting him to kiss her, an act that would presumably bring him under her spell forever, but in the end, the man escapes, giving the world this lyric as testimony of the event. Mick's mention of 1902 may stem from his familiarity with O'Neill's (1903) anthology and the song's first published version, though that text contains neither the words to the song nor the melody that Mick employs. What is more important to Mick is the fact that the event took place in Kerry, at least as far as his narrative explanation is concerned. It reflects, he suggests, the Kerry of the somewhat recent past (i.e., his own childhood), when witches were a hazard and poverty prevailed. It is a Kerry that Mick feels linked to, retrievable to him now only through song. For the bulk of Mick's listeners, however, this explanation is wholly unnecessary: the Irish songs of Mick's repertoire seem to have held a kind of iconic significance in themselves as unmistakable reminders of Mick's Gaeltacht past and the Irish tradition that such areas maintain for the benefit of the entire nation.

Like *Bean Dubh an Ghleanna,* many of Mick's songs are set in Kerry, or understood to have occurred in that county, even if the song's text does not say so. *The Valley of Knockanure* (see below) mentions the place-names Gortnagleanna, Tralee, Feale, and Lea and commemorates historical events that took place in the region. *Eileen McMahon, The Days of My Youth, Oh Why Did I Leave My Home and Why Did I Cross the Sea?* and *The Rose of Tralee* (see below) all, similarly, contain Kerry references. Other songs are understood by Mick to refer to Kerry, particularly in its historical significance as a remote refuge from foreign invasion and as a perennial source of emigrants. Our conversation that evening made these associations clear, as Mick remarked:

> M: They were giving land to anyone:
> > That's why they were very populated back then.
> > But they had to leave it all,
> > > and go *straight* back to America,
> > > because they had no living at all there,
> > > no, no, no living.

Thus, it is not surprising that audiences tended to interpret Mick's rendering of *Little Thatched Cabin* as the story of a Kerryman and, further, to elide that Kerryman with their own resettled friend and neighbor Mick Lyne.

EXAMPLE 7.2

Far beneath a hill's shadow stands a little thatched cabin,
Where first shone the light of my life's early morn.
It stands a little by the side of a river,
And there 'neath the same roof my father was born.

It was there at her knee that my mother first taught me
The duties of right and the errors of wrong,
And it was there that I first drove the cows to the meadow,
A barefooted boy I ever lived on.

Oh I care not for ever, a whole lifetime I've wandered.
I've seen the evil and panics of all.
But one thing I've learned and I'll never forget it:
The little thatched cabin, the best home of them all.

As I grew to manhood I started life's journey
I prayed that my fortune would lie in that world.
Oh what a day, and my heart is an old one,
The little thatched cabin, the best home of them all.

But now I'm growing old, and the fortune's smiling on me.
When I think on my boyhood, it grieves me to shame.
I'd give all the gold that's in this wide world,
To be back in that little thatched cabin again.

Although this song makes no explicit mention of Kerry, it is clear that both Mick and his audience viewed it as a Kerryman's testimony. I remember that once, after Mick had sung this song at a pub, a man asked him if his boyhood home had a thatched roof. It did indeed, and Mick's father had also been born "'neath the same roof." One of the conditions of resettlement, however, was that the family's original house was sold by the government (to a wealthy doctor from Dublin, who used it as a summer residence). Resettlement had its price, and perhaps Mick's audiences were aware of the sacrifices Mick had made for a better situation in Meath. Yet it is also a fact that many houses in the vicinity of Tandragee also had thatched roofs and that this song could well have been about a person from a little thatched cabin nearby. Still, Kerry and thatch both connote for many Irish of Mick's generation the epitome of picturesque traditional life, lived amid the lilting syllables of Gaeltacht speech and the unhurried pace of western life. Mick's son-in-law from Liverpool once remarked to me, "Your arms get tired in Kerry, having to tip your hat or wave at every person who passes by in a car." And for many who listened to Mick's song, part of the enjoyment of the event lay in seeing in Mick and in his repertoire an embodiment of Kerry, a piece of the fading Ireland of old. For Mick himself, and for his audiences, his songs are an emblem of a life of the past, a way of revisiting in memories a world otherwise lost to him.

The Kerry significance of Mick's repertoire was evident in his and Lizzy's comments about *The Rose of Tralee.*

L: Would you like him singing *The Rose of Tralee*?
T: Sure, Yeah.
L: Well, seeing's he had a daughter in it.

The song as performed that night is presented below.

EXAMPLE 7.3

The pale moon was rising upon the green mountains,
The sun was declining beneath the blue sea
When I strayed with my love to the pure crystal fountain,
That stands in the beautiful Vale of Tralee.

She was lovely and fair like the roses and the summer,
It was not her beauty alone that won me;
Oh no, it was the truth in her eyes, they were darling,
That made me love Mary, the Rose of Tralee.

The cold shades of evening her mantle were spreading,
And Mary all smiling sat listening to me;
The moon through the valley her pale ray was shedding,
When I won the heart of the Rose of Tralee.

[Mick and Lizzy together:] She was lovely and fair like the roses
    and the summer,
It was not her beauty alone that won me;
Oh no, it was the truth in her eyes, they were darling,
That made me love Mary, the Rose of Tralee.

At first, I was not sure what Lizzy meant by saying that Mick "had a daughter in it" when she referred to this song. *The Rose of Tralee* is a well-known literary ballad, composed by William Pembroke Mulchinock (1820–64) about his love, Mary O'Connor (Healy 1977: 60). As the conversation following the song made clear, Lizzy was referring to the annual Rose of Tralee beauty pageant and festival, by that time in its fortieth year. Pageant contestants come from across the world but must demonstrate a Kerry connection. Mick's daughter Noreen once won the contest during the 1970s as the contestant from Liverpool, and this fact seems to increase Mick's title to the song in Lizzy's eyes. The story that they told regarding the song itself is set in Kerry but in an unspecified final location. Immediately after the song, Lizzy supplied me with her version of the narrative behind the song.

L: This was, you're asking about a folk song.
T: Yes.

L: This was a very high society sort of fellow.
   He was his uncle's son of the house,
   and she was a maid in the house.
T: Aha.
L: Right. And he was courting her.
M: Ah my.
L: She started, I think she had a child from him.
   And I'm not terrible sure what they,
      his family was very much against it.
   But, eh, when she died,
      she died in Kerry.
   When she died,
      he was poor.
   He was the only son of this fairly wealthy house.
   And he wrote that song about her.
   But she has, eh,
      Nobody knows where the Rose of Tralee is buried.
M: No, somewhere in Kerry.
   She's buried in an unmarked grave and there's—
L: Even though *every* year there's the Rose of Tralee [beauty pageant]
   there's nobody knows where Mary the Rose of Tralee is buried.
   The song was composed by the boyfriend
M: That's right:
L: "The truth in her eyes" that were—
M: That's right, *[sings]* "That made me love Mary."
   He gave her—she died of *grief.*
L: Yeah.
M: Poor Mary.
L: I don't know what she died of, but nobody knows where she's buried.
M: And every year there's a big celebration down in Kerry—
L: And nobody knows.
M: They can't find out where she is buried—a mystery.

Mick and Lizzy's explication gives an entirely different tone to the song as performed. Rather than portray a lover's fond memory, as one might at first assume from the words alone, the song becomes an ironic contrast to the tragedy

that will eventually befall Mary and her beau. Although the tale of class difference, familial pressures, out-of-wedlock birth, and death lies outside the lyric's
words, Mick and Lizzy found it evidenced in the lines they quoted from the
text: "the truth in her eyes" and "that made me love Mary." Just how these lines
are tied to the narrative events is left unclear in their rendering for me, but it is
clear that for Mick and Lizzy, lyric and narrative are inextricably linked.

As "The Rose of Tralee" is a well-known Irish song, the prose narrative that
accompanies it is also familiar to many. On the Rose of Tralee festival website,[2] the event organizers present both the song and its narrative explanation
for interested readers to peruse. Their account differs somewhat from Mick and
Lizzy's. For one thing, the published version provides more explicit information;
the characters, for example, are named Mulchinock and O'Connor. And they
pass through a variety of travails, not, however, including the birth of an illegitimate child. The lovers are separated at the moment of their engagement by the
news that William is wanted (wrongly) for murder. He flees to India, where he is
bolstered by his memories of his faithfully waiting bride-to-be. An additional
stanza is included in the website's version to substantiate these narrative events:

> In the far fields of India, 'mid war's dreadful thunders,
> Her voice was a solace and comfort to me,
> But the chill hand of death has now rent us asunder,
> I'm lonely tonight for the Rose of Tralee.

William returns to Tralee just in time to see Mary's funeral procession (the cause
of her death is unspecified), eventually marries another woman, emigrates to
America, divorces, returns to Ireland, and lives his last years by Mary's grave at
Clogherbrien, dogged by her memory and alcoholism. The pageant's version,
then, lacks the detail of the child or Mary's broken heart, and it remains silent
concerning the point about which Mick and Lizzy were most adamant: the miss-
ing grave.

Mick and Lizzy's stress on the lost unmarked grave (a detail that would
support the idea that Mary's child was illegitimate) somehow accords the song
greater efficacy in their eyes. For them, the song's real import lies in Kerry itself and the fact that so many Kerrymen have been obliged over the centuries
to leave it. The existence of a major festival named after the song—focused on
crowning a diasporic Rose of Tralee—suggests that this understanding of the
song's essence is widespread.

It is also noteworthy that Mick's version leaves out the stanza that ties the song most concretely to its supporting narrative, that is, the one that mentions India and Mary's death. Even by the website's account, this stanza must have been composed later than the rest—after William's return to Ireland and discovery of his true love's demise. Yet its absence in Mick's version allows his song to stand for Kerry emigration in general rather than the specific departure of William and the ill luck of his subsequent life. It is the Kerry connection that makes the song important to Mick, and what he expects others to focus on as well in their interpretation of the song as he performs it.

Mick not only maintains but also limits his repertoire to keep intact its focus on Kerry. At one point during my visit, when Lizzy tried to get Mick to sing a song from outside his active repertoire, he snapped:

> M: I don't have that song!
> L: Sure, but you *know* the song anyway, don't ya, Mick?
>   How does it go again?
> M: By God, Lizzy girl, I can't be bothered remembering that one!

Being "bothered remembering a song" seems to mean that somehow the song resonates with Mick's own life: only then is it worth the work of learning and maintaining. Songs in this way are like "the company we keep": shapers as well as emblems of the selves we would like to be. Mick is not interested in letting his repertoire reflect his Meath experience, even if Meath has been his home for nearly half of his life.

At the same time, audiences sometimes wanted to link their own experiences or locale to Mick's songs, creating resistance to an interpretation focused solely on Kerry. As Lizzy put it at one point as Mick began to expound on Kerry life: "Is it a *long* tape you got there, Tom?" Other personal themes compete with Kerry as interpretive keys to understanding Mick's songs.

LYRICS AS NARRATIVES OF DISPLACEMENT

For Mick and his audience, lyric songs can, by their very existence, stand as emblems of belonging. Yet Mick's lyrics also repeatedly narrate the experience of displacement, in which this sense of belonging is challenged by the decision and experience of emigration. The emigrant song is an important genre in Ireland, as elsewhere in northern Europe, and some seven of Mick's twelve songs treat the theme. Some, like *Little Thatched Cabin* and *The Rose of Tralee* above, portray the speaker long after emigration has occurred, as he looks back wistfully on a world that has been lost. Others, like the following, chronicle the emotions and hopes of the speaker on the eve of departure.

EXAMPLE 7.4

I'm bidding farewell to the land of my youth
And the home I loved so well
With an aching heart I'm bidding farewell,
And tomorrow I'll sail far away.
O'er the ocean foam for to seek a home
On the shores of Amerikay.

It is not for the want of employment I'm going
It is not for the love of fame.
But a fortune bright, may shine over me
And give me a glorious name.
It is not for the want of employment I'm going
For to start me an ocean away.
But to seek a home for my own true love
On the shores of Amerikay.

But when I am bidding my last farewell
The tears lie drenched afar.
When I think of the friends in my own native land
And the home I am leaving behind.
For this I will die in a foreign land
And be buried so far far away
No fond mother's tear where I shall go to my grave
On the shores of Amerikay.

With its jauntier tempo and bittersweet optimism, this lyric seems to capture the outlook of youth, aware of the sacrifices that emigration entails but lacking in the real experience of sorrow that such sacrifices will create. Its representation of the reasons behind the emigration is also distinct: the speaker is leaving "to seek a home for my own true love," a motive that implies continued contact with the home district and the probability of an eventual return or, more likely, chain migration. The speaker's departure is not here a product of self-interest, in other words, but of self-sacrifice: the willing entry into exile in order to create the basis for a future life for both speaker and true love.

This same motivation is enunciated emphatically in *Three-Leafed Shamrock*, a song that Mick and Lizzy sang with particular emotion and vigor during the evening.

EXAMPLE 7.5

In the dark, a ship was anchored
On a bright St. Patrick's Day

On the quay a lass was sighing:
"Alas my love is going away."
In her hand she held an emblem
And her parting leaves were three
And her parting words were "Darling,
Look at these and think of me."

Chorus: Three-leaf shamrock I adore thee
Your three leaves I long to free
When there're brighter days in Ireland
I'll come home and marry thee.

Just before the ship had started
As she laid her land in mine
Just before that we had parted
She looked with loving eyes so kind.
To my coat she pinned an emblem
And her parting leaves were three,
And her parting words were "Darling,
Look at these and think of me."
Chorus
M: *[speaking voice]* Now, lovely.
L: *[sings]* But tonight, I am an exile
M & L: *[singing together]* Far from home and far from thee,
Next my heart I wear your token
Look on that or fail to be.
But alone the Sea of Ireland,
And your face I might never see,
When there're brighter days in Ireland,
I'll come home and marry thee.
Chorus

The image of emigration here is one of necessity: Ireland's problems force the speaker to leave. Thus, with confident candor, the speaker can declare, "When there're brighter days in Ireland, I'll come back and marry thee." This lyric is thus in a certain sense soothing and exculpatory: the person departing can be said to have no choice, and the people left behind are accorded no blame for the choice to leave. Nor is the emigrant guilty of abandonment: the departure, even if in practice permanent, will come to an end as soon as days brighten back in Ireland. Given the gloomy economic and political climate of Ireland in the past, such a promise would presumably never come to the test.

This appealing image of selfless emigration, of course, has faded somewhat in recent years. Brighter days had indeed come to Ireland at the time of our recording, with the country enjoying a rapidly expanding high-tech economy and ample employment opportunities for the young and computer literate. Today the choice of emigration is clearly an act of self-interest and self-realization, intended to gratify the ambitions or interests of the migrant. While others may benefit from this venture, it is no longer as easy to portray emigration as an act of selflessness.

So, too, a massive influx of European Union money had markedly boosted the standard of living in Ireland, and a deluxe new motorway had opened that linked Dublin in the east to Galway in the west. Its effect on Meath was to create the infrastructure for wealthy Dubliners to own country retreats or weekend getaways in the Midlands, meaning that prime lots in the area were now selling with unprecedented speed and at top prices. Strict laws aimed at controlling suburban sprawl limited new construction in the countryside, but standing houses in the vicinity had now passed to once-unlikely owners, such as Germans. "They're nothing to us," noted Lizzy, acknowledging the fact that the newcomers, although welcome to live alongside the Irish of the area, would not become part of the local culture to any real degree. Mick and Lizzy had carefully selected a neighbor to take over the farming of Mick's land, wishing to prevent its loss to developers or outsiders. Further, the high-speed traffic brought by the new road had made nighttime driving treacherous. Several of Mick and Lizzy's friends had recently been in severe driving accidents, and Mick and Lizzy were now obliged to stay home of an evening instead of stopping by one of their favorite pubs.

None of these unforeseen eventualities is ever contemplated in the rosy but undetailed image of "brighter days" in Mick's song, creating a powerful potential for irony in its performance. Yet Mick's songs—and the interpretations he and his now-limited audience bring to them—maintain silence on all such recent issues. His repertoire can only speak of the issues that masses of Irishmen of the past faced and that find expression in the lyrics as composed. And so the personal feelings of the singer and audience are narrowed to conform to those of previous generations. Mick's personal feelings about these new issues run deep, but he cannot express or explore them through his lyric repertoire.

Lyrics and the Master Narrative of Ireland

While Mick's lyrics emblematize and demonstrate his Kerry heritage, and speak to the experience—personal, familial, and collective—of migration, various of his songs also contribute to an exploration of the grand narrative of Ireland itself. In this overarching notion of the "story of Ireland," individuals can come to see themselves and their lives as reflective of a larger reality, illustrations of historical experiences or moments that have faced and shaped the entire nation. Mick clearly finds this notion satisfying, and emphasizes it in his repertoire.

"He's *steeped* in the Troubles." So Lizzy characterized Mick during our evening recording. In his personal testimony as well as song repertoire, Mick amply demonstrates this claim. Three of the twelve songs Mick performed deal with issues of war or resistance to British rule, and Mick lost his only brother in violence during the brutal War of Independence. It is with the gravity of personal experience that he performed the following version of *The Valley of Knockanure*.

EXAMPLE 7.6

You may come and speak about Easter week and the heroes of '98,
Of the gallant men who roamed the glen, in victory or defeat;
Their names were placed in history's page, their memories will endure;
Not a song was sung for our darling sons in the Valley of Knockanure.

They were Walshe, Lynes, and Dalton: men that were in their prime.
In every house, in every town, they were always side by side.
The Republic bold, they did uphold, they outlawed on the moor,
But side by side, they fought and died, in the Valley of Knockanure.

At Gortnagleanna's rugged height, three gallant men took shape,
They viewed the soft sweet wheat as the summer breeze did play.
It was not long until Lynes came on saying, "Time is not mine nor yours,"
But it was too late, they met their fate, in the Valley of Knockanure.

They took them then beside a fence, where the furze did bloom.
And like brothers so, they faced the foe, to meet with their dreadful doom.
And when Dalton was dying, aloud he cried, with a fashion proud and true:
"For our land we're dying, as we face the sky, in the Valley of Knockanure."

It was by a neighboring hillside, they listened in calm dismay.
In every house, in every town, a maiden knelt and prayed.
"They are closing in around us, with a rifle fire so sure,"
And Dalton is dead and Lynes is down, in the Valley of Knockanure.

There they lay in the hillside's clay for the love of Ireland's cause.
The cowardly clan, the Black and Tans, they showed them English law.
No more they'll feel the soft wild steel over uplands fair and high,
For side by side, they fought and died, in the Valley of Knockanure.

I then met Dalton's mother and those words to me did say:
"May the Lord have mercy on those boys who died in that glen today,
Oh but I would kiss their cold, cold lips, my aching heart would cure,
And we laid them down to rest in the Valley of Knockanure."

The golden sun was sinking, far beyond Feale and Lea.
The pale, pale moon was shining, far beyond Tralee.
The dismal stars and clouds afar had darkened over the moor,
And the banshee cried, where our heroes died, in the Valley of Knockanure.

At first glance, this song would appear to contain more narrative clues for its
interpretation than most of the other lyrics examined thus far. Composed by

Paddy Drury of Knockanure in response to historical events, the song clearly memorializes a specific battle and set of executions of Irish nationalists during an uprising (Healy 1965: 41–44). The prime heroes—Walshe, Lynes, and Dalton—are named, as are the places of the tragedy: Knockcanure, Gortnagleanna, and Feale and Lea. Yet the song focuses more on the emotional effects of the event than on the event itself. And the explication offered by Mick and Lizzy, as we shall see, moves away from the explicit narrative toward a more proverbialized rendering of Irish suffering over time. Thus, the expected narrative explanation, once given, proves only part of the means by which Mick and Lizzy interpret the song.

In terms of structure, we may note that the song's first three stanzas are devoted to depicting the heroes amid their community and ideals, closing with the men's capture and execution. Stanza 4 depicts the heroes' noble words at the execution itself. The final four stanzas portray the mourning of the community and landscape after their deaths, with a narrator persona and first-person quotations emerging in stanza 7, where the lyric speaker appears possibly identical to Dalton's mother. She intones a familiar sentiment of sorrow for her son ("If I could kiss those cold, cold lips"), one paralleled by other standard images of prayer, banshees, and sorrowful landscape. The final image of the land and nature here is one of silence and desolation: without the human spark brought by the noble heroes, the land stands mute and static.

Mick's version of the song is more lyrical and less narrative than some collected variants; where Mick's song goes into detail on the emotional aftermath of the deaths, some versions devote much more attention to the narrative events of the ambush and battle alluded to in Mick's rendition. A more narrative version, for instance, was collected from Mrs. Bridget Howard Gladree of County Mayo in 1955 and conserved at the Department of Irish Folklore at University College Dublin.[3] A published version, also more narrative, appeared in Colm Ó Lochlainn's *More Irish Street Ballads* (1965), collected in 1939. The Ó Lochlainn version is reproduced in Richard Kopp's *Rick's Music Pages* (2003). Mick's highly lyricized version of this formerly explicitly narrative song matches closely that published by James Healy (1965: 43–44) in his *Ballads from the Pubs of Ireland*. Healy's text gives no musical notation for the song (nor does Mick read music), so it is likely that Mick used the published text either directly or secondarily to supplement his knowledge of a song he already knew somewhat from oral tradition. It is noteworthy that Healy's work appeared soon after Mick's relocation to Meath, just at the time when he was likely reframing his active repertoire as a reflection of his Kerry past.

In Mick's version and understanding of *The Rose of Tralee,* the song's characters are broadened and partly redefined from the specific man and woman of the song to a proverbialized image of the emigrant and his true love. So, likewise, *The Valley of Knockanure* is broadened in its meaning to commemorate not simply the tragic death of three brave men during the War of Independence but also the experience of Irishmen in general in dealing with British rule. This broadening of significance became evident in the discussion that followed Mick's performance. At first, Mick and Lizzy were quite willing to describe the song as referring to the events of the war, as our conversation demonstrates.

> T: What year was that?
> L: I think 1917 or 1918.
> T: Okay.
> L: That's what he's giving you a lesson in history for—
> M: The Black and Tans would kill people like you.
> L: Sure they had hooks and chains with them
>   and they'd shoot you for fun at the sight of you.
> M: Ah my, quite a fight with the Black and Tans.

In this short response to my question, then, Mick and Lizzy locate the song's events concretely in the aftermath of the 1916 Easter Uprising, perhaps during the May 1917 executions, which galvanized Irish sentiment against the continuation of British rule (McCartney 1967). This event proved pivotal in modern Irish history, and Mick and Lizzy fully expected me to know about it already, as Lizzy's half-critical remark about history lessons made clear. Following the 1918 parliamentary elections, British authorities clashed with Irishmen bent on independence in the fierce Anglo-Irish war, or War of Independence, known by people of the times as the "Troubles." This same term is used also to describe the contemporary conflicts between Catholic Unionists and Protestant Loyalists in modern Northern Ireland, a historical allusion to the earlier conflict that eventually persuaded the British government to endorse Irish home rule and eventually accept Irish independence. Lizzy was quite aware of the double meaning of the term when she used it on that evening in 1998, given the ongoing conflicts then taking place in the North. In the historical situation of 1918, the

British auxiliary troops, the "Black and Tans," engaged in battle throughout the country, trying to suppress Irish resistance and hunt down groups of men responsible for guerrilla attacks on British installations. Mick, of course, has considerable personal connection with these events, as his only brother died of head injuries sustained in one of the later Kerry clashes.

Yet it was not these personal events that the couple used in the subsequent discussion to further explicate the song. Rather, they broadened the focus from the specific war to the entirety of English oppression, and then to the specific fates of Kerry and Meath within this larger history. This discussion eventually led to their collaborative account of Mick's resettlement in Meath, a topic that thus became tied to the narrative events of the song, however unforeseen that may have seemed at the outset of the discussion. The themes of war, migration, and displacement from Kerry all become part of the greater story of Ireland, of which Mick and his repertoire become prime illustrations.

The collective achievement of this understanding on the evening of our recording involved a certain degree of negotiation and competition for interpretive control between Mick and his generally outspoken wife. I initiated the competitive portion of this explanatory process through a simple question, as the transcript shows.

> T: Where did they [the Black and Tans] come into first?
> M: Well, they came into the South.
> L: They came into *all* Ireland.
> M: Into Kerry most of all.
> L: Into Kerry.
> M: Into Kerry.
>> They came in boats into Kerry.
>> They didn't come into the Midlands as bad;
>> they slaughtered them before,
>>> long before.

In this exchange, then, Mick has been able to establish Kerry as the prime victim of Black-and-Tan aggression, a notion that accords well with the contents of his song and that maintains the Kerry focus that is characteristic of Mick's repertoire. In so doing, he is able to edge out Lizzy's assertion that all Ireland (including the Midlands) suffered equally.

But Lizzy, native to Meath and equally proud of her county, quickly seeks to turn the attention away from Kerry and toward the district in which she and Mick currently reside, despite Mick's somewhat vehement protest.

L: You know why they didn't come into the Midlands?
T: Why?
M: Don't tell him.
L: Because, eh, this is the best land—

At this point, then, audience (Lizzy) and singer (Mick) appear equally in control of formulating the interpretive response to the song. Mick would maintain focus on Kerry, but in practice he is only one of the creators of the enunciated meaning. As Lizzy gains control of the floor, she initiates a new line of argument that puts Kerry, Meath, and the song in broader historical perspective.

L: Meath was,
        as you went through Trim and saw all the castles,
        King John's Castle—
M: English,
        English had them all.
L: The English had this land.
M: And Tom, they were hunted down across the Shannon by Cromwell.
L: Yeah, with a pitchfork.
M: With a pitchfork.
        Ah, the Lord save us,
        they murdered.
L: "To Hell or to Cork!"

At this point, then, the discussion has somehow shifted to the seventeenth century, when English troops overran Ireland and imposed a repressive martial law. In the process, the story of the executions at Knockanure has become one with the struggles of the 1600s, and both have become integrally tied to the county of Mick's birth, the refuge of resisters in both eras. Meath figures as the prize for which the English vied; Kerry and Cork, as the marginal tracts to which the Irish opposition fled. Mick again asserts his personal connection with these events by noting, "My relatives came from Shannon." This is an important element in his family's history, as Mick's ancestors, dispossessed by landlords, are known to have migrated to Ballinskelligs in Kerry from Clare, across the Shannon, in the seventeenth century. The family's Kerry life of small farming and fishing is thus represented as the victimized perseverance of a family following the loss of desirable farmland, a product of Cromwell's reign.

From here, Lizzy reprises the argument, drawing in greater detail the contrast between Kerry and Meath in a manner that places the images of landscape in *The Valley of Knockanure* in an uncompromisingly negative light.

> L: The land was *so* good in the County Meath,
>> All the *kings,*
>> Strongbow,
>> and all the king's children wanted it.
> It was Leinster.
>> Leinster.
>> And Meath is the—
> M: Land of the world, Lizzy.
> L: Meath's the last word in agriculture.
>> The rich was in Meath,
> And all there was down in Kerry was
>> mountains,
>> and rocks
>> and stones
>> and everything. . . .
> It was "to Hell or to Cork."

This topic shift, has turned Kerry, the shining refuge of Mick's telling, into an inferior wasteland, to which disempowered Irishmen clung. Since in both Mick's and Lizzy's eyes the song is about Kerry in particular, this characterization comments directly on the song as well. We can see in it, as in Mick's words, varying interpretations of the lyric's imagery of "dismal stars and clouds afar darkening over the moor." But we can also see a very present vying between the relative stature of Meath and Kerry, the two counties closest to the hearts of the people assembled. And Connaught, the traditional referent in the expression "to Hell or to . . ." is sidelined entirely in the interest of places that fit better with the intent and understanding of the song as a reflection of Munster history.

The turn in the argument has also served a deeper purpose in Mick's and Lizzy's interpretive work, for it leads them directly to their tying of the song to Mick's experience of resettlement. As the couple continues the discussion:

> L: The living,
>> the living was in Leinster.
>> In Leinster.
>> This is Leinster.
> M: Now, where we're living there was eight hundred acres.
> L: This here.
> M: It was divided between Meath and Kerry.
>> I'm the only Kerryman.

Mick has moved to the topic of his own resettlement and the estate that was divided to make room for land-deprived farmers like him. Mick's assertion of a binary Meath/Kerry split of the previous estate of eight hundred acres arises from the contrasts drawn by Lizzy in the discussion up to this point and does not fit the facts of the resettlement process exactly. Historical accuracy compels Lizzy to correct the statement and note that migrants from other counties were given land there as well: "Yes, and Mayo and Clare." What is most important to the discussion at hand, however, is that the situation of injustice described in the song has finally been undone, with Mick's family (dispossessed by Cromwell centuries before) finally being restored to a workable plot of land and peace restored on the island.

This topic was on the minds of most people in Ireland that evening, as the Good Friday accords of earlier that year had received a violent and dispiriting challenge from Protestant militants in the North. A few short weeks before, national referenda in both the North and the South had endorsed a new plan for lasting peace, one that had created optimism in both parts of the island. Then, however, the "marching season" had begun, and Protestant militants had killed three Catholic children with a firebomb in County Down. Mick and Lizzy, who, like most people in the South, had formerly given relatively little thought to the Troubles of the North, now saw themselves personally challenged and drawn into the conflict through the fact that they had voted in favor of the peace plan. The Reverend Ian Paisley had preached a message of Protestant defiance and aggression to devoted Orangemen encamped by the Garvaghy Road that same evening, and the euphoria of recent weeks had vanished entirely. The ongoing Troubles of the North impinged in silent but menacing fashion on the discussion of the past Troubles of the South, reminding all three of us that the song's narrative was not so distant after all. All were part of the same grand narrative, one captured in its emotional essence by Mick's songs and the experiences they depict.

It would seem obvious to associate Mick's songs with his life experiences, and as it happens, that is exactly what Mick and his audience tend to do. Mick's songs demonstrate his connection with Kerry, a land he left behind in body but not in heart. In his performances of a Kerry repertoire, Mick reminds others and himself of his enduring relation with the county of his youth, its landscape, history, and people. In his performance of emigrant songs, Mick underscores his identity as a migrant, providing both a context and a justification for his decision to resettle in Meath. Even if the emigration described in his lyrics relates to international movement rather than resettlement within Ireland, and even if most of the people in Mick's life who actually emigrated were women rather than men, his songs are interpreted as narrations of the emotional travails he endured in moving to Meath. And finally, the events of the lyrics themselves, along with Mick's personal experiences, are subsumed into the grand narrative of Ireland, a narrative that ties all Mick's songs together and that can be shared by singer and audience alike.

In this process, of course, the singer and audience enjoy great leeway in shaping a set of understandings out of the songs they share. Yet the songs themselves exert control over interpretation as well: they select the experiences and outlooks that their users can narrate, presenting certain attitudes that the users are compelled to accept as their own. In so doing, the performer and the audience experience the weight of tradition, coming to see personal experiences within the broader narrative of the collective. The personal becomes subsumed seamlessly into both proverbialized and narrativized understandings. And crucially, none of this accrued significance occurs until a performer and an audience make use of the songs. If listeners fail to listen or singers to perform, this dynamic process of negotiation, in which personal meanings are identified, shared, and maintained, cannot take place. It exists as part of the song tradition but not in any tangible form. Rather, it is part of the overall tradition of interpretation that performers and audiences share as an element of lyric singing.

Epilogue

He sang as if he knew me in all my dark despair.
And then he looked right through me as if I wasn't there.

> Charles Fox and Norman Gimbel,
> *Killing Me Softly with His Song* (1973)

The aesthetic confrontation of a lyric can prove a powerful experience. The song presents us with the subjective perceptions of another being, portrayed as if that speaker were standing before us. If we engage with the song—if we allow it to "penetrate" (as Cloten puts it in *Cymbeline* II: 3, 13)—then we are soon obliged to interpret it. The point of this study has been to suggest that this interpretive act is complex, and that it is governed by traditions associated with the lyric songs themselves. It is possible to misinterpret a song, especially if we fail to take note of the interpretive norms, the hermeneutics, that operate in the song's ambient tradition. A competent audience, on the other hand, approaches the song in a manner dictated by the song tradition, one shared by both performer and audience. This is not to say that a song may not have multiple meanings; rather, I have suggested in these pages that the *manner* in which one approaches the interpretive task is normative, foregrounding certain choices, opening certain interpretive possibilities, downplaying or avoiding others. This system leads to a set of normative interpretations, not to any singular or monolithic meaning.

In the thoroughly silly movie *Galaxy Quest* (1999), the has-been cast members of a long-beloved, cult-status television series about space explorers meet for the first time with authentic space aliens. The problem is that neither side understands the other. The television cast thinks the aliens are simply addled fans; the aliens think that the cast members are really the heroic scientists and officers they had seen perform wonderful deeds in the television reruns they had intercepted in deep space. Their interpretive frameworks, based on assumptions specific to their own frames of reference, fail to account for the realities of a very different aesthetic and cultural system. In the course of the film, the two sides must sort out what is reality, fantasy, and ideal.

In many ways, the study of lyric song has experienced similar difficulties. It is an easy and nearly automatic tendency to interpret songs the way that one has always interpreted songs, without necessarily asking whether that mode of interpretation is operative in the culture or tradition of the singer or song itself. Unless these interpretive acts are brought up in open discussion, it is often difficult for individuals to see where their assumptions differ from those of the performers or audiences who produced or received the song in the first place. In this study, I have tried to indicate some of the complexities that obtain in the act of interpretation within cultures and some of the specificities that can render cross-cultural interpretation problematic. I have also tried to suggest ways in which the process is actually quite simple at its heart: by varying, normative recourse to three interpretive axes, individuals and communities discover, share, and maintain the meanings of the songs they sing.

I hope that this study will encourage others to explore such issues of interpretation in specific song traditions and perhaps also in other genres of oral tradition, custom, or material culture. And I also hope that the observations presented here will enrich readers' and listeners' experience of the evocative and beautiful lyric songs of northern Europe.

NOTES TO CHAPTER 1

1. Orrajaura, modern Northern Sámi Oarrejávri, can be translated "Squirrel Lake." Orthography as in Olaus Sirma's original manuscript, as reproduced in Honko, Timonen, and Branch 1993: 316–17. For transcription and partial translation into modern Northern Sámi, see Gaski, Solbakk, and Solbakk 2004: 60–61. All translations, unless otherwise noted, are mine.

2. Goethe's translation runs as follows:

Finnisches Lied

Käm der liebe Wohlbekannte,
Völlig so wie er geschieden,
Kuß erkläng an seinen Lippen,
Hätt auch Wolfsblut sie gerötet;
Ihm den Handschlag gäb ich, wären
Seine Fingerspitzen Schlangen.

Wind! o hättest du Verständnis,
Wort' um Worte trügst du wechselnd,
Sollt auch einiges verhallen,
Zwischen zwei entfernten Liebchen.

Gern entbehrt ich gute Bissen,
Priesters Tafelfleisch vergäß ich
Eher, als dem Freund entsagen,
Den ich Sommers rasch bezwungen,
Winters langer Weis bezähmte.
    (Goethe 1810)

NOTES TO CHAPTER 3

1. Turi's published book reflects the collaboration of Turi and Emilie Demant-Hatt, a Danish ethnographer. It was Demant-Hatt who organized the prose that Turi produced into the chapters as they appear in *Muitalus samiid birra*. For more discussion of this relation and its significance, see Kuutma 2003.

2. Translations are based on those of E.G. Nash in the English translation of *Muitalus*, emended to more accurately reflect Turi's original language and its connotations.

3. www.piobaireachd.com/library/glengary.htm; accessed July 31, 2003.

4. Cumha a Chliarach/The Bard's Lament: www.piobaireachd.com/library/bard.htm; accessed July 31, 2003.

NOTES TO CHAPTER 7

An earlier version of this chapter was published as "Interpreting Lyric Meaning in Irish Tradition: Love and Death in the Shadow of Tralee," *Oral Tradition* 17, no. 1 (2002): 87–107.

1. All quotations and transcriptions from Mick and Lizzy Lyne are taken from the transcript of our taping session at their farm in Longwood, County Meath, July 19, 1998. Used by permission of the interviewees. Although Mick has since passed away, I retain the present tense when referring to his views in this text. Many thanks to Dineen Grow for helping to identify, transcribe, and translate *Bean Dubh an Ghleanna*.

2. Rose of Tralee Festival website: www.roseoftralee.ie; accessed July 31, 2001.

3. Many thanks to Ríonach ui Ógáin of the Department of Irish Folklore at University College, Dublin, for sharing this version with me.

Abrahams, Roger D. 1970. *A Singer and Her Songs: Almeda Riddle's Book of Ballads.* Music ed., George Foss. Baton Rouge: Louisiana State University Press.

Acerbi, Giuseppe. 1802. *Travels through Sweden, Finland, and Lapland, to the North Cape, in the Years 1798 and 1799.* London: J. Mawman.

Aðalbjarnarson, Bjarni, ed. 1962. *Heimskringla.* Reykjavik: Hið Islenzka Fornritafélag.

Aðalsteinsson, Jón Hnefill. 2001. "The Varðlokkur of Guðríður Þorbjarnardóttir." *Northern Lights: Following Folklore in North-Western Europe. Essays in Honour of Bo Almqvist.* Dublin: University College Dublin Press. Pp. 97–110.

Ala-Könni, Erkki. 1986. "'Jos minun tuttuni tulisi'-runoon liittyvä sävelmistö." In *Suomen kansanmusiikki: Tutkielmia neljältä vuosikymmeneltä,* ed. Erkki Ala-Könni. Kaustinen: Kansanmusiikki-instituutti. Pp. 185–89.

Anderson, Benedict. 1983. *Imagined Communities: Reflections on the Origin and Spread of Nationalism.* London: Verso.

Anderson, Flemming G. 1985. *Commonplace and Creativity.* Odense, Denmark: Odense University Press.

Apo, Satu. 1981. "Suomalainen kansanrunous." In *Suomen kirjallisuuden historia,* ed. Kai Laitinen. Helsinki: Otava. Pp. 13–80.

Asplund, Anneli. 1983. *Kantele.* Helsinki: Suomalaisen Kirjallisuuden Seura.

Astington, John. 1993. "Malvolio and the Eunuchs, Texts and Revels in *Twelfth Night.*" *Shakespeare Survey* 46: 23–34.

Baum, Paull F. 1960. "The *Beowulf* Poet." *Philological Quarterly* 39: 394–99. Rpt. Joseph F. Tuso, ed., *Beowulf.* New York: W.W. Norton, 1975. Pp. 174–78.

Bellman, Carl Michael. 1790. *Fredmans epistlar.* Facsimile reprint. Stockholm: Bonnier, 1984.

Bendix, Regina. 1997. *In Search of Authenticity: The Formation of Folklore Studies.* Madison: University of Wisconsin Press.

Bergin, Osborn, trans. and ed. 1970. *Irish Bardic Poetry: Texts and Translations, Together with an Introductory Lecture.* Dublin: Dublin Institute for Advanced Studies.

Bernard, J.H., and R. Atkinson, eds. 1898. *The Irish Liber Hymnorum.* London: Henry Bradshaw Society.

Best, R.I., and M.A. O'Brien, eds. 1967. *The Book of Leinster, formerly Lebar na Núachongbála.* Vol. 5. Dublin: Dublin Institute for Advanced Studies.

Biblia sacra: Iuxta Vulgatam Clementiam. Matriti: Biblioteca de Autores Cristianos, 1977.

Blair, Hugh. [1765] 1996. *A Critical Dissertation on the Poems of Ossian.* In *The Poems of Ossian and Related Works,* ed. Howard Gaskill. Edinburgh: Edinburgh University Press. Pp. 345–99.

Blume, Clemens. 1910. "Hymnody and Hymnology." In *The Catholic Encyclopedia,* vol. 3. New York: Robert Appleton Company. Online copyright 2003 Kevin Knight. www.newadvent.org/cathen/07596ahtm, accessed August 11, 2003.

Bradbury, Nancy Mason. 1998. "Traditional Referentiality: The Aesthetic Power of Oral Traditional Structures" In *Teaching Oral Traditions,* ed. John Miles Foley. New York: Modern Language Association. Pp. 136–50.

Bragg, Lois. 1993. *The Lyric Speakers of Old English Poetry.* Rutherford: Fairleigh Dickinson University Press.

Britten Austin, Paul, trans. 1990. *Fredmans Epistles and Songs.* Stockholm: Proprius.

Bromwich, Rachel, trans. 1982. *Dafydd ap Gwilym: A Selection of Poems.* Llandysul: Gomer Press.

———. 1986. *Aspects of the Poetry of Dafydd ap Gwilym.* Cardiff: University of Wales Press.

Brorson, Kerstin. 1985. *Sing the Cows Home.* Seattle: Welcome Press.

Brown, Carleton, ed. 1924. *Religious Lyrics of the XIVth Century.* Oxford: Clarendon Press.

Brown, Peter. 1981. *The Cult of the Saints: Its Rise and Function in Latin Christianity.* Chicago: University of Chicago Press.

Buckley, Ann. 1999. "Representations of Musicians in John Derricke's *The Image of Irelaunde (1581).*" In *Music, Words, and Images: Essays in Honour of Koraljka Kos,* ed. Vjera Katalinič and Zdravko Blaz'ekovič. Zagreb: Hratsko Drus'tvo Skladatelja.

Bunting, Edward. [1840] 1969. *The Ancient Music of Ireland: An Edition Comprising the Three Collections by Edward Bunting Originally Published in 1796, 1809, and 1840.* Dublin: Waltons' Piano and Musical Instrument Galleries, Publications Department.

Bynum, Caroline Walker. 1982. *Jesus as Mother: Studies in the Spirituality of the High Middle Ages.* Berkeley: University of California Press.

Byrne, Donn. 1924. *Blind Rafftery and His Wife Hilaria.* New York: Century.

Cabrol, Dom Fernand. 1929. *Mon missel.* Quatrième édition. Tours: Maison Alfred Mame et Fils.

Cahill, Edward. 1996. "The Problem of Malvolio." *College Literature* 23: 62–82.

Cameron, Alexander. 1894. *Reliquiæ Celticæ: Texts, Papers, and Studies in Gaelic Literature and Philology.* Vol. 2. Inverness: Northern Counties Newspaper and Printing and Publishing Company.

Canal, José Maria. 1963. *Salve Regina Misericordiae: Historia y leyendas en torno a esta antifona.* Temi e Testi 9. Rome: Edizioni di Storia e Letteratura.

Cannon, Roderick D. 2002. *The Highland Bagpipe and Its Music.* Edinburgh: John Donald Publishers.

Carmichael, Alexander, trans. and ed. 1914. *Deirdire and the Lay of the Children of Uisne.* 2d ed. Paisley: Alexander Gardner.

———. 1928. *Carmina Gadelica: Hymns and Incantations.* Vol. 2. Edinburgh: Tweeddale Court.

Carney, James, trans. and ed. 1967. *Medieval Irish Lyrics.* Berkeley: University of California Press.

Chappell, William. [1859] 1965. *The Ballad Literature and Popular Music of the Olden Time.* New York: Dover.

Child, Francis James, ed. 1883–98. *The English and Scottish Popular Ballads.* 5 vols., 10 pts. Boston: Houghton Mifflin.

Coffin, Tristram. 1957. "'Mary Hamilton' and the Anglo-American Ballad as an Art Form." *Journal of American Folklore* 70 (277): 208–14. Rpt. in *Readings in American Folklore,* ed. Jan Harold Brunvand. New York: W.W. Norton, Pp. 309–18.

Collan, Karl, et al. [1857–71] 1988. *Valituita Suomalaisia Kansan-Lauluja, Pianon mukasoinnolle sovitettuja.* Kuopio: Kuopion kanpunginhallitus.

Collinson, Francis. 1966. *The Traditional and National Music of Scotland.* London: Routledge and Kegan Paul.

Connellan, Owen, trans. and ed. 1860. *Imtheacht na Tromdhaimhe; or, The Proceedings of the Great Bardic Institution.* Transactions of the Ossianic Society for the Year 1857. Vol. 5. Dublin: Ossianic Society.

Cook, Albert S., ed. 1909. *The Christ of Cynewulf: A Poem in Three Parts.* Boston: Ginn and Company.

Cotter, Geraldine. 1983. *Geraldine Cotter's Traditional Irish Tin Whistle Tutor.* Cork, Ireland: Ossian Publications.

Cowell, Sidney Robertson. 1957. "Introduction." In *Songs of Aran: Gaelic Singing from the West of Ireland.* Ethnic Folkways Library Album No. FE 4002. New York: Folkways Records and Service Corp.

Cowling, George H. 1964. *Music on the Shakespearean Stage.* New York: Russell & Russell.

Craig, Hardin, ed. 1961. *The Complete Works of William Shakespeare.* Glenview, Ill.: Scott, Foresman.

Crane, Thomas F., ed. 1925. *Liber de Miraculis Sanctae Dei Genitricis Mariae.* Ithaca: Cornell University Press.

Cranford, Chris. 2003. Cranford Publications website. www.cranfordpub.com/langan/BeanDubh.htm, accessed August 19, 2003.

Daly, Dominic. 1973. "Introduction." In *Abhráin atá Leagtha ar an Reachtúire: Songs Ascribed to Raftery,* by Douglas Hyde. Shannon: Irish University Press. Pp. vii–xii.

Davies, Oliver. 1996. *Celtic Christianity in Early Medieval Wales: The Origins of the Welsh Spiritual Tradition.* Cardiff: University of Wales Press.

Davies, R. T., ed. 1963. *Medieval English Lyrics: A Critical Anthology.* London: Faber and Faber.

Delargy, James H. 1945. *The Gaelic Story-Teller: With Some Notes on Gaelic Folk-Tales.* London: Cumberlege.

Dillon, Myles. 1948. *Early Irish Literature.* Chicago: University of Chicago Press.

Dronke, Peter. [1968] 1996. *The Medieval Lyric.* Rev. ed. Cambridge: D. S. Brewer.

DuBois, Thomas A. 1995. *Finnish Folk Poetry and the Kalevala.* New York: Garland.

———. 1996. "Native Hermeneutics: Traditional Means of Interpreting Lyric Songs in Northern Europe." *Journal of American Folklore* 109 (433): 235–66.

———. 1999. *Nordic Religions in the Viking Age.* Philadelphia: University of Pennsylvania Press.

———. 2000. "'That Strain Again!' or, *Twelfth Night*, a Folkloristic Approach." *Arv* 56: 35–56.

Duffin, Ross W. 2004. *Shakespeare's Songbook.* New York: W. W. Norton.

Dumézil, Georges. 1943. *Servius et la fortune: Essai sur la fonction sociale de luange et de blâme et sur les éléments indoeuropéens du cens romains.* Paris: Gallimard.

Dundes, Alan. 1966. "Metafolklore and Oral Literary Criticism." *Monist* 60: 505–16.

Edwards, Huw M. 1996. *Dafydd ap Gwilym: Influences and Analogues.* Oxford: Clarendon Press.

Elson, Louis. [1900] 1970. *Shakespeare in Music: A Collation of the Chief Musical Allusions in the Plays of Shakespearem with an Attempt at Their Explanation and Derivation, Together with Much of the Original Music.* Freeport, N.Y.: Books for Libraries Press.

Enäjärvi-Haavio, Elsa. 1935. "Lyyrilliset laulut." In *Suomalaisen muinaisrunouden maailma*, ed. Martti Haavio. Porvoo: WSOY. Pp. 112–75.

Espeland, Velle. 1974. *Svartbok frå Gudbrandsdalen.* Oslo: Universitetsforlaget.

Europaeus, D. E. D. [1847] 1931. *Pieni Runon-seppä eli Kokous paraimmista Inkerinmaan puolelta kerätyistä runo-lauluista. Suomen Kansan Vanhat Runot.* Vol. 3. Helsinki: Suomalaisen Kirjallisuuden Seura, 1908–98. Pp. 503–22.

Farrell, Robert T., ed. 1974. *Daniel and Azarias.* London: Methuen.

Ferguson, Donald A., ed. 1978. *From the Farthest Hebrides.* London: Macmillan.

Foley, John Miles. 1990. *Traditional Oral Epic: The Odyssey, Beowulf, and the Serbo-Croatian Return Song.* Berkeley: University of California Press.

———. 1991. *Immanent Art: From Structure to Meaning in Traditional Oral Epic.* Bloomington: Indiana University Press.

———, ed. 1998. *Teaching Oral Traditions.* New York: Modern Language Association.

———. 2002. *How to Read an Oral Poem.* Urbana: University of Illinois Press.

Ford, Patrick, trans. and ed. 1977. *The Mabinogi and other Medieval Welsh Tales.* Berkeley: University of California Press.

Forkner, Ben, ed. 1980. *Modern Irish Short Stories.* New York: Viking. Pp. 74–82.

Fox, Charles, and Norman Gimbel. 1973. *Killing Me Softly Wih His Song.* Vocalist, Roberta Flack. Atlantic Records.

Fox-Good, Jacquelyn A. 1998. "'Ring-Time': Sexual and Musical Play in *As You Like It*." *Ars Lyrica* 9: 139–56.

Frith, Simon. 1998. *Performing Rites: Evaluating Popular Music.* Oxford: Oxford University Press.

Fulton, Helen, trans. 1996. *Selections from the Dafydd ap Gwilym Apocrypha.* Llandysul: Gomer Press.

Galaxy Quest. Dir. Dean Parisot. Distributed by Dreamworks SKG, Los Angeles, 1999.

Gantz, Jeffrey. 1981. *Early Irish Myths and Sagas.* Harmondsworth: Penguin Books.

Gaski, Harald, ed. 1996. *In the Shadow of the Midnight Sun: Contemporary Sámi Prose and Poetry.* Kárášjohka: Davvi Girji.

———. 2000. "The Secretive Text: Yoik Lyrics as Literature and Tradition." In *Sámi Folkloristics,* ed. Juha Pentikäinen. Turku: NIF Publications. Pp. 191–214.

Gaski, Harald, John T. Solbakk, and Aage Solbakk, eds. 2004. *Min njálmmálaš árbevierru: Máidnasat, myhtat ja muitalusat.* Kárášjohka: Davvi Girji.

Gaskill, Howard, ed. 1996. *The Poems of Ossian and Related Works, by James Macpherson.* Edinburgh: Edinburgh University Press.

Gibson, John G. 1998. *Traditional Gaelic Bagpiping, 1745–1945.* Edinburgh: NMS Publishing.

Gollancz, Israel, ed. and trans. 1892. *Cynewulf's Christ: An Eighth-Century English Epic.* London: David Nutt.

Goethe, Johann. 1810. *Finnisches Lied.* Rpt. *Gedichteportal.de,* "Gedichte von Goethe— Seite 4." www.thokra.de/html/goe4.html#a103, accessed August 27, 2003.

Goertzen, Chris. 1997. *Fiddling for Norway: Revival and Identity.* Chicago: University of Chicago Press.

Gordis, Robert. 1974. *The Song of Songs and Lamentations: A Study, Modern Translation and Commentary.* New York: Ktav Publishing.

Gray, Douglas, ed. [1975] 1992. *English Medieval Religious Lyrics.* Oxford: Oxford University Press.

Greenberg, Noah. 1961. *An Anthology of English Medieval and Renaissance Vocal Music.* New York: W. W. Norton.

Gregory, Lady Augusta, trans. and ed. 1903. *Poets and Dreamers: Studies and Translations from the Irish.* Dublin: Hodges, Figgis and Co.

———. trans. and ed. 1904. *Gods and Fighting Men: The Story of the Tuatha de Danaan and of the Fianna of Ireland.* London: John Murray.

Grendon, Felix, ed. 1909. "The Anglo-Saxon Charms." *Journal of American Folklore* 22 (84): 105–237.

———. 1919. *The Kiltartan Poetry Book: Prose Translations from the Irish.* New York: G. P. Putnam's Sons.

Grundström, Harald, and A. O. Väisänen, eds. 1958. *Lappische Lieder: Texte und Melodien aus Schwedish-Lappland. Lapska sånger: Texter och melodier från svenska Lappland.* 2 vols. Uppsala: Lundequistska Bokhandeln; Copenhagen: Einar Munksgaard.

Grundtvig, Svend, Axel Olrik, and Hakon Grüner Nielsen et al., eds. 1853–1976. *Danmarks gamle Folkeviser.* 12 vols. Copenhagen: Samfundet til den danske literaturs fremme.

Gummere, Francis B. 1901. *The Beginnings of Poetry*. New York: Macmillan.

———. 1907. *The Popular Ballad*. Boston: Houghton Mifflin.

Hardiman, James. [1831] 1971. *Irish Minstrelsy; or, Bardic Remains of Ireland, with English Poetical Translations*. London: J. Robins. Rpt. Shannon: Irish University Press.

Harvilahti, Lauri. 1992. *Kertovan runon keinot: Inkeriläisen runoepiikan tuottamisesta*. Helsinki: Suomalaisen Kirjallisuuden Seura.

Hautala, Jouko. 1954. *Suomalainen kansanrunoudentutkimus*. Helsinki: Suomalaisen Kirjallisuuden Seura.

Healy, James N. 1965. *Ballads from the Pubs of Ireland*. Cork: Mercier Press.

———. 1977. *Love Songs of the Irish*. Dublin: Mercier Press.

Henry, Patrick L. 1966. *The Early English and Celtic Lyric*. London: George Allen & Unwin.

Henrysson, Sten. 1993. *Samer, präster, och skolmästare: Ett kulturellt perspektiv på samernas och Övre Norrlands historia*. Umeå: Centrum för arktisk forskning.

Herder, Johann Gottfried. [1765] 1992. "Essay on a History of Lyrical Poetry." In *Johann Gottfried Herder: Selected Early Works, 1764–1767*, ed. Ernest A. Menze and Karl Menges; trans. Ernest A. Menze and Michael Palma. University Park: Pennsylvania State University Press. Pp. 69–84.

———. [1765] 1992. "Fragments of a Treatise on the Ode." In *Johann Gottfried Herder: Selected Early Works, 1764–1767*, ed. Ernest A. Menze and Karl Menges; trans. Ernest A. Menze and Michael Palma. University Park: Pennsylvania State University Press. Pp. 35–51.

———. 1778–79. *Volkslieder*. Leipzig: Weygand.

Heusler, Andreas. 1941. *Die altgermanische Dichtung*. Potsdam: Akademische Verlagsgesellschaft Athenaion.

Honko, Lauri. 1963. "Itkuvirsirunous." In *Suomen kirjallisuus I: Kirjoittamaton kirjallisuus*, ed. Matti Kuusi. Helsinki: Otava. Pp. 81–128.

———. 1974. "Balto-Finnic Lament Poetry." *Studia Fennica* 17: 9–61.

Honko, Lauri, Senni Timonen, and Michael Branch, eds. 1993. *The Great Bear: A Thematic Anthology of Oral Poetry in the Finno-Ugrian Languages*. Helsinki: Suomalaisen Kirjallisuuden Seura.

Huldén, Lars. 1994. *Carl Michael Bellman*. Stockholm: Natur och Kultur.

Hull, Vernam, ed. 1949. *Longes Mac n-Uislenn: The Exile of the Sons of Uisliu*. New York: Modern Language Association.

Hyde, Douglas, ed. 1893. *Abhráin grádh chúige Connacht: Love Songs of Connacht, being the fourth chapter of the Songs of Connacht*. Baile-Átha-Cliath: Gill.

———. 1895. *The Story of Early Gaelic Literature*. London: T. F. Unwin.

———, ed. [1903] 1973. *Abhráin atá Leagtha ar an Reachtúire. Songs Ascribed to Raftery*. Shannon: Irish University Press.

———. [1901] 1903. *Casadh an tSúgáin. The Twisting of the Rope*. In *Poets and Dreamers: Studies and Translations from the Irish*, by Lady Gregory, trans. Lady Gregory. 3d ed. Dublin: Hodges, Figgis & Co. Pp. 200–215.

Hymes, Dell. 1992. "Use All There Is to Use." In *On the Translation of Native American Literatures,* ed. Brian Swann. Washington, D.C.: Smithsonian Institution Press. Pp. 83–124.

Ilomäki, Henni. 1990. "Tekeväin on meiän tetri: Näkökulmia inkeriläisen morsiamen naiseuteen." In *Louhen sanat: Kirjoituksia kansanperinteen naisista,* ed. Aili Nenola and Senni Timonen. Helsinki: Suomalaisen Kirjallisuuden Seura.

Iser, Wolfgang. 1989. *Prospecting: From Reader Response to Literary Anthropology.* Baltimore: Johns Hopkins University Press.

Jauss, Hans Robert. 1974. *Toward an Aesthetic of Reception.* Trans. Timothy Bathi. Minneapolis: University of Minnesota Press.

Jeffrey, David. 1975. *The Early English Lyric and Franciscan Spirituality.* Lincoln: University of Nebraska Press.

Johnson, Samuel. [1775] 1924. *Journey to the Western Islands of Scotland.* Rpt. as: *Johnson's Journey to the Western Islands of Scotland and Boswell's Journal of a Tour to the Hebrides with Samuel Johnson, LL.D.,* ed. R.W. Chapman. London: Oxford University Press.

Johnston, Dafydd, trans. 1993. *Iolo Goch: Poems.* Llandysul: Gomer Press.

Jones, James H. 1961. "Commonplace and Memorization in the Oral Tradition of the English and Scottish Popular Ballads." *Journal of American Folklore* 74 (292): 97–112.

Jones-Bamman, Richard W. 1993. "'As long as we continue to joik, we'll remember who we are.' Negotiating Identity and the Performance of Culture: The Saami Joik." Ph.D. diss., University of Washington.

Katz, Robert L. 1963. *Empathy: Its Nature and Uses.* New York: Free Press of Glencoe.

Kjellström, Rolf, Gunnar Ternhag, and Håkan Rydving. 1988. *Om jojk.* Hedemora, Sweden: Gidlunds Bokförlag.

Klaeber, Fr., ed. 1950. *Beowulf and the Fight at Finnsburg.* 3d ed. Lexington: D.C. Heath.

af Klintberg, Bengt, ed. 1965. *Svenska trollformler.* Stockholm: Wahlström and Widstrand.

Knuuttila, Seppo, and Senni Timonen. 2002. "If the One I Know Came Now." In *Myth and Mentality: Studies in Folklore and Popular Thought,* ed. Anna-Leena Siikala. Studia Fennica Folkloristica 8. Helsinki: Suomalaisen Kirjallisuuden Seura. Pp. 247–71.

Kolehmainen, Ilkka, and Vesa Tapio Valo, eds. 1990. *Kreeta Haapasalo: Ikoni ja ihminen.* Kansanmusiikki-Instituutin julkaisuja 31. Kaustinen: Kansanmusiikki-Instituutti.

Kopp, Richard. 2003. *Rick's Music Pages.* www.acronet/~robokopp/eire/youmaysi.htm, accessed August 19, 2003.

Krass, Andreas. 1998. *Stabat Mater Dolorosa. Lateinische Überlieferung und volkssprachliche Übertragungen im deutschen Mittelalter.* Munich: Wilhelm Fink Verlag.

Kretz, Leif, Sten Åke Nilsson, and Torkel Stålmarck. 1994. *Bellman sedd och hörd.* Stockholm: Norstedts.

Krnjevic', Hadiza. 1991. "Notes on the Poetics of Serbo-Croatian Folk Lyric." *Oral Tradition* 6 (2–3): 174–85.

Krohn, Ilmari, et al. 1933. *Suomen kansan sävelmiä.* Vol. 3. Jyväskylä: Jyväskylän Kirjapaino. Online version: virtuaaliyliopisto.jyu.fi/esavelmat/haku.php#list, accessed July 19, 2005.

Krohn, Kaarle. 1931. *Tunnelmarunojen tutkimuksia.* Helsinki: Suomalaisen Kirjallisuuden Seura.

Kuhn, Hans, ed. 1983. *Edda: Die Lieder des Codex Regius nebst verwandten Denkmälern.* Heidelberg: Carl Winter, Universitätsverlag.

Kuntz, Andrew. 1996–2005. *The Fiddler's Companion: A Descriptive Index of North American and British Isles Music for the Folk Violin and Other Instruments.* www.ibiblio. org/fiddlers/index.html, accessed July 8, 2005.

Kuusi, Matti, ed. 1963. *Suomen kirjallisuus I: Kirjoittamaton kirjallisuus.* Helsinki: Otava.

Kuutma, Kristin. 2003. "Collaborative Ethnography before Its Time: Johan Turi and Emilie Demant Hatt." *Scandinavian Studies* 75 (2): 165–80.

Laitinen, Heikki. 1990. "Torpparinvaimo Greeta Haapasalon matkat kautta koko Suomen Suuriruhtinaskunnan ja aina Pietariin ja Tukkolmaan saakka." In *Kreeta Haapasalo: Ikoni ja ihminen,* ed. Ilkka Kolehmainen and Vesa Tapio Valo. Kansanmusiikki-Instituutin julkaisuja 31. Kaustinen: Kansanmusiikki-Instituutti. Pp. 5–66.

Launis, Armas, ed. 1930. *Suomen Kansan Sävelmiä. Neljäs jakso. Runosävelmiä II. Karjalan runosävelmät.* Helsinki: Suomalaisen Kirjallisuuden Seura.

Leslie, R. F., ed. 1961. *Three Old English Elegies.* Manchester: University of Manchester Press.

Lippus, Urve. 1995. *Linear Musical Thinking: A Theory of Musical Thinking and the Runic Song Tradition of Baltic-Finnish Peoples.* Studia Musicologica Universitatis Helsingiensis 7. Helsinki: Department of Musicology, Helsinki University.

Logan, James. 1845. *The Clans of the Scottish Highlands.* London: Ackermann.

Lomax, John A. 1915. "American Folk Song." Rpt. in *Folk Nation: Folklore in the Creation of American Tradition,* ed. Simon J. Bronner. Wilmington, Del.: Scholarly Resources. Pp. 105–26.

Long, John H. 1955. *Shakespeare's Use of Music: A Study of the Music and Its Performance in the Original Production of Seven Comedies.* Gainesville: University of Florida Press.

Longfellow, Henry Wadsworth. [1855] 1985. *My Lost Youth.* In *The Norton Anthololgy of American Literature,* vol. 1, 2d ed., ed. Nina Baym et al. New York: W. W. Norton. Pp. 1285–86.

Lönnrot, Elias. 1835, 1849. *Kalevala, taikka vanhoja Karjalan runoja Suomen kansan muinoisista ajoista.* Helsinki: Suomalaisen Kirjallisuuden Seura.

———. [1840–41] 1982. *Kanteletar, elikkä Suomen Kansan vanhoja lauluja ja virsiä.* Helsinki: Suomalaisen Kirjallisuuden Seura.

Lord, Albert B. 1960. *The Singer of Tales.* Cambridge, Mass.: Harvard University Press.

Louhivuori, Jukka, and Rauno Nieminen, eds. 1987. *Paimenen säveliä: Teppo Revon paimensoittusävelmiä.* Helsinki: Suomalaisen Kirjallisuuden Seura.

Luria, Maxwell S., and Richard L. Hoffman, eds. 1974. *Middle English Lyrics: Authoritative Texts, Critical and Historical Backgrounds, Perspectives on Six Poems*. New York: W.W. Norton.

Lysaght, Patricia. 1986. *The Banshee: The Irish Death Messenger*. Boulder, Colo.: Roberts Rinehard Publishers.

McCartney, Donal. 1967. "From Parnell to Pearse (1891–1921)." In *The Course of Irish History*, T.W. Moody and F.X. Martin. Cork: Mercier Press.

Mac Giolla Léith, Caoimhín, ed. 1993. *Oidheadh Chloinne hUisneach. The Violent Death of the Children of Uisneach*. Irish Texts Society, vol. 56. London: Irish Texts Society.

MacGregor, Duncan. 1897. *Saint Columba: A Record and a Tribute*. Edinburgh: J. Gardner Hitt.

MacKay, Angus. 1839. *A Collection of Ancient Piobaireachd or Highland Pipe Music*. Edinburgh: Mac Lachlan.

MacKay, Ian. 2002. "The Art of Piobaireachd." Posted at www/piobaireachd.com/library/tunehistories, accessed August 27, 2003.

McKenna, Catherine A. 1991. *The Medieval Welsh Religious Lyric: Poems of the Gogynfeirdd, 1137–1282*. Belmont, Mass.: Ford & Bailie.

McLane, Maureen. 2001. "Ballads and Bards: British Romantic Orality." *Modern Philology* 98: 423–43.

———. 2002. "On the Use and Abuse of 'Orality' for Art: Reflections on Romantic and Late Twentieth-Century *Poiesis*." *Oral Tradition* 17 (1): 135–64.

MacNeill, Seumas. 1968. *Piobaireachd: Classical Music of the Highland Bagpipe*. Edinburgh: British Broadcasting Corporation.

MacNeill, Seumas, and Frank Richardson. 1987. *Piobaireachd and Its Interpretation*. Edinburgh: John Donald.

Macpherson, James. *See* Gaskill 1996.

Meletinsky, Eleazar M. 1998. *The Elder Edda and Early Forms of the Epic*. Trieste: Edizioni Parnaso.

Meredith, Peter, ed. 1997. *The Mary Play, from the N. Town Manuscript*. 2d ed. Exeter: University of Exeter Press.

Mills, Margaret A. 1991. *Rhetorics and Politics in Afghan Traditional Storytelling*. Philadelphia: University of Pennsylvania Press.

Monsen, Erling, trans. and ed. 1990. *Heimskringla or the Lives of the Norse Kings*. New York: Dover.

Moore, A.K. 1951. *The Secular Lyric in Middle English*. Lexington: University Press of Kentucky.

Narayan, Kirin. 1995. "The Practice of Oral Literary Criticism: Women's Songs in Kangra, India." *Journal of American Folklore* 108 (429): 243–64.

Naylor, Edward W. [1896] 1965. *Shakespeare and Music, with Illustrations from the Music of the 16th and 17th Centuries*. New York: AMS Press.

Nenola, Aili. 1974. "Lucky Shoes or Weeping Shoes: Structural Analysis of Ingrian Shoeing Laments." *Studia Fennica* 17: 62–91.

———. 1981. "Itämerensuomalaiset itkuvirret." In *Kansanmusiikki*, ed. Anneli Asplund and Matti Hako. Helsinki: Suomalaisen Kirjallisuuden Seura. Pp. 44–52.

———. 1982. *Studies in Ingrian Laments*. FF Communications no. 234. Helsinki: Suomalainen Tiedeakatemia, Academia Scientiarum Fennica, 1982.

Nenola, Aili, and Senni Timonen, eds. 1990. *Louhen sanat: Kirjoituksia kansanperinteen naisista*. Helsinki: Suomalaisen Kirjallisuuden Seura.

Nic Domhnaill Gairbhí, Máire. 2000. *A Traditional Music Journey 1600–2000, from Erris to Mullaghban*. Nure, Co. Leitrim: Drumlin Publications.

Ng, Alan. 2005. *Irish Traditional Music Tune Index*. www.irishtune.info, accessed July 8, 2005.

Niles, John D. 1983. *Beowulf: The Poem and Its Tradition*. Cambridge, Mass.: Harvard University Press.

Nomos. 1996. *Set You Free*. Sound recording. Green Linnet GLCD 3120, 1996.

Nordal, Sigurður, ed. 1933. *Egils saga Skalla-Grímssonar*. Reykjavik: Hið Islenzka Fornritafélag.

Nygard, Holger O. 1958. *The Ballad of "Heer Hallewijn," Its Forms and Variations in Western Europe: A Study of the History and Nature of a Ballad Tradition*. Folklore Fellows Communications 169. Helsinki: Suomalainen Tiedeakatemia.

Nyström, Marianne. 1994. *Myt och sanning om Carl Michael Bellman*. Stockholm: Catlssons.

Ó Canainn, Tomás. 1978. *Traditional Music in Ireland*. London: Routledge and Kegan Paul.

O'Conor, Charles. 1766. *Dissertations on the History of Ireland*. Dublin: G. Faulkner in Parliament-street.

O'Flynn, Criostoir, trans. and ed. 1998. *Blind Raftery: Selected Poems*. Indreabhán, Conamara: Cló Iar-Chonnachta.

O'Keefe, J. G., ed. 1913. *Buile Suibhne (The Frenzy of Suibhne), being The Adventures of Suibhne Geilt, a Middle-Irish Romance*. Irish Texts Society, vol. 11. London: Irish Texts Society.

Ó Lochlainn, Colm. 1965. *More Irish Street Ballads*. Dublin: Mercier Press.

Ó Máille, Tomás, ed. 1916. *Amhráin Chearbhalláin. The Poems of Carolan, Together with Other N. Connacht and S. Ulster Lyrics*. Irish Texts Society, vol. 17. London: Irish Texts Society.

O'Neill, Francis O. 1903. *O'Neill's Music of Ireland*. Chicago: Lyon & Healy.

Opland, Jeff. 1976. "*Beowulf* on the Poet." *Mediaeval Studies* 38: 442–67.

O'Reilly, Edward. [1820] 1970. *A Chronological Account of Nearly Four Hundred Irish Writers, with a Descriptive Catalogue of Their Works*. Dublin: Iberno-Celtic Society. Rpt. Shannon: Irish University Press.

O'Sullivan, Donal. 1958. *Carolan: The Life, Times and Music of an Irish Harper*. 2 vols. London: Routledge and Kegan Paul.

Parry, Thomas. 1952. *Gwaith Dafydd ap Gwilym.* Cardiff: University of Wales Press.

Pentikäinen, Juha. 1978. *Oral Tradition and Worldview.* FF Communications 219. Helsinki: Suomalainen Tiedeakatemia.

Percy, Thomas. 1765. *Reliques of Ancient English Poetry.* 3 vols. London: J. Dodsley.

Pope, John C., ed. 1981. *Seven Old English Poems.* New York: W.W. Norton.

Porter, James. 1976. "Jeannie Robertson's 'My Son David': A Conceptual Performance Model." *Journal of American Folklore* 89 (351):7–26.

Porthan, Henrik Gabriel. [1766–1778] 1983. *De Poësi Fennica. Suomalaisesta runoudesta.* Trans. Iiro Kajanto. Helsinki: Suomalaisen Kirjallisuuden Seura.

Propp, Vladimir. 1993. "The Russian Folk Lyric." In *Russian Folk Lyrics,* trans. and ed. Roberta Reeder. Bloomington: Indiana University Press. Pp. 1–56.

Ramnarine, Tina. 2003. *Ilmatar's Inspirations: Nationalism, Globalization, and the Changing Soundscapes of Finnish Folk Music.* Chicago: University of Chicago Press.

Reinholm. H.A. 1834–76. *Suomen Kansan Laulantoja.* Helsinki: Suomalaisen Kirjallisuuden Seura.

Renwick, Roger deVan. 1980. *English Folk Poetry: Structure and Meaning.* Philadelphia: University of Pennsylvania Press.

Reynolds, Dwight. 1991. "The Interplay of Genres in Oral Epic Performance: Differentially Marked Discourse in a Northern Egyptian Tradition." In *The Ballad and Oral Literature,* ed. Joseph Harris. Cambridge, Mass.: Harvard University Press. Pp. 292–317.

Robinson, Richard. *Casadh an tSugain.* www.leeds.ac.uk/music/Info/RRTuneBk/gettune/00000c05.html, accessed June 21, 2005.

Salminen, Väinö. 1917. *Länsi-Inkerin häärunot.* Helsinki: Suomalaisen Kirjallisuuden Seura.

Sävborg, Daniel. 1997. *Sorg och elegi i Eddans hjältediktning.* Stockholm Studies in History of Literature 36. Stockholm: Almqvist & Wiksell International.

Sayers, William. 1992. "Varia VII. The Deficient Ruler as Avian Exile: Nebuchadnezzar and Suibhne Geilt." *Ériu* 43: 217–20.

Schefferus, Joannes [Johan Scheffer]. 1673. *Lapponia, id est regionis Lapponum et gentis nova et verissima descriptio, in qua multa de origine, superstitione, sacris magicis, victu, cultu, negotiis Lapponum, item animalium, metallorumque indole, quae in terris eorum proveniunt, hactenus incognita produntur, & eiconibus adjectis cum cura illustrantur.* Frankfurt: Typis J. Andreae, ex officina C. Wolffii.

———. 1704. [English version]. *The History of Lapland: Containing a Geographic Description and a Natural History of that Country; With an Account of Their Inhabitants, Their Original, Religion, Customs, Habits, Marriages, Conjurations, Employments, &c.* London: Tho. Newborough and R. Parker.

Scott, Walter. [1805] 1830. "Lay of the Last Minstrel." In *The Poetical Works of Walter Scott, Together with the Minstrelsy of the Scottish Border.* New York: Leavitt and Allen. Pp. 311–54.

Seng, Peter J. 1967. *The Vocal Songs in the Plays of Shakespeare: A Critical History.* Cambridge, Mass.: Harvard University Press.

Shaw, John, ed. and trans 2000. *Brìgh an Òrain: A Story in Every Song: The Songs and Tales of Lauchie MacLellan*. Montreal: McGill Queen's University Press.

Shields, Hugh. 1981. "A Singer of Poems: Jimmy McCurry of Myroe" *Ulster Folklife 27*: 1–18.

———. 1991. "Popular Modes of Narration and the Popular Ballad." In *The Ballad and Oral Literature*, ed. Joseph Harris. Cambridge, Mass.: Harvard University Press. Pp. 40–59.

———. 1993. *Narrative Singing in Ireland: Lays, Ballads, Come-All-Yes and Other Songs*. Dublin: Irish Academic Press.

Siikala, Anna-Leena. 1990. "Singing of Incantations in Nordic Tradition." In *Old Norse and Finnish Religions and Cultic Place Names*, ed. Tgore Ahlbäck. Scripta Instituti Donneriani 13. Stockholm: Almqvist & Wiksell International. Pp. 191–205.

———. 1992. *Suomalainen samanismi: Mielikuvien historiaa*. Helsinki: Suomalaisen Kirjallisuuden Seura.

Silverstein, Theodore, ed. 1971. *Medieval English Lyrics*. London: Edward Arnold.

Skjöldebrand, A. F. 1801–2. *Voyage pittoresque au Cap Nord*. Stockholm: C. Deleen and J. G. Forsgren.

Stafford, Fiona. 1996. "Introduction: The Ossianic Poems of James Macpherson." In *The Poems of Ossian and Related Works, by James Macpherson*, ed. Howard Gaskill. Edinburgh: Edinburgh University Press. Pp. v–xxi.

Stein, Edith. [1917] 1964. *On the Problem of Empathy*. Trans. Waltraut Stein. The Hague: Martinus Nijhoff.

Sternfeld, Frederick W. 1963. *Music in Shakespearean Tragedy*. London: Routledge and Kegan Paul.

Stevick, Robert T., ed. [1964] 1994. *One Hundred Middle English Lyrics*. Urbana: University of Illinois Press.

Stoor, Krister. 2003. *To Joik Is to Live*. Audio CD. Umeå: UMUFCD-002.

Storm, Gustav, ed. 1880. *Monumenta historica Norwegiae: Latinske kildeskrifter til Norges historie i middelalderen*. Kristiania: A. W. Brøgger.

Suomen Kansan eSávelmát. http://virtuaaliyliopisto.jyu.fi/esavelmat/haku.php#list, accessed July 19, 2005.

Szomjas-Schiffert, Gjörgy, ed. 1996. *Singing Tradition of Lapp Shamans. Lapp sámánok énekes hagyománya*. Budapest: Akadémiai Kiadó.

Thomas, Gwyn, trans. 2001. *Dafydd ap Gwilym: His Poems*. Cardiff: University of Wales Press.

Timonen. Senni. 1989. *Pohjois-Karjalan lyriikka*. Kalevalaseuran vuosikirja 68. Helsinki: Suomalaisen Kirjallisuuden Seura.

———. 1982. *Näin lauloi Larin Paraske*. Helsinki: Suomalaisen Kirjallisuuden Seura.

———. 1990. "Orja, ruhtinatar, ja vapauden ongelma: Naisten omaelämäkeralliset laulut Inkerissä ja Siperiassa." In *Louhen sanat: Kirjoituksia kansanperinteen naisista*, ed. Aili Nenola and Senni Timonen. Helsinki: Suomalaisen Kirjallisuuden Seura. Pp. 189–208.

————. 2004. *Minä, tila, tunne: Näkökulmia kalevalamittaiseen kansanlyriikkaan.* Helsinki: Suomalaisen Kirjallisuuden Seura.

Tolkien, J. R. R. 1936. "*Beowulf*: The Monsters and the Critics." *Proceedings of the British Academy* 22: 245–95.

Turesson, Gunnar. 1960. *Värmländska kulturtraditioner: Äldsta dikten och musiken.* Stockholm: Tidens Förlag.

Turi, Johan. [1910] 1911. *Muittalus samid birra. En bog om lappernes liv.* [Modernized: *Muitalus samiid birra.*] Trans. and ed. Emilie Demant. 3d ed. Stockholm: Nordiska Bokhandeln.

————. 1931. *Turi's Book of Lappland.* Trans. E. Gee Nash. New York: Harper.

Utriainen, Terhi. 1998. "Feminine and Masculine in the Study of Balto-Finnic Laments." In *Gender and Folklore: Perspectives on Finnish and Karelian Culture,* ed. Satu Apo, Aili Nenola, and Laura Stark-Arola. Studia Fennica Folkloristica 4. Helsinki: Suomalaisen Kirjallisuuden Seura. Pp. 175–200.

Vatanen, Maura. 1961. *Kokkovirsi.* Sound recording at the Sound Archives of the Finnish Literature Society, SKSÄ 141: 2. Reproduced on the CD *The Kalevala Heritage.* ODE 849–2, Ondine Inc. 1995. Track 3.

Vauchez, André. 1993. *The Laity in the Middle Ages: Religious Beliefs and Devotional Practices.* Ed. Daniel E. Bornstein; trans. Margery J. Schneider. Notre Dame: University of Notre Dame Press.

Vikis-Freibergs, Vaira. 1989. "The Boyar's Beautiful Daughters: A Structural Analysis of Stanza Sequence in Latvian Folk Songs." In *Linguistics and Poetics of Latvian Folk Songs: Essays in Honour of the Sesquicentennial of the Birth of Kr. Barons,* ed. Vaira Vikis-Freibergs. Kingston: McGill-Queen's University Press. Pp. 312–41.

Virtanen, Leea. 1994. "Women's Songs and Reality." In *Songs beyond the Kalevala: Transformations of Oral Poetry,* ed. Anna-Leena Siikala and Sinikka Vakimo. Studia Fennica Folkloristica 2. Helsinki: Suomalaisen Kirjallisuuden Seura. Pp. 330–42.

Virtanen, Leea, and Thomas DuBois. 2001. *Finnish Folklore.* Studia Fennica Folkloristica 9. Helsinki: Suomalaisen Kirjallisuuden Seura.

Vries, Jan de. 1970. *Altgermanische Religionsgeschichte.* Berlin: De Gruyter.

Walker, Joseph Cooper. 1786. *Historical Memoirs of the Irish Bards.* Dublin: Luke White.

Whitelock, Dorothy. 1939. "*Beowulf,* ll. 2444–2471." *Medium Ævum* 8.

————. 1951. *The Audience of Beowulf.* Oxford: Clarendon Press.

————, ed. 1967. *Sweet's Anglo-Saxon Reader in Prose and Verse.* Oxford: Clarendon Press.

Williams, Ifor. 1972. *The Beginnings of Welsh Poetry.* Cardiff: University of Wales Press.

Woolf, Rosemary. 1968. *The English Religious Lyric in the Middle Ages.* Oxford: Clarendon Press.

Wordsworth, William. [1807] 1979. "The Solitary Reaper." Rpt. in *The Norton Anthology of English Literature,* 4th ed., ed. M. H. Abrams. New York: W. W. Norton. Pp. 220–21.

Wrenn, C. L., ed. 1953. *Beowulf with the Finnesburg Fragment.* Boston: D. C. Heath.

————. 1967. *A Study of Old English Literature.* New York: W. W. Norton.

Wretö, Tore. 1984. *Folkvisans upptäckare: Receptionsstudier från Montaigne och Schefferus till Herder.* Acta Universitatis Upsaliensis Historia litterarum 14. Stockholm: Almqvist & Wiksell, International.

Yeats, William Butler. [1897] 1980. *The Twisting of the Rope.* In *Modern Irish Short Stories,* ed. Ben Forkner. New York: Viking Press. Pp. 74–82.

Zeller, Rose. 1939. *Die Gudrunlieder der Edda.* Tübinger germanistische Arbeiten 26. Stuttgart: W. Kohlhammer.

Zupitza, Julius, ed. 1959. *Beowulf, Reproduced in Facsimile from the Unique Manuscript MS. Cotton Vitellius A. XV.* Early English Text Society 245. London: Oxford University Press.